WEST HIGHLAND WHITE TERRIERS

AN OWNER'S COMPANION

Roger Wright

The Crowood Press

First published in 1992 by
The Crowood Press Ltd
Ramsbury, Marlborough
Wiltshire SN8 2HR

British Library Cataloguing in Publication Data

A catalogue record for this book is available from the British
Library.

ISBN 1 85223 667 1

Line-drawings by Annette Findlay.

Dedication
To all my dogs, past, present and
future, who unlike humans are not
fickle with their loyalty and love.

Throughout this book, 'he', 'him' and 'his' have been used as
neutral pronouns and are intended to refer to both sexes, human
or canine.

Typeset by Acorn Bookwork, Salisbury, Wiltshire
Printed in Great Britain by Redwood Press Ltd, Melksham, Wilts

Contents

Acknowledgements

I am grateful to all those who have passed on to me their knowledge over the years, in particular, to the late 'Teddy' Clarke (Edgemoor), and Mrs Jean and Miss Lesley Taylor (Checkbar). Likewise, to top professional handler Frank Kellett (Minerstown) and Mrs Joan Langstaff (Sprotboro), who continue to impart their wisdom and advice.

Thanks are also due to Mrs Millie Jennings (Doonrae) for all her help with ancient pedigrees and research, to Paul J. Holdcroft for technical assistance, to Mrs Burrows at Thomas Fall's for the prompt help and advice with old photographs, and to all those who supplied photographs from their personal collections for use in this book.

A special thank you is owed to Chris and Mary Kernick (Makerch), for all their wonderful help generally, and especially to Chris for the benefit of his expertise and advice on the photography throughout this book.

On a more personal note, thanks to Ray Platt (Tamzin), one of the best dog men I know, who took me under his wing when I started, teaching, encouraging and guiding me in his down-to-earth, practical way. The debt of knowledge and advice which continues to mount, even today, can never be repaid. But the more important loyalty and friendship through thick and thin, can at least be returned.

Finally, thanks to Mum and Dad for their love and support and to Gareth and Jaclyn for a new direction.

1

Origins and History

A small bold breed and steady to the game
Next claims the tribute of peculiar fame!
Train'd by the tribes on Britain's wildest shore,
Thence they their title of Agasses bore.
Small as the race that useless to their lord
Bask on the hearth and beg about the board,
Crook-limbed and black-eyed, all their frame appears
Flanked with no flesh and bristled rough with hairs
But shod each foot with hardest claws is seen,
The sole's kind armour on the beaten green;
But fenced each jaw with closest teeth is found,
And death sits instant on th' inflicted wound.
Far o'er the rest he quests the secret prey,
And sees each track wind opening to his ray:
Far o'er the rest he feels each scent that blows
Court the live nerve and thrill along the nose.

John Whitaker, 1771

For pluck and pith and jaws and teeth,
And hair like heather cowes,
Wi' body lang and low and strang,
At hame in cairns or knowes.

He'll range for days and ne'er be tired,
O'er mountain, moor and fell;
Fair play, I'll back the brave wee chap
To fecht the de'il himsel'.

Then see him at the ingle side,
Wi' bairnies roond him laughin'.
Was ever a dog sae pleased as he,
Sae fond o' fun and daffin'?

Dr Gordon Stables, 1879

Col. Malcolm's eleven.

In any present-day writings of origins and history, the author has to rely heavily on earlier works, art, literature and on logical assumption, based on the insight the collation of that material gives.

In determining the accuracy of these early works, we have to put our faith in those who were closer to events than we, and who put pen to paper or brush to canvas, when the events were fresh in their minds.

Research into the origins and history of dogs is a fascinating study and one which could be carried on indefinitely, as 'new' or previously unseen material comes to hand. As a source of enlightenment it cannot be overlooked. To the dedicated fancier it should be the foundation stone to a better understanding of the breed in general and an influence on the dogs that are kept, bred, shown or judged.

That the breed has a long history is well documented. The preceding poems are a testament to the fact that a small, game, hardy terrier, with a harsh coat existed as early as the eighteenth century. But other information, vague as it sometimes is, takes us back further.

In her book *The West Highland White Terrier* (*see* Further Reading), the late Mrs D. Mary Dennis recalls how she received a letter from

India stating that '. . . the ships of the Spanish Armada carried small white dogs of the West Highland type to catch the rats . . .', and that '. . . after a disastrous naval battle in the sixteenth century, several of the galleons . . . were wrecked on the coasts of the Western Isles of Scotland.' I am sure that the inference here is not that the origins of the breed lay in Spain. But that if these white dogs were the ancestral forerunners of the breed, it is likely that the ships picked them up, as vermin killers, on an earlier voyage along the Scottish coast.

Col. Edward Malcolm of Poltalloch, in his writings on the breed in *Cassell's New Book of the Dog* by Robert Leighton (*see* Further Reading), related the story of how, almost 400 years ago, James I of England and VI of Scotland, wrote to Edinburgh to have half a dozen 'earth dogges or terrieres' sent carefully as a present to France. Col. Malcolm also wrote: 'We may take it then, that in 1600 the Argyllshire terriers were considered to be the best in Scotland.' There is no proof that these terriers were West Highland Whites and it should be noted that *The Cairn Terrier* by J.W.H. Beynon, Alex Fisher and Peggy Wilson (*see* Further Reading), which has been revised by Doreen (Bunty) Proudlock, carries the same story.

Col. Malcolm is universally recognized as one of the founders of

Col. Malcolm with six Poltallochs.

the breed, but he himself stated that his grandfather Neill Malcolm (1769–1837) and father John Malcolm (1805–1893), developed the breed.

Holland Buckley stated in *The West Highland White Terrier* (*see* Further Reading), that the British Museum has '. . . abundant evidence of the antiquity of the breed', in the National Manuscripts. And that he had:

> '. . . not only seen papers in Versailles but pictures of the Cairn terriers . . . which bore the imprint of the time of Louis the Great . . . and . . . were identical in every way with a modern West Highlander, with the exception that some were prick-eared and others drop-eared or semi-erect.'

Mrs Cameron-Head, a great early supporter of the breed with her Inverailort kennel, in conversation with the renowned author Arthur Croxton Smith OBE, recalled how her maternal grandmother, born in 1800, a daughter of Norman Macleod, seventh Laird of Drynoch, used to talk of how her father and grandfather always kept a white and sandy pack, which takes the 'Drynoch Terriers', as they were known on Skye, back to the eighteenth century at least.

In Clifford L.B. Hubbard's book *Dogs in Britain* (1948), it says that 'As a show dog the West Highland White Terrier has only been known for about fifty years, but as a sporting Terrier of Scotland, the breed has been familiar for centuries . . . descended from white, cream and sandy Cairn Terriers . . .'.

The art world holds more historical evidence of the breed. Edwin Landseer seems to have had a certain feeling for the Highlander type. He shows two West Highlanders in an engraving published in 1836. Again, in 1839, he shows an early West Highland White in a group of sporting dogs and from the same year comes the famous *Dignity and Impudence*, showing a Bloodhound side by side with a Highlander.

That a dog something like a West Highland White Terrier existed centuries ago seems to be an established fact. But to discover just how it was developed and established before the mid-nineteenth century to become the breed we know today, may be nigh on impossible. So much of the information is lacking and many of the facts we know are subject to controversy and counter-argument or shrouded by the mists of time.

'Varminty' – certainly. (Original photo by Chas Reid.)

Arguments will rage in favour of one breed or another being the ancestral predecessors of the others. Clearly, it seems that after studying the facts as we know them, and bearing in mind the periods in time of which we speak, it can be logically assumed that Scottish, Skye, Cairn, Dandie Dinmont and West Highland White Terriers were all descended from the same ancestral stock: that of the Highland Terrier, to which Dr John Caius, in a book written in Latin around 1570, made special reference.

In the centuries before dog shows were started in 1859, the main criteria for the sporting men, chiefs, lairds and their gamekeepers were that their terriers could do a good day's work, keeping down the vermin, seeking out the fox from its lair or the badger from its set, and tod (otter) hunting.

Taking into account the lack of roads and communication networks at that time, it is hardly likely that they would travel far to mate their bitches. And even less likely that much detail of the fancy, as we know it, would have been of the slightest interest to them. As Col. Malcolm wrote:

'But men kept their dogs in the evil pre-show days for work and not for points, and mighty indifferent were they whether an ear cocked up or lay flat to the cheek, whether the tail was exactly of fancy length, or how high to a hair's breadth it stood . . . In those days two things – and two things only – were imperatively necessary: pluck, and capacity to get at the quarry.'

9

Bearing in mind the quarry being pursued and the job required, it is logical to assume that a certain type, size, and possibly colour, would be bred for, and that if a dog of a similar type to their own good bitch was within reach, then that dog would be used. These different types would be compounded over generations, thus separating the common type of ancestral stock into different, but still related, types of terrier, which would eventually evolve into quite separate and distinct breeds.

There are many historical roads down which the researcher could travel, each offering its own short-cut to the same destination, that of the origin. In his book *Dogs of Today* Major Harding Cox maintained that '. . . whereas the Cairn is the founder of its own ancient type, the "West Highlander" has been produced by an original cross between the little dog of Skye (no, not what is now known as the "Skye Terrier") and the Scottish (late Aberdeen) Terrier.' He also says that the Cairn was the typical terrier of the Island of Skye,

Carna, circa *1900*.

which begs the question as to how the name Skye Terrier '. . . was allotted to a show-manufactured animal, such as never was within a thousand miles of the Hebrides.'

This is somewhat supported by the fact that the Cairn was earlier known as the 'Working Type of Skye' and, later, the 'Short-coated Prick-eared Skye' or, later still, the 'Prick-eared Skye Terrier'. The early 'Scotch Terrier' was much more like a Highlander than it is today. It was generally longer on the leg, with a shorter, thicker head and was nearer in size and build to our breed. The colour varied from black to white, with pied, wheaten and other intermediate colours all common. Ian Kettle, the Cairn Terrier breed historian, told me that he has seen a red or rusty-coloured dog, native to the Island of Skye, which looks to this day like a Cairn/Scottish Terrier cross.

The argument that the Cairn is the common ancestor of all the terrier breeds of Scotland, save a little doubt in the case of the Dandie Dinmont, is a strong one. Through the efforts of a few, who took the trouble to keep and improve the whites, creams, sandies and other pale colours, there is so little doubt that the West Highland White is a direct descendant of the Cairn, that any argument against it is rendered untenable.

If there should be any lingering doubts as to the origin of the white coat, these can be easily dispelled. It is well documented that white and other pale-coloured Cairns were born, but were destroyed at birth until a few like Col. Malcolm decided to keep them. Col. Malcolm makes several references to the fact that dogs should not be down-marked for having a little colour on them, and he was doubtless referring to the possibility of some of the coloured variety showing themselves. Croxton Smith maintains that they are 'more properly cream', and in Bell's *Quadrupeds* (1837), it describes Cairns as 'generally dirty white'.

Further support, if any were necessary, on colour, the physical proximity of the breeds or the required type, can be found in extracts from general comments by prominent Cairn judges of the day. Charles McNeil, MFH, writing in 1911, had this to say:

> Tremendous strides have been made in the Cairn Terrier during the last year. The boom in them . . . has brought to light a number of animals ranging from bad Scotties to good Cairns. . . . I think in another year or so we shall see as nice a little Terrier as possible, uniform in size and probably also in colour, as there is evidently a very strong tendency to go for pepper and salts and sandys. . . .

11

Much has been written about the type . . . and I am sure the outcome will be a charming Terrier, absolutely a type of its own and one the merest novice would never mistake for a small Scottie. Prospective fanciers of this breed will do well to carry in their eye a small West Highlander, when purchasing a Cairn, and then they will be as near as they can go to true type.

The point at which the various breeds took on a separate and more uniform type seems to coincide with the advent of dog shows in 1859. By about 1900, several Scottish sportsmen were breeding white terriers, and different strains were known variously as: Poltalloch, Roseneath, Pittenweem and even White Scottish Terriers. These white fanciers would eventually combine to form a single breed, the West Highland White Terrier.

By far the most influential of these figures was Col. Malcolm. The Cairn Terrier breeders habitually destroyed any white, creamy, or lighter-coloured pups at birth, thinking them to be less hardy and game, or possibly a liability on the snow-covered hills. The Malcolms disagreed and set about keeping the light colours, pioneering the breed in the first instance as working terriers. Later Col. Malcolm bred and further developed these whites, creams and light sandies into a distinct strain and type, which resembled more closely the breed we know today. They were known by the name of Poltalloch Terriers.

The canine author Arthur Croxton Smith wrote in 1930, using his first-hand information, that,

A sporting writer twenty years ago imagines them as a composite variety made up of many breeds. I am quite sure that no competent breeder would have imagined any such vain thing if he had had the privilege of visiting Colonel Malcolm's kennels in the year 1900, for he would have perceived at once that the trained eye had been exercised for many canine generations in getting the dogs all of a type. There was no suggestion of a mixture about them.

Col. Malcolm must have been a very determined and dedicated man, as can be seen in his writings. Although he had no ambition to become a 'doggy man', his determination was borne solely out of a love of the breed he had developed and nurtured.

Many of the early shows scheduled all Terriers native to Scotland under the heading of 'Scotch' or 'Scottish Terriers'. In Birmingham, in 1860, a 'White Skye' was a winner of one of the scheduled classes for 'Scotch Terriers'. Then at the Crystal Palace Show, 1899, Dr Flaxman showed a team of Roseneath Terriers, and Lady Forbes was amongst the winners with a 'White Scottish Terrier'.

Between 1899 and 1900 a 'White Scottish Terrier Club' was formed, with Dr Flaxman as president and Lady Forbes as secretary, and any of the aforementioned white terriers used that name for registration. But the white terrier fraternity were by no means in full agreement with the name and, in 1904, they united with the purpose of attaining breed recognition at the Kennel Club.

In 1905, with Col. Malcolm as chairman, the White West Highland Terrier Club was formed. In September of the following year, the Kennel Gazette gave details of the application to recognize both the breed and the club. The following month, the issue contained notice of the application of a southern club seeking to be named The West Highland White Terrier Club. After considering both applications at its meeting on November 20, 1906, the Kennel Club committee decided that the breed was to be called The West Highland White Terrier and that 'The Scottish Club, if they wish, can be registered as The West Highland White Terrier Club, and the South of England might be registered as The West Highland White Terrier Club of England.'

Registrations started in 1907, with three dogs and four bitches. By the end of the first year, sixty-three dogs and seventy-nine bitches, making a total of 142 had been registered as West Highland White Terriers.

Similarly, the Cairn Terrier had been registered as 'short-coated prick-eared Skye Terriers'. When, in 1908, Mrs Alastair Campbell began to advocate the claims of this terrier, showing them at Cruft's in the Skye Terrier Classes, the Skye Terrier people were enraged. In August 1909, Lady Aberdeen wrote to *Country Life* saying that she had some of these Short-coated Prick-eared Skyes and that her father, the late Lord Tweedmouth, had used this breed, along with long-coated Skyes, for hunting in Inverness-shire. She suggested that they be called West Highland White Terriers, as in her opinion they were practically the same as the ones already registered as such. After a meeting with the Skye fraternity, the Kennel Club stepped in, hinting that 'Cairn Terrier' might be appropriate. This was accepted in 1910, and explains why Cairn Terriers were not recognized as such until three years after West Highland Whites, the breed for which they were heavily responsible.

It is interesting to note that neither of the first respective champions of the two breeds, who are both praised as being great dogs, great sires and responsible for laying the foundation of their breeds, were first registered as such. The first West Highland White Champion, Morven, was initially registered as a White Scottish Terrier. The first Cairn Champion, Gesto, was the last Cairn to be listed under 'Prick-eared Skye'.

In modern times, the idea of interbreeding may seem a little quaint, but if we remember that interbreeding of Cairns and West Highland White Terriers was practised until 1925, with white puppies being registered as West Highland Whites and any others as Cairns, it clarifies the fact that in the not too distant past, when the breeds were used for working, it was quite acceptable. There are many examples of this mixed lineage which serve to highlight the point made of common ancestry, and to explain some of the 'faults' we encounter, for no apparent reason, from time to time.

The West Highland Terrier dog Conas plays a hugely important role in both breeds, both in siring top-quality progeny and as an example of common ancestry. The first Cairn to gain his title, Gesto, was sired by Sgithanach Bhan, who was by Conas out of Deochiel, who were all West Highland White Terriers. The first West Highland White to gain his title, Morven, had Conas as a great-grandsire.

Conas mated to Rada produced another West Highland White in 1907. The interesting point here is that a grandsire of Conas, Callum Dhu, and a grandsire of Rada, Seafield Rascal, were both early Scottish Terriers.

One of the most notable Cairns, Harviestoun Raider, had a grandam Glenmor Grugach (Cairn) who was sired by Ross-shire Helvellyn (WHW) out of Deilie (Cairn). Helvellyn's sire was Atholl (WHW), who was by Ch. Morven (WHW). Two of Deilie's grandparents were the aforementioned Conas and Rada and a third grandparent, Smallburn Daisy, was another early Scottish Terrier.

With this kind of early mixture there is little need to wonder why the occasional modern-day West Highland White carries a little coat colour. Col. Malcolm expressed his views on the subject by saying:

> Attention to breeding as to colour has undoubtedly increased the whiteness, but, other points being good, a dog of the West Highland White Terrier breed is not to be rejected if he shows his descent by a slight degree of pale red or yellow on his back or his ears.

It appears that some of the earlier fanciers wanted pure whiteness always, forsaking some of the physical attributes of the breed that had so recently come to their notice. In *Hutchinson's Popular & Illustrated Dog Encyclopaedia*, edited by Mr Walter Hutchinson, it says,

> Later, however, this useful working Terrier of Scotland was bred to be an entirely different type. There is no doubt that this was achieved by crossing the Sealyham with the West Highland White. . . . the West Highland White's metamorphosis from a smart, active, sound, white Cairn Terrier to a long-bodied, short-legged creation was due to such a cross . . .

If this were true, it would explain the references to northern and southern types, which, although not as evident in the present day because of all the interbreeding of these types, still exists. It would also account for our inclination to prefer a certain type, and our disbelief at some of the results of our carefully controlled breeding programmes.

Is it possible that the breeding of so long ago can still affect our breed today? I think that with some things, because they have been perpetuated, the answer is yes, quite easily. In other ways, the chances are remote, but still possible. I recall a conversation with Doreen 'Bunty' Proudlock who, for many years was the Cairn Terrier breed historian, and is also one of the most knowledgeable people on dogs today. The story is that, in 1975, on a visit across the Atlantic, she stayed at the home of some well-known Cairn breeders. She knew that there was a litter of Cairn puppies about five weeks old but was never invited to see them. Towards the end of her stay, she asked if she could be allowed to see the puppies, which on sworn secrecy she was allowed to do. The owners had been horrified when the pups were born and had been afraid to let anyone see them, fearing for the consequences, for all the Cairn puppies, out of the owner's Cairn bitch by their own Cairn dog (with not another dog for miles), were white – to all intents and purposes West Highland White Terriers!

At the beginning of this chapter, I said that research into the origins and history of the breed was a fascinating and educational pastime. What I have penned is but a dot on the horizon in comparison with what could be learned by an ongoing study. I hope that this piece has whetted your appetite.

History of the Show Dog

1907–1917

Note: The date shown in brackets after a dog's name is the year in which he gained his title.

From the breed's recognition in 1907 until the outbreak of the First World War, the breed made good strides, gaining popularity, new fanciers and friends along the way. Between 1907 and 1916 West Highland White Terrier registrations totalled 3,947 with twenty-seven of those being champions.

Good dogs were difficult to come by in the early days and much of the good stock came from north of the border, from whence it originated.

The dog Conas again comes into play being the first traceable West Highland White Terrier blood and a getter of good stock. He sired five West Highland Whites of repute, three sons and two daughters. The best of all was the famous daughter Ch. Runag (1910) said to be the model of what a West Highland White should be in shape and character. The other daughter Cabaig was the dam of Brogach, described at the time as a biggish terrier with great bone and substance, moderate in colour and long enough in back. He in turn was the sire of Ch. Morven (1907). Of the three sons, Ch. Oransay (1908) was owned by the Countess of Aberdeen, and another son, Balloch Bhan, sired Am. Ch. Baughfell's Talisker and Inverailort Roy. The third son sired Ch. Highclere Rhalet and Chief of Childwick. Rhalet won seventeen CCs and was himself a prodigious sire, being responsible for three champions.

Ch. Morven, who was one of five champions owned by Colin Young, is said to have been far and away the best West Highland White of his time, both in the show ring and as a stud. Born on 28 March 1905, he won his first CC at seven and a half months of age and, in 1907 (the year he became the breed's first champion), he won five CCs. He was beaten only once during that year when Col. Malcolm judged at SKC and Morven left the ring without a card. The Countess of Aberdeen owned a Morven daughter, Ch. Cromar Snowflake (1907), and was a stalwart supporter of the breed. Atholl, a Morven son, never became a champion because of his poor colour, but proved his worth as a sire.

Many of the early show kennels exhibited both Cairns and West

Ch. Morven (1907). (Photo by Thomas Fall.)

Highland Whites, registering them according to their colour. Errington Ross was one who campaigned both breeds under the banner of Glenmohr. He won a certificate with the Cairn Glenmohr Rascal, who was by Harviestoun Raider, but was more successful with the whites. Ch. Glenmohr Model (1910), who was by Atholl, reputed to be Ch. Morven's best son, and Ch. Glenmohr Guanag (1914), both owned by Mr C. Viccars, gaining their titles. The Mercia kennel of Miss Viccars dates back to 1913, and under that name three Cairn champions were made up. Miss Viccars also held a great interest for West Highland Whites, and her Childwick kennel was very prominent in the early days. As with the two Glenmohrs and Ch. Kiltie (1909), five of the six champions to carry the kennel name were registered as being owned by Mr C. Viccars. First of those five was Ch. Rosalie of Childwick (1913); the sixth and last was Ch. Chiel of Childwick (1924), owned by Mr A.J. Warren. When the Kennel Club decided in 1924 that all interbreeding of Cairns and West Highland Whites should cease, Miss Viccars was one of the strongest opponents. About that time, she gave up her West Highland Whites and concentrated on her Cairns.

Other pre-1917 notables included Holland Buckley and his daughter Mrs Barber, who shared the success of their Ch. Scotia Chief and

17

A group of Mrs Cameron Head's prizewinners. (Photo by Thomas Fall.)

other good dogs in the Scotia kennel. Mrs Cameron Head was a great supporter, the best of her Inverailort kennel is recognized as Inverailort Roy. Mrs Lionel Portman had Ch. Swaites Cruachan holding the kennel banner and Swaites Gaisgeach to carry the Morven line at stud. Mrs Lucas did a lot of winning with her Highclere dogs. Mrs Cecil Clare bought many good dogs, including Ch. Morven, and Mr J. Campbell's Ornsay kennel at North Berwick produced many champions.

In 1916 came the first of fifty-eight champions from the Wolvey kennel, forty of these home bred, and the emergence of Mrs May Pacey whose name was to become synonymous with West Highland White Terriers worldwide. She had done some winning with Wolvey MacNab, a son of Atholl, and had made a start in the breed she was to dominate. The first champion, Ch. Wolvey Piper (1916), was bred in Skye by Simon McCloud and was joined in 1916 with a second champion, Ch. Wolvey Rhoda.

Some of the sale fees for dogs at the time are quite staggering. American interest resulted in some dogs crossing the Atlantic: Ch. Glenmohr Model, Ornsay Rhoda, Ch. Scotia Chief, Charm of Childwick, and Ch. Kiltie who was sold for £400 in 1909!

Between the Wars

From the beginning of the First World War to 1920, there were no more shows. All breeding was suspended until 1919, and because food was hard to get, many of the pioneering early kennels disbanded. At the end of the War, it was left to the few surviving kennels to pick up and start again.

Things were slow to get going, but gradually and surely they did. Mrs Lucas's Ch. Highclere Rhalet (1920) was the first champion to be made up after the war and played a big role in siring plenty of good stock, which was needed as the effects of war, lack of food and the breeding ban had seriously depleted the stocks. There were four other champions in 1920: Ch. Charming of Childwick, Ch. Highclere Romp, Ch. White Sylph and Ch. Wolvey Skylark.

Mrs Pacey felt that the breed came to its best between the First and Second World Wars and, certainly, this period saw the emergence of many new kennels who would breed and show dogs that have since become legendary. The years between the wars were the 'champagne years' for the Wolvey kennel. Of the 125 champions who gained their titles between 1920 and 1939, thirty-two were Wolveys (out of a total of fifty-eight Wolveys in all). Ch. Wolvey Patrician (1926) showed his worth in the show ring and at stud: he sired Ch. Ray of Rushmoor (1929) and was the grandsire of Ch. Wolvey Poacher (1933), who were later to be two of the most important stud-dogs of their time.

Ch. Highclere Rhalet (1920).

Ch. Wolvey Poacher (1933).
(Photo by Thomas Fall.)

Mr J. Campbell had managed to keep going, and continued to produce many good dogs, making up Ch. Ornsay Sporran in 1925.

Of the new kennels, Mrs E.H. Spottiswoode's Gwern kennels collected six champions in the 1920s. The first two of Mrs O.R.

Ch. Wolvey Prefect, Ch. Wolvey Pintail (both 1936) and Wolvey Peacock. (Photo by Thomas Fall.)

Ch. Wolvey Patrol (1927) and Ch. Wolvey Patrician (1926). (Photo by Thomas Fall.)

Williams's ten Cooden champions were Ch. Cooden Sapper and Ch. Cooden Suzanne, both made up in 1926. Ch. Clint Cocktail (1932) and Ch. Clint Cheek (1931) were regarded by many to be the best of Mrs Hewson's Clint kennel. In 1926, Mrs D.P. Allom and her Furzefield kennel came to the fore with Ch. Furzefield Patience. The next two of Mrs Allom's champions were both courtesy of Mrs Williams's breeding in Ch. Cooden Safety (1928) and Ch. Cooden Stonechat (1930) (the latter was owned in partnership with Mrs A.W. Bird). Mr and Mrs Warren's Ophir kennel had two highly successful years making up Ch. Ophir Chiel and Ch. Ophir Nancy in 1928, and following up with Ch. Ophir Rowdy (1929). That same year, Miss V.M. Smith-Wood's Ch. Ray of Rushmoor and Ch. Rita of Rushmoor headed the list of eight Rushmoor champions between 1929 and 1940. With her Brean kennel, Mrs E.O. Innes made up six champions in five years, starting in 1933 with Ch. Brean Taurie. Close sources at the time reckoned Ch. Brean Glunieman to be the best and on photographic evidence alone he looks like a dog that could do well today.

When Dude O'Petriburg was made up in 1934 it was the start of a

Ch. Clint Cheek (1932).
(Photo by Thomas Fall.)

'Heads and Tails.' Three Brean champions belonging to Mrs Innes,
1937. (Photo by Thomas Fall.)

Ch. Brean Glunieman (1934). (Photo by Robinson.)

long and fruitful association with the breed for Mrs A. Beels. Mrs Pacey's Ch. Wolvey Pintail (1936) had a show career to dream about. She was only shown three times. According to Mrs Pacey's own account, Pintail won the CC and Best of Breed at her first show, National Terrier, and then went on to Best in Show. The next day at

Ch. Phancy O' Petriburg (1961). (Photo by Thomas Fall.)

23

Ch. Wolvey Pintail (1936). (Photo by Thomas Fall.)

LKA (Ladies' Kennel Association) she did the same again, and was made up at WELKS (West of England Ladies' Kennel Society) on her third outing, this time winning only Best Bitch!

Miss A.A. Wright (no relation to the author) bred some great dogs at her Calluna kennel. Ch. Calluna Clos (1935) and Ch. Calluna Ruairidh (1937) were the first two, and the latter was the sire of Miss M. Turnbull's Ch. Leal Flurry (1938). With this dog and Ch. Leal Sterling (1938), Miss Turnbull started a long association with the breed. Both these ladies continued their interest well into my own era. I well remember Miss Turnbull sitting at the ringside at many shows, probably passing out the awards in her mind. Miss Wright gave me one of my most cherished memories when she awarded Ch. Rotella Royal Penny Reserve Best in Show and Rotella Royal Standard Reserve Best Dog, when she judged The West Highland White Terrier Club of England Show in 1979.

Mrs G. Ellis's Lynwood kennel had its first champion in Ch. Jenifer (1935), which was the start of another long association lasting well into the 1950s.

Owing to the Second World War, there were no shows from 1940 to 1946, but breeding was not banned. Although food was in short supply, some kennels managed to keep going and, once again, it would be up to them to lift the breed out of the gloom.

The Post-War Years

When war was looming many of the kennels had trimmed down their stock. Mrs Pacey had sent some dogs to Africa and America and given away many others. Other kennels had done likewise. But a few of the established kennels who had managed to keep going started again, along with an ever-increasing number of new ones.

Four new champions were made up in 1947. The Hon. Torfrida Rollo's Ch. Timoshenko of the Roe had won his first CC the previous year and was the first of seven champions bred or owned by the Kendrum kennel. Ch. Alpin of Kendrum (1962) is behind much of the breeding of today, particularly through the kennels of Birkfell and Quakertown. The first post-war champion in the breed belonged to Miss E.E. Wade. Ch. Freshney Fiametta (1947), handled by Miss Wade's father Arthur Wade, won six CCs and Best in Show All Breeds at Cambridge in 1947. Miss Wade had six champions in quick succession. Ch. Hookwood Mentor (1948) was the first to carry the kennel name and he went on to be one of the top sires.

Hookwood Irma (1947).
(Photo by Thomas Fall.)

Among the progeny who proved his worth were Ch. Barrister of Branston and Ch. Brisk of Branston (both 1950), Ch. Cruben Dextor, Ch. Hookwood Sensation and Ch. Lynwood Branston Blue (all 1951). Mrs Finch's Ch. Shiningcliff Simon (1947) was the first of nine Shiningcliffs. He was Best Terrier in Show at Cruft's 1950 and went Best in Show All Breeds at Glasgow the same year.

Mrs D. Mary Dennis's Branston kennel had been active before the Second World War and, in 1948, came Ch. Baffle of Branston the first of twenty-five Branston champions, making this kennel third in the UK all-time list. Her own favourite was the aforementioned Ch. Barrister of Branston, who was to sire ten champions. Mrs Dennis is the author of her own book *The West Highland White Terrier* (*see* Further Reading), which is on the bookshelf of every discerning owner. Her husband, the late Brunel Dennis, had the idea of compiling an album showing a photographic record of the breed going back into the nineteenth century. This album became a reality through Mr Dennis's efforts and is kept regularly updated. Mr Dennis was a former chairman of The West Highland White Terrier Club of England.

Ch. Bandsman of Branston (1960). (Original photo by C.M. Cooke.)

*Ch. Raventofts Fuschia
(1955). (Photo by Thomas
Fall.)*

Dr and Mrs Russell made up their first champion, Ch. Cruben Crystal, in 1948 and four more Cruben champions were to follow, the last in 1959. Many Crubens went abroad, particularly to America. Probably the best remembered of all is Ch. Cruben Dextor (1951), who was one of those to continue his show career in the States. Mrs Allom had made a new start making up Ch. Furzefield Pax in 1949, with Ch. Furzefield Preference (1950), Ch. Furzefield Provost (1951) and Ch. Furzefield Pilgrim (1952) following in quick succession. All these four, plus Ch. Hookwood Mentor, Champions Isla and Maree of Kendrum, Ch. Lynwood Blue Betty and Ch. Lynwood Timothy, were sired by Furzefield Piper, making him one of the most prolific untitled dogs in history. Piper, according to comment of the time, would have been a certain champion, but for losing a tooth in a fight.

Ch. Nice Fella of Wynsolot, owned by Mrs E.A. Green was Reserve Best Terrier at Cruft's 1956 and went on to sire some champions. Mrs K. Sansom's Ch. Quakertown Quality (1954) by Ch. Calluna the Poacher had been the first Quakertown champion. Ch. Alpin of Kendrum (by Quakertown Quizzical) sired Ch. Quakertown Quistador (1964) who won sixteen CCs, Terrier Groups and Best in Shows. The Quakertown breeding is very much alive today, and many of the 'northern line' exponents such as Birkfell, Erisort, Domaroy, Cregneash and my own Rotella have Mrs Sansom's breeding in their pedigrees. Mrs Sansom was a charming lady of the 'old school', a tireless worker on behalf of the breed, and a former chairman of The West Highland White Terrier Club of England, to which she was made an Honorary Life Member. To my mind, her like are sadly missed these days.

Ch. Sollershot Sun-up (1958) was one of five Sollershot champions in eight years for Mrs D.J. Kenney-Taylor before she disbanded her kennel in 1965. Her Ch. Sollershot Soloist is remembered as an outstanding dog of his time.

With their first champions in 1954 (Famecheck Lucky Charm), 1962 (Birkfell Solitaire), 1963 (Lasara Lee) and 1966 (Incheril Amaarylis), Misses Cook and Cleland, and Mrs B. Graham and Mrs E. Berry respectively, are still active today. (*See* Chapter 12.)

Mrs. G.M. Barr's Stoneygap kennel had great success starting in 1952 with Ch. Hasty Bits right through to Ch. Stoneygap Bobbin of Gillobar (owned by Mr Fraser) in 1962. Mrs M.W. Pearson has been a great supporter of the breed for many years. Ch. Rivelin Rustle

Slitrig Solitaire (1954). (Photo by Thomas Fall.)

(1958) and Ch. Rivelin Rhumba (1964) were among many notable dogs from this kennel. Mrs Pearson was, until recently, one of the longest-serving members of The West Highland White Terrier Club of England committee and a former secretary of that Club.

Miss Jeanette Herbert had her first champion Ch. Mairi of Kendrum (bred by the Hon. T. Rollo) in 1954. After many years of dedication, top professional handler Ernie Sharpe steered her Ch. Glenalwyne Sonny Boy (1975) into the record books by winning thirty-three CCs, a breed record until 1989. The same breeder and handler also had another champion in 1978 with Glenalwyne Shieldhu. Miss Herbert is the secretary of The West Highland White Terrier Club and a Championship Show judge in the breed.

Mrs J. Beer was the owner of the world-famous Whitebriar kennel. Ch. Whitebriar Jimolo (1963) was the first of many owned or home-bred champions. Francis Rundle handled Ch. Whitebriar Jonfair (1971) to huge success for owner Mr John Hodsoll. Later, in partnership with Miss Maureen Murphy, the Whitebriars were always to be seen amongst the winners. Ch. Domaroy Saraband of Whitebriar was one of two litter-brothers that dominated the show scene in 1978, the other was Ch. Domaroy Saracen. Since Mrs Beer's passing, the Whitebriar tenets have been upheld by Miss Johnson and her closely related Wistmills.

Mr and Mrs B. Thompson had four champions carrying the Waideshouse name. Ch. Waideshouse Woodpecker (1963) was typical of the great stock produced here. Mrs A. Sagar dedicated herself, it seems, to breeding lovely dogs for other people. The home-bred Ch. Rhianfa Rifleman (1964) was owned by Fred Sills the professional handler. In 1968, Mrs Estcourt made the most of another of Mrs Sagar's breeding by making up Ch. Rhianfa's Up and Coming of Estcoss, and Miss Catherine Owen of the Gaywyn kennel had a marvellous run of success with Ch. Rhianfa Take Notice in 1972.

Mrs Sylvia Kearsey has proved the worth of her Pillerton kennel on both sides of the Atlantic. Her Pillerton Pickle (by Ch. Calluna the Poacher, out of Blainey of Branston), whom she bought from Mrs Beels in 1961, produced in her first litter Ch. Pillerton Pippa (1965) who won her first CC and Best of Breed at Cruft's that year, and Ch. Pillerton Peta (1966). Also in 1966, came Ch. Pillerton Peterman, who is, as Mrs Kearsey says herself, the one that everybody remembers, and why not? He was an outstanding dog, winning nine CCs and the title of Top Dog (1966), before passing on his great virtues by siring nine English champions. The remaining three

Ch. Pillerton Peterman (1966).

Ch. Pillerton Prejudice (1973).

home-bred English champions are Ch. Pillerton Peterkin (1971), Ch. Melwyn Pillerton Picture (1972) and Ch. Pillerton Prejudice, who was one of Ch. Pillerton Peterman's best daughters, winning Best in Show at The West Highland White Terrier Club of England Show 1973. In 1975, after forming a partnership with the Biljonblue kennel with W. Ferrara and J. Price, Mrs Kearsey moved to Pennsylvania taking Champions Prejudice, Pip and an eleven-and-a-half-year-old Peterman with her. Ch. Pillerton Peterman had already sired six All Breed Best in Show winners in America, so was well known there, and he continued to do so right up to his passing at the age of thirteen. In 1983, Mrs Kearsey returned to England bringing Peterman's last son and a grandson, hopefully to continue in the same vein.

Besides owning Ch. Melwyn Pillerton Picture, the Melwyn kennel of Mr and Mrs Pritchard has bred two champions of its own: Ch. Melwyn Milly Molly Mandy and Ch. Melwyn Mastermind. I also remember another lovely one of their breeding, Melwyn Maggie May, who won umpteen Reserve CCs. Always staunch supporters of the breed, Mr and Mrs Pritchard have served or worked on behalf of The West Highland White Terrier Club of England for many years. Mrs Pritchard had the honour of judging the breed at Cruft's 1990, where her Best of Breed was Ch. Olac Moonpilot, who of course went right through to win Best in Show.

Ch. Whitebriar Jillian (1968) bred by Mrs Beer, was Mrs M. Coy's first champion. Since then Mrs Coy has bred three champions under the Cedarfell banner, the last of these in 1973. The standard-bearer for the kennel has to be Ch. Cedarfell Merry-N-Bright (1971), the only one who was bred and owned. This dog won ten CCs and was a Group and Best in Show winner. He also sired, amongst others, Ch. Glenalwyne Sonny Boy, who held the breed record for many years with thirtythree CCs.

Miss C. Owen has owned four champions in the breed. Ch. Alpingay Sonata was the first in 1968. Ch. Rhianfa Take Notice (1972) was acquired with one CC in hand at eighteen months of age, and was successfully campaigned to his title. The next two, Ch. Gaywyn Gypsy and Ch. Gaywyn Bradey of Branston were both made up in 1973 and sired by Ch. Alpingay Sonata. Miss Owen is an author and great authority on the history of the breed. Though not currently active in the show ring, she keeps well in touch and is still a great supporter.

Michael Collings now concentrates on his celebrated Welsh Ter-

Ch. Whitebriar Jolson (1987).
(Photo by Chris Kernick.)

riers, but he has made up three champions in our breed under his Purston prefix, namely: Ch. Ardenrun Andsome of Purston (1973), Ch. Purston Peter Pan (1974) and Ch. Millburn Merrymaid (1977). He also bred Ch. Purston Petite (1973) for Mr and Mrs Parr, and other CC winners. Mr Collings sent many dogs to America, which were very successful over there.

The latter part of the 1960s saw the Highstile kennel of Mr and Mrs Bertram come to the fore. Ch. Highstile Prank and Ch. Highstile Poppet (both 1967) were followed by Ch. Highstile Priceless (1969). Always breeding the same good type, Mr and Mrs Bertram exported several top-quality dogs, which went on to be top winners in their new homes. In 1982, the Highstiles made a comeback (actually they'd never been away), with Highstile Paladin who won two CCs in that year and gained his title with a further two CCs in 1983, before going on to Sweden. There, he quickly gained his Swedish title and became a notable sire. Mr Bertram finished at the pinnacle of a judge's career by awarding CCs at Cruft's in 1989. Sadly, as I write this résumé, I learn that Mr Bertram has passed away. He will leave behind the memories of a quiet, unassuming man, with a sharp wit, a wry smile, a dry sense of humour and some outstanding dogs.

The late Mrs Margaret Webster started a run of five English champions, either home bred or owned, with Ch. Kirkgordon

Morning Song in 1978. The third one Ch. Kilbranon Crispin (1982) was the only one who was home bred, but the Kilbranons were nevertheless an unmistakable type. She finished the run of champions with a flourish, when in 1987 Ch. Cameron at Kilbrannon (1986) was Best of Breed at Cruft's.

I well remember Mrs Thelma Lees making up Ch. Carillyon Cadence in 1975. The other title winner, Ch. Carillyon Caravel of Clarinch (1978), bred by Mrs Lees and owned by the late Mrs Buchanan, was a real showgirl. Carillyon Courage, I thought, was a real 'top drawer' dog. By the time he was eighteen months old he had already won two CCs and one Reserve CC and was a certain champion, but tragically he died soon after. Another one of Mrs Lees' breeding who has made a name for himself, this time at stud, is Carillyon Clancy (by Ch. Erisort Special Request, out of Ch. Caravel), owned by Mrs McDonagh. He has sired Ch. Haweswalton Merry Go Round (1989) and Ch. Haweswalton Rhapsody (1990).

Keith Hodkinson bred four English champions in the 1970s: Ch. Erisort Special Request (1974), Ch. Domaroy Erisort Serenade (1977), and Ch. Erisort Something Special and Ch. Erisort Sleighbelle (both in 1979). The latter was owned in partnerhip with Barbara Hands. He also bred litter-brothers Erisort Statesman and Erisort Senator of Ashgate (owned by Sue Thomson), both of whom won two CCs. In fact, Erisort Statesman had won his two CCs in double-quick time, when virtually overnight Keith decided to stop showing dogs. Ch. Erisort Special Request was hardly used at stud until he was eight years old, and he was infertile just over a year

Ch. Erisort Special Request (1974).

Ch. Erisort Something Special (1979).

later. However, despite his limited stud use, he sired five English champions and won the Top Stud-Dog award a few years later. Of late Keith is taking renewed interest in the breed.

Ch. Checkbar Finley MacDougal (1974). (Photo by Anne Roslin-Williams.)

Happy times. Lesley Taylor with Ch. Tervin Peregrine at Checkbar,
and Keith Hodkinson with Ch. Morenish Fanny Macdougal. Seen
after Lesley had handled both dogs to win a memorable double at
Darlington in 1978. (Photo by Mc Farlane.)

Last, but by no means least, is the Checkbar kennel. Although registered as being owned by Mrs Jean Taylor, this kennel was a family concern with daughter Lesley and father Willie in full support. Between 1969 and 1978, the Checkbars were always amongst the winners or thereabouts. Champions Checkbar Remony Rye and Donsie Kythe (both 1969) were followed by Ch. Checkbar Tommy Quite Right (1971), Ch. Finlay MacDougal (1974) and Ch. Tervin Peregrine at Checkbar (1978). In between times, Lesley handled Miss Grieve's Ch. Morenish Fanny MacDougal (by Finlay) to her title. The spirit of competition and the warmth which emanated from the 'Taylor clan' epitomized all the good things about showing dogs, which is all too often lacking these days. When tragically first Jean and, soon after, Lesley passed away, it was a great loss, not only to me personally but to the future of the breed. Lesley in particular, being only in her early twenties, had so much to offer.

2

The Breed Standard

In this chapter, I have included the current Breed Standards of the United Kingdom and the United States of America. The original UK Breed Standard of 1908 is reproduced in Appendix 1 (*see* page 250). Of these three Standards, I consider the latter two to be superior, and particularly helpful to the newcomer. I urge readers to study all three and, for interest, to make cross-references.

If taken literally, there are parts of the Standard which could easily be misconstrued. For instance, if we take the description of ears as 'small' in its literal sense, we could misinterpret this to mean the smaller the better. That is just one example and the Standard contains other such unclarified descriptions. In all cases, including the one given above, the conclusion to be reached is that the part of the dog described, must be relative to the proportions and balance of the whole dog. To help readers form a true mental picture of the various aspects of the Standard and the Standard as a whole, I would advise that they take particular care to note the punctuation and use of words or phrases, and to study the drawing of the West Highland White Terrier shown on page 42. The Standard can read quite differently if certain punctuation is ignored: descriptions can be exaggerated or taken out of context if the reader is vague about the relevant points and construction.

The UK Breed Standard

(Reproduced by permission of the Kennel Club of Great Britain)

General Appearance

Strongly built; deep in chest and back ribs; level back and powerful quarters on muscular legs and exhibiting in a marked degree a great combination of strength and activity.

Characteristics

Small, active, game, hardy, possessed of no small amount of self-esteem with a varminty appearance.

Temperament

Alert, gay, courageous, self-reliant but friendly.

Head and Skull

Skull slightly domed; when handled across the forehead presents a smooth contour. Tapering very slightly from skull at level of ears to eyes. Distance from occiput to eyes slightly greater than length of foreface. Head thickly coated with hair, and carried at right angles, or less, to axis of neck. Head not to be carried in extended position. Foreface gradually tapering from eye to muzzle. Distinct stop formed by heavy, bony ridges immediately above and slightly overhanging eye, and slight indentation between eyes. Foreface not dished nor falling away quickly below eyes, where it is well made up. Jaws strong and level. Nose black and fairly large, forming smooth contour with rest of muzzle. Nose not projecting forward.

Eyes

Set wide apart, medium in size, not full, as dark as possible. Slightly sunk in head, sharp and intelligent, which, looking from under heavy eyebrows, impart a piercing look. Light coloured eyes highly undesirable.

Ears

Small, erect and carried firmly, terminating in sharp point, set neither too wide nor too close. Hair short and smooth (velvety), should not be cut. Free from any fringe at top. Round-pointed, broad, large or thick ears or too heavily coated with hair most undesirable.

Mouth

As broad between canine teeth as is consistent with varminty

37

expression required. Teeth large for size of dog, with regular scissor bite, i.e. upper teeth closely overlapping the lower teeth and set square to the jaws.

Neck

Sufficiently long to allow proper set on of head required, muscular and gradually thickening towards base allowing neck to merge into nicely sloping shoulders.

Forequarters

Shoulders sloping backwards. Shoulder blades broad and lying close to chest wall. Shoulder joint placed forward, elbows well in, allowing foreleg to move freely, parallel to axis of body. Forelegs short and muscular, straight and thickly covered with short, hard hair.

Body

Compact. Back level, loins broad and strong. Chest deep and ribs well arched in upper half presenting a flattish side appearance. Back ribs of considerable depth and distance from last rib to quarters as short as compatible with free movement of body.

Hindquarters

Strong, muscular and wide across top. Legs short, muscular and sinewy. Thighs very muscular and not too wide apart. Hocks bent and well set in under body so as to be fairly close to each other when standing or moving. Straight or weak hocks most undesirable.

Feet

Forefeet larger than hind, round, proportionate in size, strong, thickly padded and covered with short harsh hair. Hindfeet are smaller and thickly padded. Under surface of pads and all nails preferably black.

Tail

5 to 6 inches long, covered with harsh hair, no feathering, as straight as possible, carried jauntily, not gay or carried over back. A long tail undesirable, and on no account should tails be docked.

Gait/Movement

Free, straight and easy all round. In front legs freely extended forward from shoulder. Hind movement free, strong and close. Stifle and hocks well flexed and hocks drawn under body giving drive. Stiff, stilted movement behind and cow hocks highly undesirable.

Coat

Double coated. Outer coat consists of harsh hair, about 5 cms (2 ins) long, free from any curl. Undercoat, which resembles fur, short, soft and close. Open coats most undesirable.

Colour

White.

Size

Height at withers approximately 28 cms (11 ins).

Faults

Any departure from the foregoing points should be considered a fault and the seriousness with which the fault should be regarded should be in exact proportion to its degree.

NOTE Male animals should have two apparently normal testicles fully descended into the scrotum.

Scale of Points

General appearance and size .... 20 points
Coat and colour .... 10 points
Skull .... 5 points
Eyes .... 5 points
Muzzle and Teeth .... 15 points
Ears .... 5 points
Neck .... 5 points
Body .... 10 points
Legs and Feet .... 10 points
Tail .... 5 points
Movement .... 10 points

TOTAL ..... 100 points

There is no easy way of understanding the Breed Standard and being able to relate that understanding to a particular dog or dogs; it comes with experience and involvement in the breed. Over a period of time (which differs in length from person to person) you will develop 'a feel' for the breed, so that you will be able to make an evaluation, to a great extent almost subconsciously. From this point on, given that the appetite for learning is there, you can increase your knowledge and understanding, and the application of it. The more experience you gain the more likely you are to have a better perception of the Standard in relation to the dogs you show, breed and judge. For all aspects of the 'dog game' involve a continuous learning process, and if you can truly accept this fact then you are sure to reappraise your beliefs, however slightly, as your knowledge, experience and understanding develops. There are those who will never admit to changing any of their views and think that it is somehow important that they do not, but this is the attitude of the closed mind, and I would dismiss it, for there is always more to learn!

Fortunately, there is a wealth of knowledge to be gleaned from the Breed Standard, even by the novice. There are parts which are very specific and other parts which are not so, and these are commonly referred to as grey areas. It is generally within these grey areas that differing interpretations are to be found, although there are some who seek to change even the specific parts to suit their own mistaken beliefs or the stock they own. (These mistaken beliefs will be dealt with in the section on interpretation, *see* below.)

I have always felt that such rewriting of the Standard is quite wrong, for the Standard, albeit the revised version, was written by the founders of the West Highland White Terrier before I and almost anyone else as far as I know, were born, and it will be here as a word picture of the perfect specimen long after us all.

When the Kennel Club last revised the Standard in 1986, they sought to streamline the text by leaving out unnecessary words and restructuring other parts. Some of the changes are regrettable in that they have resulted in the omission of some of the specific features and descriptive language, which helped the reader to conjure up that mental picture of the perfect West Highland White. The perfect specimen has yet to be born, and it is towards this goal that we all strive. One of the measurements of our success should be how close, in our own honest judgement, we can come to this perfection.

After studying the Standard, it should be noticed that the West Highland White Terrier is a breed without exaggeration: not one part of the dog is overdone in any way. We are, of course, making our judgements on the dogs of the present day with all the fashions and fads of trimming and presentation, and so on, but we should still be comparing the dog in question to that perfect dog contained within the Standard.

Another very important point to be borne in mind is the original use of the breed, as a catcher and killer of otter, badger and vermin supreme and the natural habitat of his origin in the uncompromising weather and terrain of the West Highlands of Scotland. For no matter what variation of *haute coiffure* is in fashion, the breed must always possess the capability to be that same intelligent, game, hardy type of the working terrier.

Interpretation of the UK Breed Standard

That each individual has a different perception of the same Standard is accepted. Without this difference of opinion there would be little point in dog shows, for the same dogs would carry off all the prizes, although if everyone was in agreement the breed as a whole would probably be more consistent. However, I do not think the views of the knowledgeable and experienced are so diverse. That may sound contradictory, but when conversing with some that seemingly hold

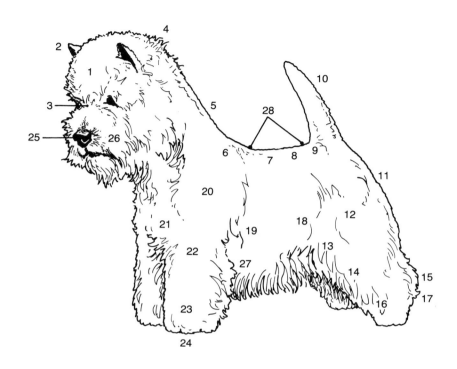

The points of a dog.

1. Skull.	11. Buttocks.	21. Brisket.
2, Ears.	12. First thigh.	22. Forearm.
3. Junction of skull and muzzle (stop).	13. Stifle.	23. Pastern.
4. Occiput.	14. Second thigh.	24. Toes.
5. Neck.	15. Point of hock.	25. Nostrils/nose.
6. Withers.	16. Pastern.	26. Muzzle.
7. Saddle.	17. Hock.	27. Point of elbow.
8. Loin.	18. Flank.	28. Topline of back.
9. Croup.	19. Rib-cage.	
10. Tail or stern.	20. Shoulder.	

different views, it is quite often the case that, minor differences apart, broad agreement is reached.

The great danger for the breed is the way some individuals express views, which sometimes leads the listener or reader into mistaken beliefs. This is particularly true of judges' critiques, when, in their wish to write something new or highly congratulatory, they use fancy rhetoric which not only exaggerates some positive point of the dog (which needs no exaggeration), but hinders rather than helps the reader's appreciation of the dog in question.

During the course of this interpretation, and the book as a whole, I shall try to highlight some of these points and the fallacies they have promulgated.

Head and Skull

Some breeds have become known as 'head breeds' because to a great extent the importance of the head takes precedence over all other parts of the dog. Thankfully, this is not and, it is hoped, never will be the case in our breed. Nevertheless, the head of a West Highland White Terrier is very important, and one of the areas that causes most confusion, over-exaggeration, misunderstanding and misintepretation for exhibitors, breeders and judges alike.

We are looking for a broad, smooth, *slightly* domed skull (not big domed or apple-headed), that tapers *slightly* from the ear to the eye and *gradually* along the foreface from the eye to the muzzle.

'Distance from occiput to eyes *slightly* greater than length of foreface.' To know these relative distances you have to be sure of the starting and finishing points. The position of the eyes is obvious; the occiput is the lump at the back of the head where the vertebral column joins the skull, not, as one well-known Championship Show breed specialist judge once told me, the forehead! So from the occiput to the eyes is a bit longer than the rest of the foreface. A common misinterpretation is that the muzzle should be short or the shorter the better; not so. If you go down that road with your breeding, you will encourage bad mouths, because as you over-shorten the foreface or muzzle, there is less space for all the teeth to fit, which results in a cramped mouth and misplaced teeth. The breed should be neither long-nosed (dolichocephalic) nor short-nosed (brachycephalic), but fall between those two (mesocephalic).

'Distinct stop.' These two words cause more problems of interpretation than any other I can think of. From time to time, in critiques, you will read 'Deep stop', and even worse, 'Deepest of stops'. The latter implies the deeper the better, which again is quite wrong. The Kennel Club definition of 'stop' is: 'The step up from muzzle to skull; indentation between the eyes where the nasal bone and skull meet'. On a good head, the stop should be clearly perceptible (the Standard says 'distinct', which means the same). That does not mean that the head should have a stop rising like a cliff-wall or that the skull should overhang. The term 'stop' is used to define the place where the saggital crest (foreface) ends and the skull outline drops down to the nasal bones, and is so used in many other breeds, such as the Rough Collie (which to the layman appears to have no stop, although in fact its Standard says that it should). This 'stop' is formed by the heavy, bony ridges above and slightly overhanging the eye, not the area between the eyes. To get a better impression of this, just feel your own eyebrows, which are heavy, bony ridges. 'And a *slight* indentation *between* the eyes.' Much of this indentation can be felt as a groove which runs vertically between the eyes, formed by the nasal bones and the zygomatic arches. The lowest point of this indentation is where it meets the skull and this is, presumably, the exact point of the stop.

If our breed were to have a deep stop or if breeders were to follow the 'deepest of stops' implication, and breed for a deeper stop, the true expression of the breed, so apparent in a good head, would be lost and the breed would display a Pointer or Boxer stop, with a dished face, totally altering the expression, which is abhorrent to any serious West Highland White Terrier fancier.

In fact the foreface should be well made up, rather than falling away. Often the strength in the foreface will come with age and maturity, but even young puppies should not be what could be described as 'weak' in this area, for it would give a snipy appearance.

The nose should be black and will be faulted if it is not, unlike the nails and pads, where the Standard says 'preferably black'. The nose should be 'fairly large', but not ridiculously so, and it must stay in proportion. Although it says 'nose not projecting forward', the nose does extend beyond the end of the muzzle, but only very slightly.

In concluding the interpretation of this very important part of the Standard, I would urge you to remember that the West Highland White is a breed without exaggeration; bear in mind his original use and let these points be the basis for your own better judgement.

Eyes

That the eyes should be set wide apart lends more importance to the need for good width in the skull and a strong muzzle in order that the eyes may be so placed. And if the heavy, bony ridges are evident in the correct degree, the eyes will have that 'slightly sunken' appearance that can be complemented by the heavy eyebrows. No colour is given for the eyes, which are described as 'as dark as possible', in the original Standard (1908), it recommended dark hazel and there lies the clue: dark hazel, the darker the better. Similarly, in the current Standard, there is no guide to the shape of the eye, which should be almond-shaped. Dark eye-rims are not always seen these days, but when they are present they complement a good eye and add that little bit more definition to the whole expression, which could be vital in the show ring. Any serious deviation from these points, such as round, full (bulging), or light eyes (light hazel, amber or yellow), should be penalized in proportion to its degree.

The eyes are one of the major components necessary to give the desired expression. The Standard says 'sharp and intelligent, which . . . impart a piercing look'. Whilst this correctly describes the desired expression, add to this alert, excited, happy, courageous, and perhaps you will have a better understanding. The eyes can say so much, but you will agree that all these adjectives and more would describe the mixture of emotions that combine to help give the required 'varminty' (mischievous) expression so desired, often seen, and always admired in the West Highland White Terrier.

Ears

Equally important to the overall expression are the ears, which should be relatively small, but in proportion with the particular head on which they are placed and with the dog overall. Ears that look correct and in balance on one dog may not be quite so well suited to another and vice versa, although both sets would be perfectly acceptable within the Standard. Over-large, thick, broad and misplaced ears spoil an otherwise good head and expression; they are easily noticed and should be guarded against. Black or dark skin pigmentation inside the ear has always been regarded as preferable and certainly adds a further touch of quality. The hair on the top of the ears is trimmed to give a sharp-pointed, inverted V-

correct ear-set

set on too high
(pixie-eared)

Ear placement.

set on too low (donkey-eared)

shape. They should be placed correctly on the top outer edge of the skull, carried firmly and pricked up, alert with expectation; good ears used properly put the finish on a good head and expression.

Mouth

Remembering its original working use, it is no wonder that the breed evolved to have a broad mouth with teeth that are large for its size. If the teeth were smaller, the capacity for killing its quarry would be that much more diminished. Narrower in mouth and muzzle and the teeth would become cramped and possibly misplaced. A full complement of teeth is forty-two, which are made up as

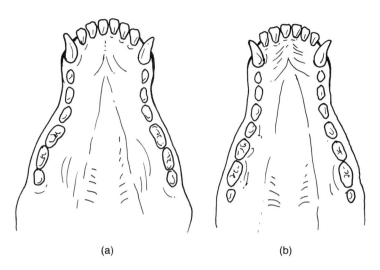

(a) Top jaw: six incisors, two canines, six premolars, six molars (total
of twenty teeth). (b) Bottom jaw: six incisors, two canines, eight
premolars, six molars (total of twenty-two teeth).

illustrated in the drawing above. In the UK, less importance is
placed on the number of molars and premolars than on the teeth at
the front of the mouth (the incisors and canines), which should have
the correct 'scissor bite': top incisors should tightly overlap the
lower incisors, with the canine teeth interlocking.

In Europe and Scandinavia, they will tolerate no more than four
molars or premolars missing; any more than this and the dog
(however good a specimen he might be apart from this), is either not
eligible for show or penalized to such a degree that the chances of
winning anything are remote. Germany in particular views any
missing teeth very seriously.

On the subject of molars and premolars only, I accept that teeth
are an important aspect of the dog, but it is one amongst many. It is
a much-written fact that many of the present-day wolves in the wild
do not now have full mouths. The change in environment and
feeding habits seem to have set evolution in motion, removing the
need for these teeth. As the wolf is the forerunner to the domestic
dog, is it fair to insist that all these show dogs, which have been
domesticated for a century or more, must have forty-two teeth?

47

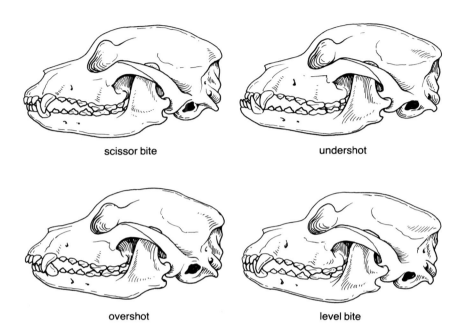

scissor bite   undershot

overshot   level bite

Types of bite.

It seems so obviously wrong that a dog who is inferior in many other ways can be placed over a better dog by virtue of his possessing an extra molar or premolar. Surely judgement should be based on the strengths and failings of each dog when compared to the Standard, with each fault or virtue being viewed in proportion to its degree.

Black lips and gums, although no longer stipulated in the Standard, are still good to see; they add definition and a further touch of quality to the mouth as a whole.

To my mind, one of the major omissions in the current Standard is the lack of a definite number of incisors. With no guide, it could be argued that five incisors between the canines are acceptable – heaven forbid! Of course, those with past experience know that there should be six incisors between the canines in both the top and lower jaws, but the exclusion of that information may lead to a different interpretation in years to come.

Neck

The neck should be sufficiently long to allow the proper, proud head carriage, but not so long that it looks exaggerated (swan-necked). Too long a neck is almost, but not quite, as bad as too short a neck, which gives the appearance of stuffiness and is most likely to be the result of upright shoulder placement. Strong and muscular, the neck should gradually thicken towards the base, where it should merge almost imperceptibly with the shoulders.

Forequarters

If any one part of a West Highland White Terrier claimed more importance than the rest, it would surely be the forequarters, because as a whole, the correctness of this part affects so many other parts. Without good forequarters, the construction of the dog is bound to be wrong elsewhere, restrict movement and seriously affect the overall general appearance.

The shoulder blades should slope backwards and, where they meet the backbone, should be well-knitted in, but not quite touching. They should lie close to the chest wall with the elbows well-tucked in, so that when running a hand from behind the ears down to the back, they should allow a smooth transition with little, if any, feel of disjointedness. I agree with Mrs D. Mary Dennis, who in her book on the breed says the best description of shoulders she ever heard was from Dr Russell of Cruben fame who maintained that 'good shoulders resembled more nearly the neck of a champagne bottle than that of a beer bottle.'

The joint of the scapula and humerus should be placed forward, almost at a right angle so that the legs are placed under the body in a direct line with the shoulder blades, allowing a correct, long, free stride. You may see from time to time dogs being 'stacked up' in the show ring with the forelegs placed forward like a rocking horse. This is either a fault of the handler's or an attempt to cover a fault in the dog; it is, of course, incorrect.

The correct depth and width of the chest between the forelegs (brisket) varies with age. Puppies and young stock may not have fully developed here, particularly in depth, which comes with maturity. Usually as the dog matures it will fall in brisket to the required depth, which is roughly in line with the elbow. Width is more difficult to ascertain and will depend again on the overall

1. Scapula or
   shoulder blade.
2. Humerus.
3. Radius.
4. Ulna.

Correct shoulder placement (layback).

proportions and balance of the dog. Nevertheless it is very important. Too wide here and the dog would not be able to carry out its working function, following its quarry into the cracks and crevices of the great boulders of its native terrain. Too narrow in front and there would not be sufficient room in the chest for the size of heart and lungs needed for stamina, and the all-important gameness would be reduced. As a general rule, I like to be able to place the four-finger width of my hand between the front legs: either a close or slightly loose fit I find correct; anything much more spacious is too wide, anything much tighter or cramped is too shallow.

The forelegs should be as straight as possible. The Standard says 'straight', but that in itself is slightly misleading because the shape of bones and joints in the leg decide its straightness, so 'as straight as possible' is a clearer definition. That said, I am giving no credence to crookedness in the forelegs, which should be penalized to its degree. The forelegs should have strong, round bone of good

50

1. Scapula or
   shoulder blade.
2. Humerus.
3. Radius.
4. Ulna.

Incorrect shoulder placement. Too straight (upright).

substance but not overdone, because if this is apparent throughout the dog, he will look coarse and heavy. Neither should the bone be so light that it makes the dog look weak and shelly. Viewed from all angles, the foreleg should be vertical and perpendicular to the body. When presented in the show ring the forelegs are best described as looking like shirt sleeves. Serious faults here include: too wide or narrow, Queen Anne (fiddle) front, feet turning out or in, bowed front, out at the elbows. The forelegs should be free and move parallel to the axis of the body so that when moving in a straight line and viewed from the rear, it is not possible to see beyond the hindquarters to the shoulders.

Faults in the forequarters can have a consequential effect on other parts of the dog: if the shoulders are upright, the neck will probably be shorter, the back longer, the head carriage could be affected and the length of stride will be shorter giving rise to a pit-a-pat, stilted movement. Excessive width or narrowness in front will be easily

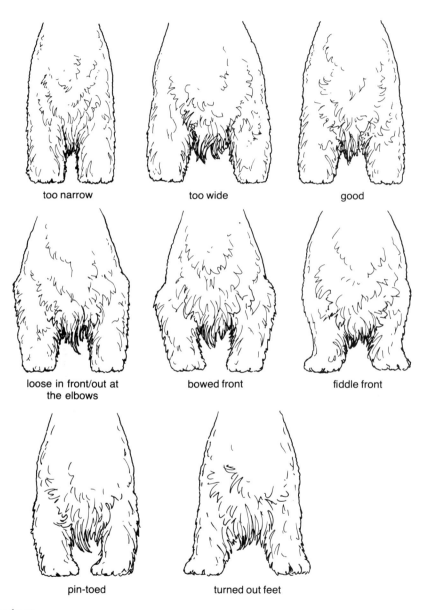

too narrow   too wide   good

loose in front/out at   bowed front   fiddle front
the elbows

pin-toed   turned out feet

The front.

seen. The fault referred to as 'out at the elbows' may cause a looseness in the front and in the movement. Any seriously mis-shaphen forelegs will be easily seen and detract from the dog both when standing and moving.

Body

When standing in front of, and looking down on to, the dog, the body area from the shoulder to the tail should be wedge-shaped. This shape is derived from the combination of the closely fitting shoulder blades, the ribs, which are well-arched in the upper half only, and then flatten out down the sides of the dog (if you picture the shape of a magnet, that would give you a guide), and the broad loins. You may see the ribcage described as 'big-ribbed' or 'big spring of rib' or even 'barrel-ribbed', all of which are completely wrong in a West Highland White Terrier. As a minimum, the depth of the chest should extend to the elbow, the back ribs, again, should have plenty of depth, and the distance from the last rib to the upper thigh should be as short as possible without affecting the free movement of the body, thus making the loin short. When assessing the length of back, it should be remembered that even though the dog may have a good shoulder placement and correct tailset, ribs that are too short will make the loin longer, so that the dog still appears long in back. One of the first and easily remembered things we learn is that the breed should have a short back, so it is surprising that the Standard has never said 'short-backed'. What it does say is 'compact', the definition of which is closely or neatly packed together; dense, solid. The two are not quite the same, which will help to explain how the term 'short-backed' can be misconstrued. Short back does not mean the shorter the better, for the elements of proportion, balance, type and size should be consi-dered when making this judgement. What may look short in one dog may not be quite so in another; everything is relative.

Hindquarters

The hindquarters should have enough width across the top to give the desired 'wedge shape'; without the necessary width the body will look narrower and longer, in show parlance 'like a milk bottle'. 'Thighs very muscular' means well-pronounced and hard to the touch. The same applies to the second thigh, which, although smaller, should be just as well-defined, a point that is often over-looked. A good turn of stifle defines a bent and well-flexed hock that is set under the body ready to push the dog off into movement (*see* Gait/Movement).

Feet

Poor feet can spoil a dog in more than just the appearance of the foot itself; it can affect posture and movement. Forefeet are larger than the hind ones, but all should be round in shape and tight, like a cat's foot. All too commonly seen these days are weak pasterns giving a flat-footed appearance and consequent loss in the spring of step. The pads of the feet should be thick to give a good cushion to the legs and feet; remembering the original use of the breed and the fact that it is an active dog, good padding is essential. Black pigmentation of pads and nails is preferred and along with good all-round pigmentation should be striven for, but here it is not a serious fault. From time to time, even a dog with the best of pigmentation will lose some colour, quite often in winter, but also if he is not in the peak of condition.

Tail

'5 to 6 inches long (13 to 15 cms)'. When standing alert with tail erect, the tip of the tail should be level with the top of the head between the ears, or slightly lower. There should be no excess hair

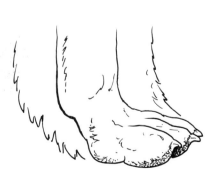
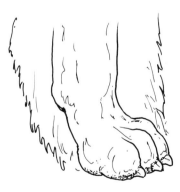

incorrect: flat, weak foot   correct: tight, cat foot

The feet.

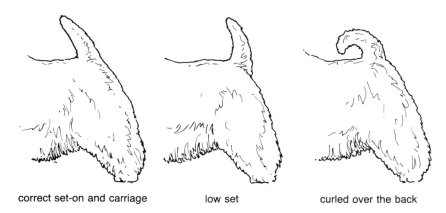

| correct set-on and carriage | low set | curled over the back |

Tail set.

on a tail when it is correctly trimmed to be 'carrot-shaped' which is in keeping with its formation of being thicker at the root and gradually tapering to its point. As straight as possible, carried confidently either straight up or slightly toward the head, but not over the back. The set-on should be in line with the spine. Tails that are low set, thin, too long or too short, twisted or bent, carried low or over the back should be frowned upon and penalized in proportion to their degree.

Gait/Movement

This is one of the main areas of disagreement within the fancy and one that is more open to personal opinion than most. One regularly sees a particular dog's movement described in a critique as 'excellent', 'terrific', 'super', and so on, and having been at the ringside and watched the dog move, one wonders if the judge was looking at the same dog – such is the difference in assessment.

The Standard says 'free, straight and easy all round' and I feel that a well-constructed dog who is showing himself off with a willingness to go, is apparent to all. The forelegs should be freely extended giving a pattern in the length and force of stride to the remainder of the dog. If there is a fault in the shoulder placement, such as exaggerated uprightness, the dog will be 'tied at the shoulder' which will restrict the length and, possibly, the shape of stride in the foreleg. The hindquarters are the 'engine room' and should

55

display such power that when the stride begins from a position close under the body, with the hocks well-flexed, they will propel the dog forward with noticeable force. Many find the 'close' description of movement confusing, particlarly when dogs are downgraded for moving too close. In years gone by, I for one have questioned some of the more experienced fanciers on this point with conflicting replies. After much thought, over a long period of time, my conclusion is that the West Highland White Terrier hind action will incline to a closer movement, in comparison with the wider 'leg at each corner' look of some of the other terrier breeds, such as the Wire Fox Terrier or Lakeland Terrier, whose movement would be quite wrong in our breed, making the dog look awkward and restricted. This closeness should never be confused with allowing touching of the hocks or, worse, crossing of the hind legs. Much depends on the pace at which the dog moves: if   is too slow, it is difficult to note the extension, power or propulsion; too fast and the legs tend more to the centre of gravity (this is described as single-tracking). When on the move, the back should remain level at all times. One of the more common faults, which is heavily penalized, is the crossing over of the legs either in front or behind, or both; this is termed 'plaiting' or 'weaving'.

Two actions which are mistakenly accepted as being correct are the 'hackney' step in the forelegs, which may to some look attractive but in fact does not allow the necessary extension in front, and more commonly, a high lifting action at the end of the stride in the hind legs, which again may look impressive but is an over-exaggeration and a waste of energy to the dog.

In essence, when a good dog is seen moving well it will display that impression of fluency, strength, power and activity with an apparently effortless combination of its attributes.

Coat and Colour

The crowning glory, rarely seen to perfection, and in the show dog at least, requiring many hours of time and effort. There are very few who can reach the dizzy heights, even with an outstanding dog, if the coat is not in good order. The outer coat is harsh and kept about 2in (5cm) long. I would advise all to consult a tape measure to see exactly how long 2in (5cm) are, and bear in mind that measurement of the coat is taken from where the hair breaks through the skin to its very tip. I stress this point because there is much debate concern-

56

ing the 'modern' way of trimming and the assertion that coats are too short. Sometimes they are, but in the main I have seen little evidence to support the argument that this is a growing trend. The undercoat (which resembles fur) is equally important both for protection against inclement weather and also in the show ring, as it combines with the outer coat and helps knit together the so desired close-fitting jacket. The hair on the head, legs and undercarriage is longer, and on the head softer without being fluffy or resembling cotton wool. In the 1986 Standard, the description of the coat changed from 'hard' to 'harsh'. This has caused consternation to many, but for myself I think it is no bad move as long as we observe the change for what it is and do not allow it to justify acceptance of soft coats.

The colour, as described in the very name of the breed, is white, although you may come across a small degree of wheaten or light-brown top coat from time to time. Quite often, this is a result of over-zealous trimming, occasionally a result of an incorrect diet, or it can be hereditary. In the first two instances, this coat colour may have just shown itself in a dog who has hitherto had a lovely white coat, and it can be relatively easily corrected by careful light trimming or changing the diet, depending on the cause. In the last instance, the coat colour, because of its inherent nature, will probably have been apparent throughout the dog's life and will continue to be so. However, depending on the seriousness of the colouring, improvement can be made with very careful trimming and presentation. (*See* Chapter 8, page 147.) I would hold that a dog with a double coat of the correct texture with some slight colouration or wheaten tipping would always take preference over a dog of equal quality with a soft, fluffy coat which is abhorrent to the breed.

Size

I am not a size fanatic. The Standard says 'about 11 inches (28 cms) at the withers', which gives a degree of latitude. Again we come back to proportion, balance, type, and the overall quality displayed. Personally I do not think we have a size problem in the breed: we see a few that are too big and coarse and equally some that are small and weedy, but by and large the size of dogs in the show ring today comes within the parameters described in the Standard. Over the years, I have noticed that almost subconsciously and collectively the exhibitors and breeders say to themselves that the breed is getting too big or too small, and in the following years the trend will be in the opposite direction, but still within the parameters of the Standard. Just pose yourself a hypothetical question: you have a choice of two dogs, the first of top quality but a touch big or small, the second is good for size but mediocre in make and shape. Which one would you choose? My experience has shown that it is difficult to do well with a male that is under 11in (28cm) as they do not seem to find favour; bitches, however, do find favour at the smaller end of the scale, provided always that they have quality, not only in the finer points of construction, but in good bone and substance. It would seem, therefore, that the males at the smaller end of the scale are not acceptable, and it is a fact that we refer to an outstanding male specimen as a 'stallion type' and that the smaller ones do not fit into that category. Likewise, bitches that are at the higher end of the acceptable height scale often have a difficult passage to attain success at the top level, the reason being that they sometimes lose some of their femininity and take on a doggy look. These are, of course, generalizations and there are many exceptions to the rule.

In a nutshell, my opinion is that, unless the dog is massively tall or minutely small, as long as he has quality in good proportion, type, balance, showmanship, and style, he should be good enough for the show ring, and perhaps amongst the winners.

The American Breed Standard

(Reproduced by kind permission of the American Kennel Club)

General Appearance

The West Highland White Terrier is a small, game, well-balanced hardy looking terrier, exhibiting good showmanship, possessed with no small amount of self-esteem, strongly built, deep in chest and back ribs, with a straight back and powerful hindquarters on muscular legs, and exhibiting in marked degree a great combination of strength and activity. The coat is about two inches long, white in color, hard, with plenty of soft undercoat. The dog should be neatly presented, the longer coat on the back and sides, trimmed to blend into the shorter neck and shoulder coat. Considerable hair is left around the head to act as a frame for the face to yield a typical Westie expression.

Size, Proportion, Substance

The ideal size is eleven inches at the withers for dogs and ten inches for bitches. A slight deviation is acceptable. The Westie is a compact dog, with good balance and substance. The body between the withers and the root of the tail is slightly shorter than the height at the withers. Short-coupled and well boned. *Faults*: Over or under height limits. Fine boned.

Head

Shaped to present a round appearance from the front. Should be in proportion to the body. **Expression** Piercing, inquisitive, pert. **Eyes** Widely set apart, medium in size, almond-shaped, dark brown in color, deep set, sharp and intelligent. Looking from under heavy eyebrows, they give a piercing look. Eye rims are black. *Faults*: Small, full or light colored eyes. **Ears** Small, carried tightly erect, set wide apart, on the top outer edge of the skull. They terminate in a sharp point, and must never be cropped. The hair on the ears is trimmed short and is smooth and velvety, free of fringe at the tips. Black skin pigmentation is preferred. *Faults*: Round-pointed, broad, large, ears set closely together, not held tightly erect, or placed too low on the side of the head. **Skull** Broad, slightly longer than muzzle, not flat on top but slightly domed between the ears, it gradually tapers to the eyes. There is a defined stop, eyebrows are heavy. *Faults*: Long or narrow skull. **Muzzle** Blunt, slightly shorter than the skull, powerful and gradually tapering to the nose, which is large and black. The jaws are level and powerful. Lip pigment is black. *Faults*: Muzzle longer than skull. Nose color other than black. **Bite** The teeth are large for the size of the dog. There must be six incisor teeth between the canines of both lower and upper jaws. An occasional missing premolar is acceptable. A tight scissor bite with upper incisors slightly overlapping the lower incisors or level mouth is equally acceptable. *Faults*: Teeth defective or misaligned. Any incisors missing or several premolars missing. Teeth overshot or undershot.

Neck, Topline, Body

Neck Muscular and well set on sloping shoulders. The length of neck should be in proportion to the remainder of the dog. *Faults*:

Neck too long or too short. **Topline** Flat and level, both standing and moving. *Faults*: High rear, any deviation from above. **Body** Compact and of good substance. Ribs deep and well arched in the upper half of rib, extending at least to the elbows, and presenting a flattish side appearance. Back ribs of considerable depth, and distance from last rib to upper thigh as short as compatible with free movement of the body. Chest very deep and extending to the elbows, with breadth in proportion to the size of the dog. Loin short, broad and strong. *Faults*: Back weak, either too long or too short. Barrel ribs, ribs above elbows. **Tail** Relatively short, with good substance, and shaped like a carrot. When standing erect it is never extended above the top of the skull. It is covered with hard hair without feather, as straight as possible, carried gaily but not curled over the back. The tail is set on high enough so that the spine does not slope down to it. The tail is never docked. *Faults*: Set too low, long, thin, carried at half-mast, or curled over back.

Forequarters

Angulation, Shoulders Shoulder blades are well laid back and well knit at the backbone. The shoulder blade should attach to an upper arm of moderate length, and sufficient angle to allow for definite body overhang. *Faults*: Steep or loaded shoulders. Upper arm too short or too straight. **Legs** Forelegs are muscular and well boned, relatively short, but with sufficient length to set the dog up so as not to be too close to the ground. The legs are reasonably straight, and thickly covered with short hard hair. They are set in under the shoulder blades with definite body overhang before them. Height from elbows to withers and elbow to ground should be approximately the same. *Faults*: Out at elbows, light boned, fiddle-front. **Feet** Forefeet are larger than the hind ones, are round, proportionate in size, strong, thickly padded; they may properly be turned out slightly. Dewclaws may be removed. Black pigmentation is most desirable on pads of all feet and nails, although nails may lose coloration in older dogs.

Hindquarters

Angulation Thighs are very muscular, well angulated, not set wide apart, with hock well bent, short, and parallel when viewed from the rear. **Legs** Rear legs are muscular and relatively short and sinewy. *Faults*: Weak hocks, long hocks, lack of angulation. Cow hocks. **Feet** Hind feet are smaller than front feet, and are thickly padded. Dewclaws may be removed.

Coat

Very important and seldom seen to perfection. Must be double-coated. The head is shaped by plucking the hair, to present the round appearance. The outer coat consists of straight hard white hair, about two inches long, with shorter coat on neck and shoulders, properly blended and trimmed to blend shorter areas into furnishings, which are longer on stomach and legs. The ideal coat is hard, straight and white, but a hard straight coat which may have some wheaten tipping is preferable to a white fluffy or soft coat. Furnishings may be somewhat softer and longer but should never give the appearance of fluff. *Faults*: Soft coat. Any silkiness or tendency to curl. Any open or single coat, or one which is too short.

Color

The color is white, as defined by the breed's name. *Faults*: Any coat color other than white. Heavy wheaten color.

Gait

Free, straight, and easy all around. It is a distinctive gait, not stilted, but powerful, with reach and drive. In front the leg is freely extended forward by the shoulder. When seen from the front the legs do not move square, but tend to move toward the centre of gravity. The hind movement is free, strong and fairly close. The hocks are freely flexed and drawn close under the body, so that when moving off the foot the body is thrown or pushed forward with some force. Overall ability to move is usually best evaluated from the side, and topline remains level. *Faults*: Lack of reach in front, and/or drive behind. Stiff, stilted or too wide movement.

Temperament

Alert, gay, courageous and self-reliant, but friendly. *Faults*: Excess timidity or excess pugnacity.

Approved 13 December 1988; effective 1 February 1989.

Interpretation of the American Standard

Where necessary, any interpretation, explanation, comment or advice can be found in the interpretation of the UK Breed Standard (*see* pages 41–58); we are after all discussing the same breed of dog. Suffice it for me to reiterate my earlier comment that in my opinion the American Breed Standard is superior to the UK Breed Standard because it contains almost everything I would want from what is supposed to be a word picture.

After studying this Standard, I should like to make the following observations. It says '. . . the nose, which is large and black'. I would be happier with the UK definition 'fairly large', or words to that effect.

The description for both forelegs and hind legs is 'relatively short', which I find a little vague. Relatively short in comparison to what? I presume it means to the rest of the dog, but even that allows plenty of latitude.

The length of tail, again, is given as 'relatively short' and begs the same question. It goes on to give a guide to length in '. . . never extended above the top of the skull', but gives no indication of how much shorter than the top of the skull is acceptable. Again, I would be happier with an approximate measurement.

These are the only criticisms I would make, and they are very minor ones at that, apart from the fact that the Standard keeps making reference to a dog called a 'Westie', and yes, it is in just as common use in the UK as it is around the world. Personally I hate it. What's wrong with West Highland White Terrier?

However, the credits of this Standard are manifold. I have heard critics say that it dwells too much on the presentation of the dog, but after studying it at some length, I do not agree. The guides to presentation do not replace any part of the Standard, which in itself is very comprehensive, but is added information. This may have been frowned upon in days gone by, but in the modern era it is certainly acceptable. The rest of the Standard contains much descriptive language and goes a long way to filling the gaps which lead to misunderstandings. I find the description of gait and coat particularly illuminating.

3

Owning a West Highland White Terrier

Before owning any dog, you should consider all the advantages and disadvantages and discuss the whole matter with all the people who are to be involved with this new acquisition. You may have seen the National Canine Defence League's sticker in the back of cars that says, 'A dog is for life not just for Christmas', and it must be remembered that a dog's lifespan can be fifteen years or more. During this time, he will depend on you to feed, groom and exercise him, and look after his general well-being through all the good and bad weather, through illness, at holiday times, and so on. After the initial purchase of your dog, you are also committing yourself to the regular cost of his upkeep: food, grooming, veterinary fees and boarding fees. For this commitment, the benefits can be manifold: you will have a friend and companion through thick and thin, a permanent burglar alarm, a pal to take you for a walk (think how good you will feel for the exercise); in all, a bundle of fun and tricks that will pay back your investment of time and expense a thousand-fold.

Why this Breed?

Our breed is one of the most popular and is forever gaining in popularity. There are lots of reasons for this. Even though the breed is relatively small in stature, he is hardy and game and will find favour not only as a family pet but also as 'a man's dog'. Size is, however, very much in their favour for in today's modern society West Highland Whites will be quite happy whatever location or size of abode they live in; they are very adaptable creatures, so whether exercise is a five-mile hike each day or just a short walk around the streets, they are happy.

'Heads up.' (Original photo by Walter Guiver.)

Easy to train in all manner of things, many times have they put to shame the notion that you 'can't teach an old dog new tricks'. Combined with adaptability, the breed as a whole is very intelligent and will often surprise you in just how quickly they learn new things or alternatively pay no attention to certain noises or situations with which they have become familiar. They will quickly come to recognize the place in which they live as their domain and guard it with great purpose. For a small dog, the West Highland White has a loud bark and will let you know in no uncertain terms when you have a visitor, invited or not! As an instance of all this, I recall the first one I ever owned, a bitch named Ziggy, who was bought three months before the birth of my first daughter. I wondered how the dog would react to the baby, but from the very first day the baby came home Ziggy, without any training or instruction, would lie in a space between the baby and the door of the room, guarding against intruders. As a general rule, I would not advise families with very small children to have a dog, not least because a family's demands on your time and attention leaves you little left to devote to the dog. That said, there are many contradictory examples, as the one above shows, which serve to impress upon readers another of the qualities to be found in the breed to a great degree, that of good and equable temperament.

West Highland White Terriers are also 'good doers', and will eat all manner of good wholesome food. Once mature, the adult dog will be quite happy with being fed once a day and, because of his physical size, is not too expensive to keep (a point to bear in mind when remembering the cost over a typical lifespan of between twelve and fifteen years). No problems with casting coats either as the West Highland White does not moult; regular grooming to remove the few loose hairs that he sheds naturally is all that is necessary between trims.

For these reasons alone, it is no wonder that our breed goes from strength to strength and more owners are seen proudly showing off the 'light of their lives' to the envy and admiration of all. The only thing better than a West Highland White as your choice for a dog is two or three . . .!

What Age is Best?

Whether to have a very young puppy chosen from a litter or to have an older puppy, an adolescent or an adult dog is a decision that can be taken only by the individual, based on their circumstances and particular needs. For example, if the would-be pet owner is of mature years, it may not be practical to have an eight-week-old puppy, especially when taking into account all the trials and tribulations a young puppy can be, plus remembering that the usual lifespan of a West Highland White is twelve to fifteen years. Such a person would probably be better suited with an older dog, but only the reader can know what is best after carefully considering personal circumstances.

A young puppy, say eight to twelve weeks old, is very much a baby and has to be treated as such. It will alternate between immense activity, before quickly tiring, and sleeping until the next bout of playful exercise. It will need four to six carefully balanced meals per day and cannot be taken beyond the confines of your home until it has been inoculated at twelve weeks, even though it is not or only partially house-trained. Young puppies should not be left alone for long periods, two or three hours at most, for it is unfair and the puppy will only become lonely, bored and troublesome. To

Joining in the festive fun. Crinan Christiana plays Santa. (Photo by Chris Kernick)

summarize, a young puppy is hard work and tying. To offset these points, a puppy of this age will probably settle into the family, particularly in a family with children, more readily than an older dog. You will derive enormous pleasure from watching him as he grows, and your puppy will have no vices or bad habits, save the ones you teach or allow. I am a firm believer that, almost without exception, bad dogs are not born but made. You will have the task of training but will have the pleasure and satisfaction of knowing that it is all your own work.

For the person not wanting such a baby, or wishing to give an unwanted dog a good home, the older dog is a better choice. It may be that this dog is in need of a new home because his owner has died or has become unable to cope, or he may be a rescued dog (our breed operates a rescue scheme that takes care of dogs, who are in need of rehoming for various reasons, until a suitable new home can be found). The disadvantages of an older dog are that he may take time to adjust to his new environment and may have some bad habits or vices because of his previous training, or lack of it, or he may have psychological problems caused by ill-treatment. To his credit, the older dog will probably be inoculated and past the baby stage of feeding, and will be 'ready made' for walks, playing football, fetching the stick, and so on. He will probably be house- and lead-trained, and will no doubt be able to do all sorts of things which you will only find out in time as he surprises you.

My advice to all prospective owners is to contact the secretary of the nearest West Highland White Terrier Club (*see* Appendix 2, page 253), join the club and then ask for help in your quest. You will find the secretary only too willing to assist you with advice and the names of known, responsible breeders and exhibitors.

What Sex?

Is it better to have a dog rather than a bitch or vice versa? You may have heard the old wives' tales that dogs will roam, are not as faithful, are prone to fighting and make your home smell because they are always lifting their leg against the furniture, whereas bitches are quite the opposite? Well, this can be dismissed for what it is, a load of old wives' tales. The truth is that both sexes have their merits and their failings. Dogs do mark their territory by urinating around it, but not in the house if you have trained him properly. They will roam if they are allowed to, particularly if there is a bitch in season close by, but then so will any dog, male or female, if he is allowed that kind of freedom. Dogs are no more vicious or prone to fighting than bitches, and both sexes are faithful to their owners. The only major difference between the two sexes is that bitches have an oestrous cycle which means that they come in to season or are 'on heat' roughly every six months. A season lasts approximately twenty-one days and, during that time, great care has to be taken that she is not mated by next door's mongrel. She will have to be kept under lock and key and only allowed out to relieve herself in your own garden and be accompanied during these outings. Of course, if you intend to breed West Highland Whites, you will have to choose a female; but if you want a pet only, there is little to choose between dogs and bitches.

Whatever age or sex you choose, you will find the West Highland White to be affectionate, intelligent and loyal. They are gregarious dogs who thrive on being involved or searching out some new interest; they are terriers and, by instinct, are nosy and inquisitive, always on the alert for the next bit of sport.

Show Dog Selection

Assuming you have studied the breed at shows, read as much as you can (particularly the Breed Standard), and thought long and hard before deciding to have your own dog to show (*see* Chapter 9, page 169), where do you find a good one? The best direction to look is towards one of the established, successful breeder/exhibitors.

Before approaching any club, you must decide on the type of West Highland White Terrier that you wish to show. Each breeder will interpret the Breed Standard slightly differently, and will tend to produce dogs of a type that can be associated with that particular kennel. So it is important to go to as many shows as you can so that you discover which breeder's stock consistently appeals to you most. Breed club secretaries will be able to put you in touch with a breeder, and you may be invited to look at a litter of puppies. However, it is important to ensure that this breeder produces dogs of the type you have decided upon if you are to establish your own kennel in years to come, founded on a specific chosen type.

It may be difficult for the newcomer to know or understand the different types and strains that exist within the breed, unless they have spent a lot of time, possibly a year or two, in and around the breed. Having bought a certain type of puppy, the newcomer may subsequently change his mind about his original choice of strain and type in preference for another, especially when extra knowledge

Ch. Robbie McGregor of Wyther Park (1975). (Photo by Anne Roslin-Williams.)

and understanding allows him to choose with better judgement. Provided this is done because it is genuinely thought that the change is to 'the correct type', to which the newcomer will offer some dedication, it is both wise and acceptable. However, there is a growing trend for the newer exhibitor to swap and change for the wrong reasons. Many is the time recently that one sees an exhibitor come into the breed with a perfectly good specimen puppy of a specific type and strain. He meets with some moderate successes, but then acquires another pup of different type, which is more successful, often because unlike the original choice it is an early maturer. Suddenly the more successful type is the preferred choice, simply because at this very early stage in both the dog's life and the exhibitor's career, it wins more. This shows a basic ignorance of the whole object of breeding and exhibiting dogs. Dedicated fanciers do not chop and change their chosen type and strain; they persevere, believing in their own stock. It is not necessarily the change in either stock or opinion that is wrong, but the reasoning and concept of the 'dog game', and it is this that gives rise to fears for the breed's future.

Having selected a breeder who has a litter available, what do you look for and what questions do you ask? First of all, a good breeder will know most of what there is to know about his own stock, so his advice is invaluable. However, no one can say with certainty that an eight-week-old puppy will make the grade in the show ring, for much can happen in the intervening months to make that sort of assertion turn sour. One hears so many tales of eight-week-old puppies being expensively bought as show dogs, or because they have 'show quality'. This description is hogwash. That you may have to pay more for a puppy with a first-class pedigree from an established breeder with proven success in the show ring is not disputed, and is to be expected, but a fairer description would be 'quality bloodlines with show potential'.

You will be shown the puppy's pedigree, at which point you should ask whether this litter is the result of outcrossing or line-breeding; and whether or not the sire and dam have been mated before, and with what success. Although there may be no difference in the quality of the puppies themselves, it should be borne in mind that outcrossing results in a litter containing more of a mixture of bloodlines, whereas a line-bred litter will be more solid and predictable in its make-up. For further explanation of the principles of breeding, *see* Chapter 4, pages 74–80.

Using the degree of knowledge you have, look at the construction of the puppies and ask the breeder for his opinion. Look for the obvious: you do not have to be an expert to know whether the nose is black, the eye dark, the ears erect or the tail straight, and so on. Check that the coat is harsh and do not be tempted into taking home that 'adorable' bundle of cotton wool fluff which always seems to win hearts but is oh so wrong for the breed. The straight, hard-coated puppy will be just as lovely in a while when the furnishings have grown. Take note of temperament and showmanship: well-adjusted pups will usually come to you with their tails wagging, or carry on playing oblivious to this strange person in their midst. Watch the puppies carefully and notice the extroverts, the confident ones who carry their tails properly. If the one you are tempted to choose, or the one the breeder says is the best, is the one that goes into the farthest corner and just sits there shivering with fright, you would have to put a question mark next to its temperament. But do not ignore the breeder's advice: if you cannot see why a particular puppy is the best, just ask the breeder to explain.

You should satisfy yourself that your chosen puppy is in good health, although no good breeder will let you have a puppy knowing that it is not so. However, it is as well that you let your vet give

Puppies enjoy their show days. Barbara Hands (Crinan) and Julie Edmondson (Pepabby) are pictured in a typical puppy class.

the puppy a check-over, just to be sure that everything is fine. Most breeders will not mind if you make this health check a condition of the purchase and many now include insurance cover in the purchase price.

There are conflicting views as to when is the best time to assess the quality of puppies. Some say they can tell the minute they are born, others at four or six weeks, or even later at six months, and so on. Each has his own way, based on knowledge and an instinctive feel for his own breeding. With my own stock, I maintain that what you see at eight weeks is what you get at eight years, only smaller, and with rare exceptions apart, this has proved to be true. Puppies go through all kinds of 'ugly' stages when they look long, tall, leggy and so on. But eventually they mature and, with a bit of luck and a following wind, the breeder will be right in his first selection more often than not. Even then, that selection, although the best in that litter, may not be quite good enough. If breeding top winners was so easy it would lose some of its challenge and every litter would have a champion in the making. There has never been a perfect dog; every one has a fault, and we are constantly trying to improve what we have. I recall that famous terrier man Cyril Whitham of the renowned Townville prefix saying, 'show me a dog with three faults and you've shown me a good dog.' Many a true word has been spoken in jest.

I cannot overstate the importance of the advice given by the breeder, both on selection, and on other subjects such as rearing, handling and feeding. They will be able to tell you just what to expect of their stock at a certain age and will teach you to be patient in the weeks or months when you despair that this puppy will ever make the grade. I have heard quite a few novices expounding on how the breeder tried to palm them off with a different pup from the one of their choice, only to find some time later that the breeder's choice is the one that steals the show.

Sometimes it is possible to buy an older puppy with show potential, or even an adult. Some of the larger kennels cannot possibly keep everything, but run on promising ones until they are six months old or so. Or it could be that someone is simply giving up or cutting down, but it doesn't happen often. Any stock you buy may cost more but will be less of a risk than an eight-week-old pup. Over five to six months of age, pups have cut their second teeth so you can make sure that the mouth is good. Older ones have gone through many of the ugly stages and are starting to shape up, so there is not much guesswork. If the dog is over six months of age, it may be that he has been shown, in which case, his success to date is a guide to his potential. An older one should not be showing any signs of shyness and you can also see him being moved on a lead, when you can carefully watch the movement and showmanship.

After all I have said, it is no easy business selecting stock, for even the best-laid plans go amiss. Whatever you do, be patient; it takes time to get things right and breeders and exhibitors spend their lives trying to do just that. Finally, once again, I stress my advice to put your faith in the breeder and trust to his knowledge, experience and integrity. After all, it is in the breeder's best interests that any stock he breeds and sells with 'show potential' is seen to be of good quality.

4

Breeding

To breed a litter of good-quality healthy puppies, with all the thought and work it entails, is one of the most satisfying, fascinating and tiring experiences imaginable. Good breeding is also a necessary requirement of the breeder's quest to produce that perfect specimen of the breed, which has so far eluded all.

Responsibilities of the Breeder

In this chapter I shall not waste time expounding the arguments for or against commercial breeding, but suffice it to say that as dedicated fanciers of the breed our only reason for breeding should be to try to enhance and improve on the breed as a whole, and on our own stock in particular. To produce puppies simply for resale defeats the object of the serious fancier. It must be noted that our breed is very popular as a pet, but it is better that pet puppies come from responsible breeders who have worked hard in all areas to produce puppies of high quality, that can be admired and seen to display the type and characteristics of the breed, than from those who produce some of the poor specimens seen from time to time, displaying all that is unwanted and doing nothing for the breed at all. In my experience, close scrutiny reveals such defects as being the result of either puppy farming (where the only consideration is profit, not care for the breed), or the result of misguided pet owners producing litters by using next door's pet dog, often because lots of their friends want a little dog 'just like our Snowy'. So yes, the serious breeder does have a role to play, albeit one of a secondary consideration when parting with surplus stock, in providing good-quality animals to fill the demand for pet dogs and in educating the pet owners, so that they in turn will pass on this knowledge to others. However, I know of several owners who, while having no interest for exhibiting themselves, have bred the odd litter to good

73

effect. By taking reliable advice when buying their bitch from a good source with good bloodlines, and then taking advice when choosing a stud-dog, the resulting progeny have been of a very acceptable standard. I have no objection to such breeders who, by their efforts and willingness to learn, are genuinely (if inadvertently) striving to improve the breed.

There are many points to be taken into account when you think of breeding a litter. To begin with, you must be aware of the financial implications: there is a stud fee to be paid and, even with an uncomplicated whelping, there will be veterinary costs when the vet examines the bitch and her pups and gives the advisable post-natal antibiotic injection. There is also the cost of feeding the bitch during nine weeks of pregnancy, and then, in addition, the puppies for a minimum further eight weeks, on top-quality food and supplements. Unless you have orders for the surplus puppies, there will be the cost of advertising and, if you are obliged to keep them beyond twelve weeks of age, they will require inoculations. In addition, there is the cost of housing, bedding, toys, and so on. Finally, there is the time you will need to give, for which, if you were to be paid an average hourly rate, you would receive a very fat wage packet at the end of the term. But for the serious, dedicated breeder, seeing a happy, healthy and, it is hoped, good-quality litter is reward enough for all the trials and tribulations.

Mating

You will need to plan carefully the time you mate your bitch, taking into account that from the time of mating her to the time the puppies go to their new homes will be a minimum of seventeen weeks. Make sure you will have this period free to spend all the time necessary. For instance, have you booked a holiday, or are you away from home for some reason, maybe at a show, at the time the bitch is due to whelp? All such things have to be taken into account and the timing of this prospective litter needs careful planning.

The Art of Breeding

Breeding dogs of the highest standard, and consistently so, is almost like putting together a huge jigsaw puzzle, except no one tells you when you start that there will always be a few pieces missing, or a few extra pieces that simply do not fit.

You will notice that I have headed this section 'The Art of Breeding' and an art it surely is. Science can offer much information and assistance to the breeder, but many experienced breeders would agree that the laws of science can sometimes be turned upside down when applying them to the breeding of livestock, including pedigree dogs. Much of the success achieved by established breeders can only be attributed to the human factor: the individual who can draw on personal knowledge, experience and uncanny intuition, so that the choice of certain stud-dogs mated to certain brood-bitches will, in all probability, consistently produce stock of a very high quality. Of course, even the plans of the most enlightened minds sometimes go awry and, likewise, the complete novice will occasionally breed something quite outstanding, forever to be remembered as 'beginner's luck'. But in the main, the deciding factor is this intuition, this 'feel' for the right choice, which most would find difficult to explain.

Genetics

It is not my intention to delve deeply into the complicated subject of genetics, for there are many good works entirely devoted to this subject to which the reader can refer (*see* Further Reading, page 254). It is not essential to have a profound knowledge of genetics for the average dog breeder to make use of its principles, but an understanding of its basic workings can be invaluable.

Characteristics such as the conformation, temperament, size, pigmentation, and so on, of all living things (in this case dogs) are produced by genes. Genes are present in pairs, one having come from the father, the other from the mother. In this way, every dog receives half his characteristics from his sire, and half from his dam, whose genes are, in turn, inherited from their sires and dams, and so on throughout their lines.

You would be forgiven for assuming that these characteristics, or genes, were inherited from the sire and dam in equal parts, but this is not so. Some genes are 'visible', while others are 'hidden', some are dominant, others recessive and visible or recessive and hidden. To make things even more complicated, many genes are not completely dominant or recessive, but are dominant or recessive to a varying degree, or half-way between the two. Some characteristics or genes may remain latent for generations so that when they unexpectedly become visible by appearing in progeny, they appear to bear no relationship to the immediate parents. All this makes the equation either more fascinating or infuriating, depending on your point of view, so that unless you have in-depth knowledge of the genetic make-up of an animal's ancestry, there is no way of knowing what these hidden or latent genes are or where they came from. That said, it is far better to follow a definite plan or breeding programme than to breed haphazardly.

Many have used the principles of Mendelism, some with full understanding of these principles, and others (such as myself, at first), unwittingly. Gregor Mendel was an Austrian monk who experimented with edible peas. His findings were published in the *Journal of the Brunn Scientific Society* in 1865, but stayed unnoticed until they were rediscovered and their importance realized some thirty-five years later.

Mendelism

Mendel asserted that all individuals are made up of paired characteristics called genes, one derived from each parent. If the characteristic inherited from each parent is the same, the individual is homozygous for that characteristic and can give only that characteristic to its offspring. If the characteristic from each parent is different, the individual is heterozygous and may give either characteristic, but not both, to each individual offspring. Therefore, the appearance and physical development of an homozygous individual can only follow the development brought about by that particular characteristic contained in the gene. The heterozygous individual may show either one of the inherited pairs of characteristics only (excluding the other completely), or a combination of the two inherited characteristics, which by blending together form a different appearance than either of the two characteristics contained in the gene. Note that the blend itself is not inherited.

To summarize, Mendelism works on the basis that like begets like and, broadly speaking, this is correct. However, the fact that two West Highland White Terriers mated together will produce West Highland White puppies does not mean that two such champions when mated together will produce champions, or anything approaching that quality.

Ways of Breeding

When planning a litter or, better still, a breeding programme, there are three main routes to take: inbreeding, line-breeding and outcrossing.

Inbreeding

Inbreeding is the practice of mating together very close relations, for example father to daughter, mother to son, sister to brother. It is rarely used these days in our breed and should only be attempted by the most knowledgeable and experienced of breeders. To its credit, inbreeding is the surest and quickest way of fixing a type or strain because it cannot produce any new characteristics; instead, it concentrates what is already in the bloodlines as it doubles up all the good points. But it must be remembered that inbreeding will also double up on all the faults as well. Therefore the quality of the stock used must be absolutely outstanding not only in make and shape but, and I emphasize this point, in temperament. For even the most experienced have found that inbreeding, if practised regularly, often leads to awful problems with temperament and mental stability.

Line-Breeding

Line-breeding is the matching of pedigrees, which means mating together dogs with one or more common relations. It is by far the most popular way of breeding, and although it will normally take longer than inbreeding to fix the type or strain of your choice, it is also the safest and has been proven so for generations.

Quite often, the same common relation is seen in the pedigree repeatedly. Close line-breeding, for example granddaughter to grandfather, grandmother to grandson, uncle to niece, aunt to nephew and, less frequently because it is very close, half-sister to half-brother, is not so far removed from inbreeding, but by experience we have learned that paradoxically it is just far enough removed to dilute the concentration and, in general, eradicate the less savoury problems that can be found with inbreeding.

There is an abundance of theories on breeding and it is not for me to try to cover them all within the confines of this book. However, the Bruce Lowe System has much to its credit and expounds the virtues of line-breeding on successfully proven maternal lines. I was indoctrinated with this theory by my 'Auntie Joan' (Joan Langstaff), owner of the famous Sprotboro terrier kennels. Mrs Langstaff was born into dogs, her father owning the Sprotboro affix before she took over some forty years ago. During those forty years she has bred many champions in four different terrier breeds and is a great believer in the system of line-breeding to proven maternal lines.

The Bruce Lowe System, used widely in racehorse breeding, based on the performance of racehorses in classic races, was first applied to the breeding of dogs by the Rev. Dr Rosslyn Bruce, who was a Fox Terrier breeder. He maintained 'The general principle that good and continuously successful female lines of blood are better worth following up than more casual successes . . .'.

For example, if you were considering a grandfather to grand-daughter mating and wished to follow this principle of maternal line-breeding, the choice of sire would be one of the grandfathers on the dam's (or maternal) line, or a brother of the grandfather, or an uncle of the proposed dam, but still from her maternal line.

Another of the permutations I have used to good effect is line-breeding to the paternal line. When you are really taken with a particular dog you have seen and would like to breed something of his image, use his sire or grandsire (the paternal line), as they are the ones who were heavily responsible for his make-up. Then, if all went well and you wanted to compound that breeding further, a bitch from the progeny of that union could be mated to one of his sons from a different, but still complementary, union or even that dog himself, and so on.

The permutations within the principles of line-breeding are enormous, and it is not so difficult, even for the novice, to plan a breeding programme for three or four generations. It is the most advisable and by far the most sensible approach to the serious breeding of dogs.

Outcrossing

Outcrossing is the mixing of pedigrees, which means mating together unrelated dogs. It is used when a strain has been line-bred for some time, and is showing, perhaps, a serious recurring fault; or it is used when 'gut feeling' suggests that it is time to bring in some new blood as a prevention against such ills, rather than having to find a cure later. This is a perfectly legitimate step to take although great care has to be taken in choosing the outcross. Done in a haphazard way, as can be seen all too often, it can be quite disastrous. For example, some have chosen to use a dog quite unrelated to their own stock, sometimes for convenience (say, the close proximity of the stud-dog), but more often because the out-cross is a top-winning dog. The thinking behind this is that outcros-sing to a top-winning dog will beget top winners. Occasionally, and in the short term, this can meet with some success but if, say, this top-winning progeny is then mated to another unrelated top win-ner, the chances of further improvement are much diminished because the genetic make-up and traits of the resulting progeny are so unrelated and such a mixture. When outcrossing to this extent, the likelihood of a successful combination of the genes or strains is remote. And since the stock in the kennel will also be of such a great mixture, it would take several generations of careful line-breeding to return to a reliable type and strain. It should also be borne in mind that any male offspring from such outcrossing are unlikely to meet with any appreciable success as a stud-dog, for their mixed lineage means that they are of little use either for line-breeding or outcros-sing.

Used correctly, albeit by necessity, outcrossing need not be so traumatic, and it can improve your stock with no great loss to your chosen strain or type. When thinking of outcrossing, the choice of outcross should be as solid a line-bred dog as possible, but from a different line to your own. Try to choose a line that is of a similar type to your own (albeit unrelated) and/or one which consistently excels in the areas that you want to improve. The retained progeny from this union should then be line-bred back into your own lines so as to once again compound that line, strain and type.

There is plenty of information available to help us plan a litter or a breeding programme: pedigrees, photographs, videos, the written word, the spoken word, the quality of the stock sired by a dog you have in mind or from a similar mating as the one you are contem-plating, and so on. The trick is really to have a clear idea of what you are trying to achieve, what type, what strain or, if you have already established these, what improvements you wish to make. Here are just a few tips I have used myself, which you may find helpful.

When looking at photographs, it is much better to have untouched ones, because if they have had artwork done to them, you really cannot know what improvements have been made to the natural 'warts and all' original. Look at the photographs upside down as well as the right way up; sometimes it is amazing how you can pick out things when viewing them upside down that you would miss when viewing them the right way up. Ask as many questions as you dare, to as many people as possible, but do use some tact and discretion or you might have your nose snapped off. And do not be convinced of anything until you have seen it with your own eyes or have heard the same from several reliable sources.

In this way, you can build up a dossier of information on the stud-dog, strain, line or kennel of your interest, which is important when making decisions on breeding and exhibiting. Lastly, each time you have a mating in mind, make up a fault/virtue pedigree of the yet-to-be-born offspring. I used to write the virtues in black and the faults in red beneath as many names in the pedigree as possible. Recently, I have used the idea of coding by letters, which involves making a separate sheet for each dog and beneath its name writing a list of the various points: head, ears, neck, front, tail, temperament, and so on. Then, if one dog excels in head, for instance, write in black ink a capital 'A'; if the dog is just good in head, write a small 'a'; if he is just moderate, then in red write a capital 'Z', and if poor write a small 'z'. In this way, it is very easy to compare not only the lineage but also where you are doubling up on good or bad points. You can enlarge on this idea if you wish by using different letters for intermediate appraisals or other information, it depends how much time and information you have and how complicated you want this system to be.

The Stud-Dog

Selection

At this stage, it is assumed that you have decided which type and strain of West Highland White Terrier you want to breed and, having spent the time digesting all the information you have been able to lay your hands on, plus attending shows to watch and select or discard some of the ones on view, it now befalls you to make your final choice. You may have several suitable dogs in mind, all fairly equal in suitability of pedigree, type, strain and appeal. So what could the deciding factor be? Whether a dog is a champion or not is neither here nor there; by far the most important question at this time is does the dog stamp his mark? In other words, are his virtues visible in his progeny? If there are a number of good quality specimens sired by him, and from different dams, this is a good sign that he is a dominant sire. At this stage, the question of hereditary diseases must also be a serious consideration. If you know that a dog has sired something that is not quite sound, or that there is something of the like in his pedigree, you must put a question mark against his name. But be sure that the source of any information you obtain is reliable, because dog breeding and exhibiting, as in other forms of competition, is not without that small band of 'helpful' advisors whose motives are borne out of jealousy or avarice, or both.

Travelling distance could also be a factor in deciding on a stud-dog, although any breeder worth his salt would not care how far he had to travel to use the stud-dog of his choice. The motorway networks, being what they are nowadays, mean that what used to be regarded as major expeditions are relatively easy journeys. If the distance is a problem but you are still keen to use that particular stud, your bitch could be sent by rail or even air, but be careful to make adequate preparations and liaise in full with all the interested parties.

The stud fee, again, should not create a problem to the dedicated breeder. Stud fees in our breed are low and have been so for some time. It used to be that the stud fee was equal to the cost of a puppy, but now even the most expensive stud is only about half that figure. This is no good for the breed at all and I urge readers to liaise with others in the breed and set a minimum stud fee, in their own area at least. Once this is done, it is a simple job to raise stud fees in line with puppy prices on an index-linked basis.

After all these considerations, as I have intimated earlier, there is no written guarantee of anything, but as all the great breeders show, the extra care, time and effort more often than not pay dividends. In the end we come down to the old adage, 'You pays your money and you takes your chance.'

Keeping a Stud-Dog

If you are just starting out, or have a small set-up, it is neither advisable nor necessary to keep a stud-dog of your own. As a newcomer, you have yet to make your mark in the breed, and to become established and develop your line, you need to use one or more of the best dogs available, so you do not need a stud-dog for yourself. For the same reasons, a stud-dog at this time would hardly be a financially viable proposition (they rarely are), because it is unlikely that other breeders will be beating a path to your door. You also have to consider the problems and extra work you will have when your own bitches come in season, and the need for the facilities and space to keep them separated during your bitches' seasons.

Some of the top kennels prefer not to keep a stud-dog of their own, opting for a quieter life by keeping top-quality bitches and having the choice of any dog they wish as a suitor for them. Miss Sheila Cleland's Birkfell kennel is world-famous and has successfully produced stock of the very highest quality since the mid-1950s, and she keeps mainly bitches, the two exceptions being Ch. Birkfell Sea Squall and Ch. Birkfell Student Prince.

So unless the stud-dog is a top and consistent winner, with the very best line-bred bloodlines and has proved himself to be a dominant and prolific sire of quality stock, he is unlikely to attract enough interest for the owner to be able to retire to the Bahamas on his earnings. Even when the dog does meet these criteria, it does not follow that he will be in constant demand. In addition to all this, stud fees are low, as I mentioned earlier, which can mean a lot of work for little reward.

All in all, it is certainly wiser to wait a little while before you think of having your own stud-dog. That said, it is usually the case that most owners keep a dog first and foremost because they consider him to be a good specimen for the show ring, and as they now have a dog why not offer him at stud? If he is a good line-bred dog, and a good specimen himself, so that you do some winning with him, and you are keeping him anyway, then why not? You will get plenty of fun showing him and any stud fees he makes along the way will help towards the cost of running your kennel and pursuing your expensive hobby, but don't think of the Bahamas just yet!

Stud-Dog Management

The main criteria are good feeding, housing, exercise, training and living environment.

Keeping the stud-dog in the peak of condition is of paramount importance, and you need to be observant at all times as stud-dogs can soon lose condition. A 'complete diet' food should be enough for a dog in light work, but if he is in big demand, even spasmodically, he will need extra food with more protein. Vitamin E is thought to aid fertility and Vitamin B is given to many dogs (of both sexes), in the form of brewer's yeast tablets, as an aid to good health. But take care and remember that (and this applies to all dogs) a fit dog is not a fat dog!

A happy living environment is very important as is plenty of good exercise (preferably in the company of other kennel-mates). Except at times when it is unavoidable, the stud-dog should not be treated as different and be segregated from the rest of the kennel. Make sure that his housing and bed are draught-free and dry: no dog will thrive in draughty, damp, miserable conditions.

Training should start at an early age by getting him used to being handled both on the floor and on a table. Pop him in a box from time to time so that he accepts this as well. All this will pay dividends, not only for stud use but for the show dog too.

Keep his vaccinations up to date – particularly the one against parvovirus, which causes sterility in dogs for up to a year. Sperm counts have been proved to drop in hot weather, so those who live in hot climates are adivsed to keep dogs in cool or, better still, air-conditioned housing. Britain is rarely blessed with this problem, but it should be borne in mind during the occasional heat wave.

Stud Terms

Before putting a dog at stud you should decide what terms you are prepared to offer, as these terms, if accepted, will form an agreement between the two parties that is legal and binding. It is advisable that this agreement is written in the form of a letter sent by you outlining the terms, and a reply from the owner of the bitch accepting them. However, many stud bookings are taken by telephone and, quite often, at short notice, but at the very least the stud receipt (given on payment) should contain not only details of the fee paid but any other arrangements, such as free return (*see* pages 84 and 93). This may seem unnecessary, especially when the two parties are good friends, but it can and does save argument later should something go wrong or recollections differ.

You may find the following guidelines useful:

1. Always write down the date and time of the mating in your diary at the time of the booking.

2. If your dog is a proven sire, you may wish to ask for a small deposit in advance, as confirmation. If so, state whether this is refundable or not if the other party cancels the booking.

3. Stud fees are usually paid in full on the day, immediately after the first successful mating. Until a dog is proven at stud, I usually ask that no payment is made unless the bitch is found to be definitely in whelp, until which time I do not give a signed litter-registration form.

4. Many owners like their bitch to have two services, the second twenty-four to forty-eight hours after the first. This is acceptable provided the dog is not booked for that day or in heavy demand at the time. A second service could be necessary if it is felt that the first was not wholly satisfactory (perhaps if the bitch was not quite ready). But if the first service was all that it should be, a second one should not be required. If the bitch does not conceive, you can offer a free return (or second service free of charge), although it should be to the same bitch on her next heat. There is a popular misconception (pardon the pun) that this free return is an automatic obligation of the stud-dog owner. This is quite wrong and it must be clearly understood that once a dog is a proven sire, the fee paid is for the service of the dog, not for a guarantee of puppies.

5. The litter-registration form can be given either at the time of the mating or when the pups are born. The former has become the expected practice but can leave the door open for the unscrupulous, so use your best judgement.

All of these terms and more can vary, but the most important thing is that they are understood and agreed by all parties concerned beforehand, preferably in writing.

When to Start

If a dog is used extensively at stud when young, this is thought to lead to premature infertility. I have had a dog who mated his first bitch at the age of seven months but this is rare. The young dog is probably ready, willing and able at about ten or eleven months of age. After his first bitch, it is wise not to use him again for four to six months. It will be better all round for the dog to have a long stud life, rather than a short-term one, particularly when you consider that if he becomes successful in the show ring he is likely to attract more interest later in life.

Stud Procedure

Introducing the young and/or inexperienced dog to stud work needs patience, care and plenty of common sense.

It is much easier for the handler if the matings can be done on a table or other raised platform. However, for the first few matings the dog will be happier, and you will probably meet with more success, if the matings are done on the floor.

Ideally, the bitch should be a matron (experienced bitch) who is known to be placid and easy to mate. This will give the young dog confidence, and whatever stupid things he may do the bitch will stand in readiness for mating quite oblivious to any problems you may be encountering with the dog. It would be a disaster if the bitch was a maiden (previously unmated) and carried on jumping around and whining, as maiden bitches often do. Your dog would be likely to become upset and disillusioned with the whole affair, which could have a detrimental effect for some time afterwards.

Once you have accepted a bitch for mating and the day arrives certain pre-mating preparations should be made. It is wise not to feed either dog or bitch within a short time of the mating. Dogs asked to perform matings on a full stomach will invariably vomit the food back and will probably feel less than 100 per cent as a result. I find it useful to put the dog in a box in the mating room a few minutes before he is introduced to the bitch. He will quickly become used to this and attune his mind to the job in hand.

It is important that both dog and bitch are allowed to relieve themselves before the mating and, particularly in the bitch's case, that she has opened her bowels to prevent discomfort during the mating.

Have to hand a soft scarf or tie, a jar of petroleum jelly or other lubricant, a roll of disposable paper kitchen towel, a sponge and some mild antiseptic.

Whether the mating takes place on a floor or table, the surface should be non-slip; rubber or carpeted surfaces are best. If it is to be a table mating, the table or raised surface should be next to a wall so that there is no danger of either animal falling away. I prefer a fixed, raised surface rather than the fold-up type of grooming table. Whichever you use, make sure that it is level and does not wobble or rock. Nothing could be more confidence-shattering for a dog than a wobbly table or one that falls over during the mating. Both animals need to feel secure and safe during this important event.

Before the actual mating takes place, it is good to allow the prospective mates a short period of foreplay. Using an enclosed, secure area, or a play-pen, keep both animals on their leads but allow them a few minutes to become acquainted. At this time, it can often be seen whether the dog is keen and whether the bitch is ready. If she is, she will stand with her tail turned to one side (flagging), inviting the dog to mount her. But this is not always the case: if the bitch is frightened or apprehensive, she may refuse all the dog's advances even if she is ready.

After this period of foreplay, put the dog back into his box in readiness for the mating while you make final preparations to the bitch. Stand her on the table (or floor) facing in the direction you intend to carry out the mating. Being right-handed, I always have the bitch facing to my left. Check that there is no hair around the vulva that may cause difficulty; if there is, cut it away or grease it down. If she is ready, the bright red discharge will have turned to an almost clear pink colour, the swelling will be subsiding and the area around the vulva will feel soft. With well-washed hands and short-cut nails, take some of the lubricant on to your little finger and insert it into the vagina. This will lubricate the passage, making penetration easier for the dog and more comfortable for the bitch. If at this time the bitch should become at all fractious, it is probably as well to muzzle her with the soft scarf or tie by wrapping it around her muzzle, crossing it underneath and fastening it behind the ears. This is not always done by any means, but needs good judgement. No risk should be taken of the dog getting bitten, so if in doubt use the muzzle.

I shall explain the next phase of the mating as a right-handed handler; the opposite will apply for those who are left-handed. Stand the bitch four-square facing to your left, and have the owner or your assistant hold her head firmly but gently, either by the hair on the sides of her head or by her collar. Let the dog out of his box, but do not allow him to mount the bitch just yet. Entering from under the bitch's belly, place your left hand palm up between her hind legs with your index and middle fingers on either side of the vulva, and your thumb interlocked with the right thigh of the bitch (this will effect control on her movement). Use your right hand to move her tail sideways towards you. Allow the dog to mount and he will start to strike. He can be encouraged from an early stage with 'good boy' or 'clever lad'; it's amazing just how a dog will some-times respond to this encouragement and help you through some difficult matings when, for him, it would have been easier not to bother. With your index and middle fingers you can now feel where the dog is striking and make the necessary adjustments by moving the bitch in the required direction. If there is a great disparity in the height of the couple it may be necessary to place one of them on some extra carpet or matting.

When the dog enters the bitch, he will begin to work quite vigorously until the bulbous gland in his penis swells up and 'ties' him to the bitch. During this tie, do not allow the bitch to try and pull away from the dog, as the dog will be unable to withdraw and the bitch's pulling will be painful for him.

The 'tie' lasts for anything from a few minutes up to an hour or more, but generally about fifteen minutes. During this period (from the moment of penetration), place your right arm around the rear of the dog just under his tail and clasp the right hind leg of the bitch. Using the fingers of the left hand, stimulate the dog further by gently massaging the area beneath the penis, at the same time praising him. These post-penetration encouragements will help deter the dog that tries to dismount before the two have tied, and gives all dogs, especially young and inexperienced ones, more confidence.

The ejaculation of semen happens in three distinct stages: the first stage lasts about thirty to fifty seconds and consists of a clear watery fluid which contains no spermatozoa. Ten to twenty seconds later, the second stage starts and lasts between fifty and ninety seconds. This second ejaculation is the testicular secretion of a white, glutinous fluid which is sperm bearing. Finally, after another ten- to twenty-second gap, there is the third phase in which the prostate gland secretes a thin watery fluid which carries no spermatozoa. This phase lasts from three to forty minutes. During this time carefully move the dog's front legs from the bitch's back to the supporting level, away from you, to take the weight off her back. It may be that the dog shows a desire to turn. If so, help him by carefully lifting him around, a little at a time, until the dog and bitch are standing tail to tail. However, many dogs show no inclination to turn at all.

When the tie is complete, the dog will come away naturally and can then be placed back in his box for a short rest. I usually leave him for half an hour before allowing him some short exercise and then feeding. Immediately after the mating, the bitch will lose fluid from the vulva, which can be blotted using the disposable towel or tissue. Both dog and bitch should be sponged with a mild antiseptic for cleanliness and prevention against any possible infection. Check that the dog's penis has properly retracted into the sheath. Gentle manipulation may be required to effect this.

After the mating some breeders like to tip the bitch up by her hind legs, wheelbarrow fashion, as soon as the mating is complete, so that the 'sperm' runs up inside the bitch. This 'sperm' is, however, just the watery fluid; the sperms are already swimming to meet the eggs, of their own natural volition. But if the owner of the bitch wants to do this, and it keeps him happy, it will do no harm, but if it was really necessary I am sure dogs would have been endowed with the instinct to perform headstands.

All this makes mating dogs seem fairly easy, which of course it isn't. There are all sorts of variables and problems that can and do arise from time to time. In extreme cases, a bitch of known sound temperament may for one reason or another become so upset or unwilling as to be too difficult for the dog (particularly the young and inexperienced). It may be necessary to abandon the mating altogether or alternatively sedate her: anti-car-sickness tablets can be used for simple sedation as they are not so strong or dangerous, are readily available, easy to administer and quite often do the trick by just taking the edge off an over-anxious bitch. But follow the manufacturer's instructions and, if they do not work, consult your vet for advice. However, on no account should you agree to allow the mating of any dog or bitch who is of unsound temperament, which is quite a different matter from the one described above. Doing so will only compound the fault and pass it on to the next generation when, as serious and conscientious breeders, you are trying to eradicate such faults.

Occasionally, a dog will seem uninterested in a bitch that has come for mating, or his interest starts to wane when the mating becomes more protracted than normal. At such times, I have found that simply putting the dog on the floor while the bitch is still on the table soon arouses his desire again. If not, more drastic action can be taken: after making sure the bitch is not accessible (say on the table or, better still, in a pen) and the dog in his box, positioned so he can see the goings on, bring in another dog and let him start courting the bitch (with the pen between them). Stud-dog A is not going to allow his arch rival stud-dog B to steal his thunder, so after a minute or two, put stud-dog B away and no doubt stud-dog A will be 'chomping at the bit' to get on with the job.

The Brood-Bitch

Selection

Bitches are the foundation of a kennel. You can use any stud-dog on offer for a relatively small fee, but if the bitch or bitches you mate them to are not good enough, you are fighting an uphill battle.

Therefore, it goes without saying that you should start with the best possible stock available. Many kennels start as a result of first buying a dog as a pet and then becoming interested in showing and breeding. However, unless you have been lucky enough to buy a pet bitch who also meets with the requirements of a brood-bitch, do not be tempted into trying to build your kennel using her as the foundation. Start again with the best available bitch you can find, using the guidelines previously explained (*see* pages 68–72). She should be of the strain and type of your preference, and line-bred from a line of known good producers and self-whelpers. Unfortunately, top-quality bitches, more so than dogs, are like gold dust. Established breeders and exhibitors just do not part with what they see to be a champion in the making – they are just too valuable, not in money but as standard bearers of their kennel. From time to time, top-quality stock does become available for a variety of reasons: owners giving up, overstocking, and so on. This is a rare occurrence and your best course of action in obtaining a suitable bitch is either to have one on breeding terms or to buy one who meets all the requirements of line, type and strain, but has never been shown having been retained as a brood-bitch only. Breeding terms vary and can be whatever you agree, but usually you take the bitch, mate her to a dog chosen by the bitch's owner, whelp the bitch and pay all the outgoings in return for a puppy or puppies, or for the brood-bitch herself with the owner taking the litter or an agreed part of it. Either way, it is to be hoped that you will end up with something on which you can start your kennel.

Breeding Life

The Kennel Club and the breed clubs each have a Code of Ethics regarding the aspects of keeping and breeding dogs. The penalties for abuse of this code are severe and the criteria contained therein, with exceptions, are well founded.

A bitch should not be bred from until her second season, or until she is fourteen months of age. She should have no more than six litters in her lifetime, with a rest of a year between litters, and she should not be bred from beyond seven years of age. There are special circumstances making exceptions to these rules but in general they are applicable to all.

Management of the Brood-Bitch

Like all dogs, the brood-bitch should have a happy living environment, good housing, exercise and a balanced diet. Except when she is in season (on heat) or in the latter stages of pregnancy, she should lead a normal life in the company of the rest of the kennel. Bitches start coming into season at about six to eight months of age and thereafter every six months. This is the norm, but bitches vary with longer or shorter times between seasons. Sometimes they show no colour (blood) during a season (known as a clear season), and the season may pass undetected or may only be noticed when she begins to make designs for mating kennel-mates of either sex. Such problems of irregularity need investigation. Many are caused by hormone deficiency, but they can be the result of infection. *Beta Haemolytic Streptococcus* (BHS) is a common organism with many varieties and frequently affects dogs causing tonsilitis, high temperature, skin disorders, and so on. Although it is not serious in itself, the disease leaves behind an infectious residue in the throat, or in the vagina where it causes irregular seasons, reduces the chances of conception and is known to play a major role in Fading Puppy Syndrome (*see* pages 112–14).

The normal season lasts three weeks. The first signs that the bitch is coming into season is the enlargement of the vulva, swelling which can be slight or very obvious with a discharge of mucus that lasts for a week or so and can easily go unnoticed. This is followed by a discharge of blood, more noticeable swelling and a general hardening around the vulva which will last about another week, until the discharge of blood recedes turning almost transparent pink in colour and the area around the vulva softens. It is at this point, usually around the eleventh or twelfth day, that the bitch is ready for mating. During the third week, all these signs will gradually disappear until at the end of the third week the season is finished.

At the first sign of heat, inform the owner of your chosen stud-dog and make a provisional date for mating, which can be adjusted (assuming a degree of flexibility regarding the availability of the stud-dog) as you await the change of colour and, more importantly, the softening of the vulvar region. Some bitches will show colour throughout the whole season, so the change of colour precept is fallible. However, even when this does happen, the vulvar region will still soften mid-season and is a more reliable sign that the time for mating is nigh. Feed extra protein and a little more quantity, perhaps an extra meal from the onset of the season. This has been proved to work in the rearing of other animals in so far as it tells the system to prepare to rear offspring and the system naturally reacts by increasing hormone activity. It goes without saying that the bitch should be segregated from any males in the kennel to prevent any chance of a mismating.

There are no hard and fast rules about which is the right day to mate the bitch. They vary so much from one bitch to another: some are ready as early as the seventh day while others have been known to be mated on the twenty-first day or later and still produce good litters. I have found that with the more youthful, between the eleventh and thirteenth day is generally the norm and as they get older (four–seven years) maybe a day or two later, but look for the signs. Softening of the vulvar region and the bitch starting to show interest in her kennel-mates by pushing her rear end toward them and standing with her tail twisted to one side (flagging) are two of the best. Your vet can help you with this decision by carrying out an ovulation test. If you experience continual difficulties in getting a bitch into whelp or if she has had more than one unusually small litter, it may be due to hormone deficiency, which can be helped with hormone injections from the vet.

It is very important for all dogs, and particularly for the brood-bitch, that they do not become obese. Obesity certainly reduces the chances of conception and increases the chances of small and poor litters. If your feeding and exercise arrangements are correct, it is unlikely that this will be a problem although there are exceptions to the rule. If the bitch is overweight, change the diet to give a higher protein content and less starch.

The owner of the stud-dog may wish you to arrange for your bitch to have a vaginal culture done to make sure that she is infection free. You should not take offence at this suggestion as it must be borne in mind that an infection could be passed on to the dog, perhaps leaving him to perpetuate it in any subsequent mates. The stud-dog owner could have particular reason to wish to avoid one of the bacterial infections that affect fertility, the very last problem wanted with breeding specimens. If when you take the bitch for mating, the stud-dog, particularly an experienced one, shows little or no interest in her, it is probably the best sign of all that she is not yet ready. So if you have an experienced dog of your own let him tell you, but keep both animals on leads so that when he has given you the indication you want, you can prevent him from mounting her.

The bitch should be wormed, preferably just before she comes into season, as worm eggs can pass through the teats of the dam after the birth or through the umbilical cord before it and thus infect the newborn or unborn puppies. Should you fail to do this, it is as well to treat her for roundworms only two weeks before the whelping.

Mating the Brood-Bitch

Much of the information relevant here is covered on pages 85–8 to which the reader should refer. However, there are some important points outstanding.

Prior to the day of mating, give the bitch a good groom so that when she meets the stud-dog she looks clean and tidy. First impressions often have the greatest impact and nothing is more off-putting to the stud-dog owner than a dirty, scruffy bitch arriving to be mated. On the day of the mating, do not feed the bitch unless you really have to before the mating and, if you do, allow as much time as possible beforehand. This will alleviate problems that arise with car sickness and discomfort during the mating. Allow plenty of travelling time and let the bitch relieve herself, especially her bowels before setting off. If you are undertaking a long journey it will be necessary to stop for this purpose along the way, too. If the bitch is not used to travelling, or has a history of travelling sickness, then give the appropriate tablets. If she is used to travelling in a box, all the better as it may come in useful during the mating procedure. It is a good idea to take along your own lubricant (special types can be obtained from your vet in sachet form), also a cloth or sponge together with a mild antiseptic fluid for post-service cleaning. If the bitch is a maiden, it is as well that you carry out an internal inspection yourself using the aforesaid lubricant, before setting off. A collar and lead will be required during the mating, even if the bitch never uses one at home.

Once you arrive at your destination, allow the bitch to relieve herself a final time before the mating. The experienced stud-dog owner will have everything in hand. Each has his own way of doing things, so spend a few minutes discussing what procedure you are expected to follow – it will aid the smooth accomplishment of your aim.

Whether you should ask for one or two services is up to you. If the first service is a good one, the dog was keen to mate, and the bitch was keen to stand, even after a preliminary objection or two, I do not feel that a second mating is really necessary. But if both owners agree, it will probably do no harm to have a repeat performance twenty-four to forty-eight hours later. Bearing in mind that it is possible for the bitch to conceive to both services, I consider it dangerous to have a second service more than forty-eight hours after the first. If, for example, you decided to repeat the mating three days after the first, and the bitch should whelp three days early to the first service, then any pups that were conceived to the second service would be six days premature and their chances of survival would be in jeopardy.

Once the mating is completed, the fee has been paid, receipt, pedigree and litter registration form given, let the bitch have a short rest before setting off on the return journey. On arriving home let her exercise quietly and feed as normal before returning her to her usual kennel and routine.

5

Pregnancy and Whelping

The normal gestation period in dogs is sixty-three days (*see*, opposite), although it is quite common for a bitch to whelp up to three days early or late without cause for concern. As sperms can live inside the bitch for up to four days it is possible for conception to take place during the four days after the mating. Puppies born much beyond this margin, however, have a much lesser chance of survival.

Signs of Pregnancy

Individual breeders have their own ways of telling whether or not their bitches have conceived and how many puppies they are likely to have. Behavioural changes often occur, with the normally lively animal becoming quieter and more reserved. Teat enlargement in maiden bitches from the second week on is a good sign, but matrons will often develop this sign whether they have mated or not. Some believe that if the uterine discharge stops after mating, this is a sign that the bitch has conceived, but it has been proved to be a rather shaky belief as many bitches continue to discharge for the full term of the heat and still produce good litters. Expert hands can feel the number of heads between the twenty-first and twenty-eighth day, after which the heads will disappear up the horns of the uterus. We now have scanning machines readily available which give reliable information if taken at the right time: scans are less reliable if taken too early. There are pregnancy testing services which can be employed. Your vet will need to take a blood sample from the bitch between twenty-eight and thirty-seven days after the last mating, which will be sent away for testing. The results which are said to be at least 95 per cent accurate are usually available within a couple of days.

False or phantom pregnancies only add to the problem and happen with strongly maternal bitches even when they have not

94

Gestation table. The first column shows the mating date; the second column shows the expected whelping date.

Jan	Mar	Feb	Apr	Mar	May	Apr	June	May	July	June	Aug	July	Sept	Aug	Oct	Sept	Nov	Oct	Dec	Nov	Jan	Dec	Feb
1	5	1	5	1	3	1	3	1	3	1	3	1	2	1	3	1	3	1	3	1	3	1	2
2	6	2	6	2	4	2	4	2	4	2	4	2	3	2	4	2	4	2	4	2	4	2	3
3	7	3	7	3	5	3	5	3	5	3	5	3	4	3	5	3	5	3	5	3	5	3	4
4	8	4	8	4	6	4	6	4	6	4	6	4	5	4	6	4	6	4	6	4	6	4	5
5	9	5	9	5	7	5	7	5	7	5	7	5	6	5	7	5	7	5	7	5	7	5	6
6	10	6	10	6	8	6	8	6	8	6	8	6	7	6	8	6	8	6	8	6	8	6	7
7	11	7	11	7	9	7	9	7	9	7	9	7	8	7	9	7	9	7	9	7	9	7	8
8	12	8	12	8	10	8	10	8	10	8	10	8	9	8	10	8	10	8	10	8	10	8	9
9	13	9	13	9	11	9	11	9	11	9	11	9	10	9	11	9	11	9	11	9	11	9	10
10	14	10	14	10	12	10	12	10	12	10	12	10	11	10	12	10	12	10	12	10	12	10	11
11	15	11	15	11	13	11	13	11	13	11	13	11	12	11	13	11	13	11	13	11	13	11	12
12	16	12	16	12	14	12	14	12	14	12	14	12	13	12	14	12	14	12	14	12	14	12	13
13	17	13	17	13	15	13	15	13	15	13	15	13	14	13	15	13	15	13	15	13	15	13	14
14	18	14	18	14	16	14	16	14	16	14	16	14	15	14	16	14	16	14	16	14	16	14	15
15	19	15	19	15	17	15	17	15	17	15	17	15	16	15	17	15	17	15	17	15	17	15	16
16	20	16	20	16	18	16	18	16	18	16	18	16	17	16	18	16	18	16	18	16	18	16	17
17	21	17	21	17	19	17	19	17	19	17	19	17	18	17	19	17	19	17	19	17	19	17	18
18	22	18	22	18	20	18	20	18	20	18	20	18	19	18	20	18	20	18	20	18	20	18	19
19	23	19	23	19	21	19	21	19	21	19	21	19	20	19	21	19	21	19	21	19	21	19	20
20	24	20	24	20	22	20	22	20	22	20	22	20	21	20	22	20	22	20	22	20	22	20	21
21	25	21	25	21	23	21	23	21	23	21	23	21	22	21	23	21	23	21	23	21	23	21	22
22	26	22	26	22	24	22	24	22	24	22	24	22	23	22	24	22	24	22	24	22	24	22	23
23	27	23	27	23	25	23	25	23	25	23	25	23	24	23	25	23	25	23	25	23	25	23	24
24	28	24	28	24	26	24	26	24	26	24	26	24	25	24	26	24	26	24	26	24	26	24	25
25	29	25	29	25	27	25	27	25	27	25	27	25	26	25	27	25	27	25	27	25	27	25	26
26	30	26	30	26	28	26	28	26	28	26	28	26	27	26	28	26	28	26	28	26	28	26	27
27	31	27	May 1	27	29	27	29	27	29	27	29	27	28	27	29	27	29	27	29	27	29	27	28
28	Apr 1	28	May 2	28	30	28	30	28	30	28	30	28	29	28	30	28	30	28	30	28	30	28	Mar 1
29	Apr 2			29	31	29	July 1	29	31	29	31	29	30	29	31	29	Dec 1	29	31	29	31	29	Mar 2
30	Apr 3			30	June 1	30	July 2	30	Aug 1	30	Sept 1	30	Oct 1	30	Nov 1	30	Dec 2	30	Jan 1	30	Feb 1	30	Mar 3
31	Apr 4			31	June 2			31	Aug 2			31	Oct 2	31	Nov 2			31	Jan 2			31	Mar 4

been mated. Unmated, maiden bitches have also been known to have false pregnancies owing to excessive hormone activity. Confusion arises when even the experienced breeder is sure that their bitch is in whelp at five or six weeks and then all signs of pregnancy gradually disappear. It is generally accepted in these cases that the bitch has absorbed the puppies into her natural tissues for various reasons, such as death of the foetuses. However, it is always a puzzling and sad phenomenon.

Unless there is some hugely important reason for knowing early on whether or not your bitch is in whelp, all will be revealed in due course. I have never been an advocate of palpating bitches, scanning or whatever else. By the fourth or fifth week it will usually become apparent whether or not you have a lady-in-waiting by the obvious enlargement of the abdomen. You can measure the bitch each week to check if you want. During the later stages of pregnancy, it is possible to see the unborn puppies moving and that is the best possible sign that a litter is on the way.

Infertility

Timing of mating, hormone deficiency, bacterial infection, obesity, incorrect feeding and/or exercise have already been pointed out as possible reasons for apparent infertility. There are plenty of other reasons of which I shall mention just three which are considered more probable.

Fertility can be reduced by extreme discrepancy in age: if either parent is very young or old. Later in life, the reproductive capacity of both sexes moves into decline and puppies from an older bitch may not be as strong and sturdy as before. The numbers and activity of sperm from an older stud-dog decrease and the ova of the bitch may not shed. To minimize these risks, the best breeding stock should be in the prime of life – in our breed that would be between two and five years of age.

There is no doubt that bitches will often miss to an overused stud-dog. A point to be remembered when choosing a stud-dog for your bitch. A reputation for infertility travels fast, so however much stud-dog owners dislike turning down a service or a stud fee, there must be some regulation in the numbers of matings within a given period, particularly with the young or old stud-dog.

That sperm cells are killed by excessive acidity in the vagina is a proven fact (although the normal vaginal secretion is slightly acidic). However, as the first stage of ejaculation from the stud-dog (from the prostatic gland) is alkaline, this would normally be neutralized. Acidity can be tested by using blue litmus paper, which will turn red if excess acid is present. The pre-mating treatment for excessive acidity is to flush the vagina (douche) with a mild alkaline solution.

Care of the In-Whelp Bitch

For the first four weeks, the in-whelp bitch should be treated as normal in all respects. However, do discourage jumping or extremes of work or exercise as the pregnancy progresses. Her life should involve as little stress as possible, and, again, this becomes more important the heavier in whelp she becomes. For this reason, many never show a bitch from the time she is mated until she has raised her litter and is back in the pink of condition. There is no doubt that being shown is stressful for dogs (and owners) but, of course, individual dogs have different degrees of stress tolerance and cope with it differently. My own feelings are that if the bitch is to be shown, it should not be beyond the fourth week of pregnancy.

Puppy rearing begins in the womb, so correct feeding and exercise are vitally important. For the first four weeks the in-whelp bitch should be fed as normal on good-quality food that makes up a balanced diet providing all the essentials for well-being. If you feed the complete diet food plus brewer's yeast tablets and cod-liver oil, then little else will be required during this period. From the fifth week on, she will require extra quantities of food and more additives as her appetite increases owing to the rapid develpment of the foetuses. Give two smaller meals a day rather than one large one which may cause discomfort, increasing the intake of protein rather than starch: eggs are very useful in supplying vitamins, iron, phosphorus and other minerals. A drink of milk may be taken readily and regarded as a treat. Mashed green vegetables mixed in with the food are a helpful variation. Bone meal or calcium contains the vitamins A and D in the correct proportions and promotes good bone, strong teeth and sound muscle development. Seaweed in powder or tablet form is thought to help particularly with pigmentation. Follow the manufacturer's instructions for all these additives as, paradoxically, too much calcium, for example, has been proved to have a detrimental effect on bones and joints causing an increase in hip dysplasia, not a disease that our breed suffers from but the example shows that there seems to be a fine line between what is beneficial and what is detrimental.

Two-thirds of a puppy's birth weight is gained in the last three weeks of pregnancy. The demands put on the bitch to supply all the nutrients they need at this time are enormous and she can only give so much without dipping into her own reserves. In the last two or three weeks, as she becomes heavier and the pressure on her abdomen increases, the meals should be given three or four times a day. In the penultimate week I have always given two calcium, two seaweed and two raspberry leaf tablets together with a teaspoonful of olive oil per day. The latter two are given as an aid to easier whelping and I prefer tablets so as to be sure that the bitch is getting her requirement at this stage. I increase this dosage to three tablets each of calcium and seaweed, four raspberry leaf and two teaspoons of olive oil per day during the final week.

Whilst all this information about extra feeding is extremely important, remember my earlier words that a fit dog is not a fat dog. Although, in this case, the dog is becoming fatter by the minute, it is not to be confused with obesity, which in all dogs – but most especially in the in-whelp bitch – can be so problematic, causing difficulties in conception and whelping, and the birth of small and/ or feeble litters.

A normal, regular bowel action is important to all dogs, but in particular to the in-whelp bitch. Foods which may cause hard motions should be avoided. Bones should not be given as they cause hard, chalky motions which are difficult to pass with the resultant discomfort. If this problem should arise, it can be treated with liquid paraffin which acts as a lubricant passing through the anus. As always, clean drinking water should be available at all times, and is essential to health and helpful with bowel action.

Proper exercise should not be overlooked, and is essential for general good health, bowel action, circulation and muscle tone both within and without, so vital in the act of whelping. In the first four to five weeks, the bitch can be exercised as normal along with the rest of the kennel, although do deter her from jumping. After this time, she may well quieten down of her own accord but, if not, let her walk and run freely rather than on a lead but limit the duration and intensity of the exercise. This can be continued right up to the time of whelping. In the last couple of weeks of pregnancy, because of her size, she should be discouraged from anything but a healthy walk and will probably be happier and more comfortable being taken alone or in the company of a less energetic member of the kennel. If kept with the pack, she will probably not be able to resist the temptation of trying to join in with all their games and overtire herself.

A word about the coat and grooming. I find that to give a trim around the fourth or fifth week of pregnancy is about right, particularly if the bitch is to continue her show career afterwards. This timing has two advantages: firstly, the bitch will still feel comfortable going through the trimming session at this stage. If done much later she may well not be happy about it and I think that to put a heavily in-whelp bitch through this is unkind. Secondly, the coat will still be in reasonable order for you to work on once the litter is two or three weeks old.

Simple brushing and grooming in small doses can be carried on up to the whelping day and will make the bitch more comfortable. A week before she is due, trim the long hair from around her teats, anus and vulva. I usually cut a channel clear starting at the outside of the first row of teats and taking off all the hair right the way through to the outside of the other row, in readiness for the suckling puppies. Cleanliness is vitally important not only to the bitch but to her puppies when they are born, so if she is a bit grubby or has been running in farm fields where she may have picked up traces of pesticides or fertilizers in her coat, then give her a gentle bath during the last week and exercise her away from these hazards for the remainder of her pregnancy.

Finally, a week before the expected date, let her stay in the whelping room and get used to being in the whelping box away from the rest of the kennel. Most bitches take to this almost as though it is a relief that you have not forgotten, and soon settle down peacefully to await the big day.

Whelping Preparations

Nowadays, a fortune can be spent on various items of 'essential' equipment and ancillary items. It really depends on the depth of your pocket and knowing your probable requirements. The items you will certainly need are:

Whelping box

A plentiful supply of newspapers
Veterinary thermometer
Sharp blunt-ended scissors
Hot-water bottle or heated pad
Cardboard box
Mild antiseptic
Dull emitter heat lamp
Bottle of brandy
Patience, strong constitution, knowledge and a clear head.

The mother-to-be will appreciate a quiet place of her own to settle down to the job in hand. A good strong, properly constructed whelping box is essential. Made with the right facilities it will be invaluable, save a lot of time and trouble and last for many years. It will need to be the correct size: too small and the dam (mother) will feel cramped and uncomfortable increasing the possibility of new-born whelps (puppies) getting laid on; too large and you may have problems keeping the whole box at an even temperature, and there

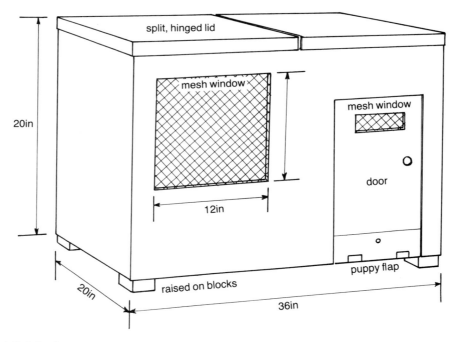

Whelping box.

is also the danger of whelps straying away from the mother in some remote corner and becoming cold. For a West Highland Terrier, a box about 36 × 20 × 20in (92 × 51 × 51cm) is suitable. It should have a hinged lid, split in half so that you can have it totally shut, totally open,or half shut, half open. A door at one end of the front for access, which should end 6in from the bottom, with a hinged, drop-down flap beneath. When the door is open but the flap closed, this will allow the dam freedom without the whelps falling out of the box or, later, the puppies following her. The other side of the front can have a wire-mesh window for observation, which should be approximately 12 × 12in (30 × 30cm). Inside the box, place guard (pig) rails around all four sections, about 2in (5cm) equidistant from the sides and the floor, as protection against the dam lying on a whelp that crawls around her off side.

I prefer the dull emitter type of heat lamp to the normal type whose bright light can upset a bitch, and it cannot be comfortable being kept in perpetual brightness. The dull emitter I use has its own support and is floor standing with a heavy base, so that it stands outside the whelping box. It also has telescopic height adjustment for heat regulation and is preferable to the type that hangs by chains above the whelping box. If you use the hanging type, take great care to secure the chains using at least two hooks for added safety lest one should fall out.

During the whelping, newspapers are the best bedding as they are warm, absorbent, readily available, easily changed and disposable. If you are lucky enough to have access to unprinted newspapers these are perfect, the only drawback with old ones being that the printing ink will rub off onto both the dam and the pups. This is a minor consideration, but for a while you will have West Highland Grey Terriers.

Do not forget to remind your vet of the imminent appearance of the litter so that if you need to call him out at some godforsaken hour of the night, he has at least been forewarned.

Signs of Labour

There are several indications that a bitch is about to start labour, but the only foolproof one is her temperature. The normal temperature for a dog is 101.4 °F (39 °C), and this will drop to between 97 and 99 °F (36.5 and 37 °C) when labour is approaching (this may happen several days before the actual whelping). It is safe to say that if the temperature is normal, the bitch is unlikely to whelp during the next twenty-four hours, so it is wise to check her temperature twice a day during the last week of pregnancy.

There are other signs which as a general rule are good indicators of imminent labour, but which are by no means guarantees. Most bitches will refuse food up to twelve hours before starting to produce their litters. Restlessness and the scratching-up of bedding are also usual occurrences but some will do these things and then after keeping you awake until the middle of the night, settle down to sleep, only to repeat the process for another day or two before finally giving birth.

The Normal Whelping

To what degree you should aid and assist during a whelping is a question of great debate. Some would argue that the bitch should be left alone to get on with it and many bitches do whelp by themselves, doing everything necessary without any problems. Others allow this natural process to happen, just keeping an eye on the events without interfering. My way, and it is shared by many, is to aid the bitch as unobtrusively as possible to ensure the safe delivery of the litter and to reduce the risks of complications and loss of whelps. After all the time, expense, thought and expectation this litter has cost, I want to be sure that should something go wrong or something need to be done, there is help to hand, and that I do not have to be wise with the benefit of hindsight, having left the responsibility for everything to nature, the dam and the lap of the gods.

Labour can be divided into two stages: the first stage can take from a few hours up to a day or more when spasmodic contractions which cannot be seen or felt by you, dilate the cervix and relax the vagina, vulva, birth passages and uterus. Until this process is complete the whelps cannot be born. The second stage is easily noticeable when the contractions become stronger and more rhythmical. The bitch will pant and be very restless but gradually the contractions will push down the lowest-lying puppy to the point of birth.

You may first see the membrane, or water bag, which may move in and out of sight with the ebb and flow of the contractions. This is the outer membrane which contains a greenish fluid, and helps to dilate the vaginal passage during birth. Inside this is another membrane which contains the whelp. Sometimes the water bag, which looks like a balloon, will break naturally during the birth (known as a dry birth), or the bitch may break it with her teeth. Inexperienced breeders sometimes break the water bag thinking it contains a puppy, but you should not do this as it may complicate the birth. Always feel a membrane when it appears: if it is soft, it is a water bag, if hard it has a puppy inside it. Once the puppy has been delivered, a further contraction will produce the placenta (afterbirth). The membrane should be broken using the nails of your fingers and removed, so that the puppy's head, mouth and nostrils can be cleaned with a towel. Of course, your hands should be scrubbed clean before you do this. A puppy can easily die from suffocation or from swallowing fluid and membrane, so it is vitally important that no time is lost. Even if only the puppy's head is born, you should wait no longer than just a couple of contractions before breaking the membrane and cleaning the mouth and nostrils. Most puppies are born with the placenta still attached by the umbilical cord, which, after waiting a minute or so, you should remove. Hold the puppy in one hand, and with the thumb and forefinger of the same hand, measure 2in (5cm) from the puppy's navel. Then, whilst gently squeezing the cord, cut it at the 2in (5cm) marker with sterilized scissors, allowing the placenta to fall into a bucket or on to some newspaper. It has been theorized that the dam should be allowed to eat the placenta as it is a source of nourishment and stimulates milk flow; equally, it has been theorized, after careful study, that the placenta is of little value. In fact, many bitches if allowed to eat them only vomit them back later, and having tried both ways I have not seen any noticeable difference.

After removing the placenta, gently but vigorously rub the puppy with the towel. This not only dries the puppy and helps prevent it becoming chilled but stimulates the circulation and internal organs of the newborn. Check the sex and weight for your records, and since such records should be kept, refer to them as dogs and bitches not boys and girls. Identify the puppies by marking each one on its tail with a different-coloured, non-toxic felt-tip pen. Finally, check for obvious outward deformities and, with great care, open the mouth to check that the puppy does not have a cleft palate (split in the roof of the mouth). Puppies with cleft palates should be destroyed because they cannot suckle properly as the milk intake is lost through the aperture in the roof of the mouth and out of the nostrils. Consequently, they will die miserably from starvation within a day or two anyway.

This may seem a lot to do but in fact it should not take more than a minute or two, and the puppy should be returned to its mother as soon as possible. She will no doubt be telling you as much all the while and should be reassured with kind words. Repeat this procedure after the birth of each puppy, recording the details once each puppy has been returned.

Newborn and young puppies can die if they catch a chill so throughout the whelping remove and replace any wet or heavily soiled newspapers and make sure that the temperature inside the whelping box is 75 °F (23.9 °C) for the first two weeks, gradually reducing to 60 °F (15.6 °C) by the end of the fourth week.

When the litter has been born, the mother will relish a bowl of warm milk and glucose, especially if she has whelped the whole litter without one, before being taken outside or to some place where she can relieve herself. You will probably have to carry her there and close doors behind you so that she cannot run straight

Contented two-week-old puppies at the milk bar. (Photo by Chris Kernick.)

back, as now and for two or three weeks she will be very reluctant to leave the puppies. During the couple of minutes she is away, you can make another check on the litter, put fresh newspapers in the whelping box and generally tidy up, so that when she returns she can settle down with her new family in comfort and take an undisturbed (by you) rest. You will probably need to do likewise but if, like me, exhausted as you may be, you are still feeling elated, you may just need to unwind before sleeping. Now you can relax in an armchair for a while and open the bottle of brandy!

Complications

As a general rule, whenever there is a difficulty with an abnormal labour, birth or whelping, professional advice should be sought. However, there are times when immediate action is necessary, probably a life-saving action.

Breech Birth

The most common difficulty is probably found with the breech birth, when the puppy is born rump, rather than head first. Mostly this will not create much extra trouble and the bitch will successfully part with the puppy and continue with her duties. When pups are born head first and in the head-down position, because the head is the largest part it naturally stretches the birth passages so that once the head is born a further contraction or two expels the rest of the puppy. In a breech birth the head is not in this position and therefore the rump may emerge leaving the head to follow through an under-dilated passage, thus making the act of producing the head difficult. Should this be the case and the bitch be straining without getting anywhere, there is no choice but to take immediate action by pulling. The placenta is almost certain to have detached from the uterine wall which cuts off the oxygen supply to the puppy, so unless the head is freed it will suffocate.

It is almost impossible to grip an unborn puppy bare-handed, since nature has made them slippery to aid the birth process. Using disposable towel, tissue paper or, better still, surgical lint, hold the puppy's body firmly, but taking care not to squeeze which could crush the fragile bones or impair the delicate organs. Gently pull as and *only* as the bitch contracts; *stop* pulling when the contraction

105

stops. This is extremely important. In this way, the head should be born without much difficulty or delay. The same procedure can be followed for normal births should the bitch be having difficulty with delivery, say, because of size.

Uterine Inertia

There are two types of uterine inertia, primary and secondary. Primary inertia is a condition where the bitch fails to have contractions at all, in which case, a pituitary injection given by the vet will usually start her off within an hour or two. If this fails, a Caesarean section will probably be required. Secondary inertia follows a prolonged labour resulting in exhaustion. Pituitary injections are useless in this case, and can be dangerous in that there is a great risk of causing a ruptured uterus. A Caesarean operation will be necessary.

Whether the cause of inertia is primary or secondary, veterinary help should be obtained immediately.

Caesarean Section

With today's anaesthetics and aftercare, Caesarean section is not the perilous operation of yesteryear. Because of their conformation and adherence to type, West Highland White Terriers are generally self-whelpers, whereas in some other breeds birth by Caesarean section is considered almost routine. In our breed by and large, this operation will be necessary only as a last resort, say, when uterine inertia has set in or when there is an obstruction preventing the birth, for example a large or badly positioned puppy. In skilled hands, the bitch will only be asleep for a few minutes, although she will be drowsy for a while afterwards. However, given that the operation meets with some success, resulting in live puppies, one of the biggest problems can be the dam's acceptance of them. Since she has not been aware of the birth process herself, she may, in her drowsy condition, be confused, aggressive towards them or unwilling to accept them as her own. If you can obtain a placenta from the vet and rub the puppies all over with it, this will help. Whether you do this or not, vigilance and great care are needed until you are sure that she has accepted them. However, most bitches do accept and rear the litter as if nothing out of the ordinary had happened. One of the most difficult decisions to make is when to ask for a Caesarean section to be performed. This is why you should try to build up a good rapport with your vet so that he understands your dilemma and so that you can discuss the facts of the matter and be guided with confidence by his advice. All too often these days, vets start talking of Caesareans almost before you have said 'Hello' on the telephone. There is no doubt that you have a difficult decision to make: if a Caesarean section is performed too early, without exploring the other avenues which may be open to you, you may discover later that it was not necessary; but if it is performed too late, you will probably lose the puppies and possibly the bitch. The old saying 'better to be safe than sorry' applies well here.

Delays

Delays may occur in labour and should be carefully monitored. In the early stages which can be quite prolonged, when contractions are slight and spasmodic, reasonable delays need not cause too much anxiety. But if the bitch has been straining with regular contractions for two hours, without producing a puppy, call veterinary assistance.

Postnatal Problems

Eclampsia

Eclampsia is caused by a lack of, or a serious draining of, calcium from the brood-bitch. It seldom affects maiden bitches. It usually occurs after whelping, sometimes a few days later, but at any time during the nursing period, particularly when the bitch is nursing a large litter. The first signs include the bitch's becoming very restless, and then hysterical, before this gives way to lethargy. After this, she may suffer convulsions and lose consciousness. This is very serious and requires immediate veterinary assistance.

Treatment   Calcium with vitamin D should be given as part of the diet during pregnancy. Affected cases must be treated immediately with large intravenous injections of calcium administered by a vet. Until the bitch has recovered, the puppies must not be allowed to feed from her, further draining her resources. Once this is done, the effect can be quite miraculous, even when a bitch has suffered unconsciousness during the period. She will suffer no ill effects and

107

will soon be back nursing her litter. Keep a careful eye on her in case the symptoms recur and supplement her feeds with calcium and vitamin D.

Mastitis

This is the inflammation of the teats after pregnancy, which is very painful and can sometimes develop into an abscess. Mastitis can also occur after a false pregnancy.

Treatment   Consult your vet, who will probably prescribe antibiotic treatment.

Post-Whelping Metritis

This is a serious condition causing a foul-smelling brown discharge (which should not be confused with the normal postnatal discharge described on page 115), and a high temperature. It most often occurs after a difficult whelping and symptoms are usually apparent within about twenty-four hours. Emergency veterinary assistance is vital.

Overheating

I have previously mentioned the required amount of heat, but have experienced exceptions to the rule. I recently had a proven, good brood-bitch, who after whelping normally and carrying out her duties for two days became very fractious and would not settle with her puppies at all. After much thought and several failed solutions I wondered if she was too hot and so switched off the heat lamp. The result was that in a matter of minutes she settled down with the litter without any further problem.

On this particular occasion, it was a warm summer's day with no cooler circulating air. The heat lamp, coupled with the heat generated by the bitch and her puppies, was just too much, and she knew best! Often, there are signs which tell you whether the bitch and her pups are happy with the heat. For instance, if the puppies are spread around the edges of the whelping box as far away from the overhanging heat lamp as possible, then the heat should be turned down and/or the lamp raised up. On the other hand, if they are huddled together directly under the lamp, yet still do not feel warm to the touch, it is quite possible that they require more heat.

Hypothermia

Hypothermia can soon set in if a puppy strays from its mother and becomes chilled. The puppy may appear cold and lifeless or, more often, be treading air with its front paws as if in slow motion. Immediate action has to be taken to warm the puppy as rapidly as possible, but do not try to feed such a puppy as the digestive system will not be able to absorb food until it has been revived. The acknowledged treatment for hypothermia in humans is immersion in hand-hot water and can be well employed here. Immerse the whole puppy apart from the head until it shows good signs of revival before drying gently but vigorously with a rough towel and finishing with a hair-drier. A variety of other revival methods used by innovative breeders have been equally successful in puppy revival, such as wrapping the puppy in tin foil and placing it inside their clothes next to the skin.

Over-Protectiveness

From time to time you may have problems with an overkeen mother. Most bitches are very protective towards their families, particularly for the first few days or even weeks. Even a docile pet can change character and threaten to bite the owner's hand when she is rearing a newborn litter. This becomes problematic when you wish to carry out some function such as cleaning the whelping box, or examining the puppies. With all bitches, it is better if these functions can be carried out while the bitch is away for exercise. When this is not possible, and it is imperative that you disturb her, do the job as quickly as possible. If you fear being bitten you should try to keep her attention in one direction, while gently but firmly taking hold of her neck to keep her still, before carrying out the necessary task. Always use gentle, soothing words when visiting the whelping box and do not invite all the neighbours round to see the puppies, however proud you might be. She should have as much peace and quiet as possible.

Orphans or Abandoned Puppies

Dealing with orphans or abandoned puppies is a difficult job. It used to be the case that when a bitch had died or refused to rear her litter for some reason, one could soon employ the services of a foster mother, lists of such being advertised in the canine press. Today this is not easy, but if you are lucky enough to have a foster mother on hand, this is the best and easiest solution to the problem. If you have another bitch with suckling young in your kennel, a good possibility exists there. Care must be taken when introducing the pups to the foster mother, but once accepted she will rear them as her own. Even a maternal bitch without a litter or milk will be a great help, she will ease the load by cleaning, keeping them warm and giving love, leaving you to feed them. Often a maternal bitch will produce milk for the orphans, even if she has not recently whelped. However, the more likely solution is that you will have to hand-rear them yourself, enlisting the help of others if possible.

Whether fostered or hand-reared, the value of colostrum or first milk cannot be overstated. Colostrum contains antibodies which help the puppies to build up immunity against infection and disease. During the first four days, it is strong and pure until the bitch's milk begins to flow around the fourth day. The colostrum will continue along with the milk for twelve days, gradually becoming weaker over that period. Therefore, if the foster mother has been suckling her own young for more than four days, or if you are to hand-rear the puppies yourself, it is a great advantage if you have access to a supply of colostrum. Some ingenious breeders have hit on the idea of starting their own 'colostrum bank' by drawing off a small amount of first milk during the first four days, into a container or plastic bag and storing it in the deep freeze. Each time a bitch has a litter, more first milk is added. When required, it is warmed and given by dropper or tube for the first few days.

Hand-rearing is an unenviable task and will stretch your powers of endurance unless you can enlist the help of some friends or family. Feed every two hours (three during the night) by dropper or bottle, or every four hours by tube. I prefer the tube not only because it is easier to use and less time-consuming, but because I can be sure exactly what the puppy has taken. (Tube-feeding takes about two minutes, dropper/bottle about ten to fifteen minutes.) In support of bottle feeding, I accept the argument that it encourages the suckling reflex, but I do not see that it matters, as once you have fed the pups until they can be weaned they stop suckling to start lapping and eating. Puppies will not suck in air if fed by tube which they certainly will do if a bottle or dropper is used. Whatever your preference, so long as it meets with success it is the right choice. To bottle-feed, a premature baby bottle with a soft nipple is best. For tube-feeding, a catheter tube and syringe can be obtained from your vet or chemist. All equipment and your hands must be scrupulously cleaned before use; after use the feeding equipment should be sterilized as an extra precaution.

There are several good proprietary brands of milk substitute available from vets and pet shops, which should be given at blood temperature. Individuals have their own home-made recipes, most of which seem to be only slight variations of the same. Here is one recipe:

1 teaspoon milk powder
1 teaspoon glucose, sugar or honey
¼ pint of cow's milk
1 teaspoon of double cream
1 pinch of salt
2 drops of children's liquid vitamins

Before using a tube, lay it against the puppy and mark the distance from the puppy's mouth to its last rib. Fill the syringe with the correct amount of mixture and join it to the tube. Insert the tube into the puppy's mouth over the tongue, then gently down the throat until you reach the marker. Slowly inject the mixture, then gently withdraw the tube. Seek the supervision of a more experienced breeder when doing this for the first time.

For the first few days of life, puppies will urinate only when stimulated, normally by the bitch's licking. You will have to take over by imitating the rhythmic, stroking action with a finger. All puppies will defecate naturally after every feed as the build-up of food in the stomach starts an involuntary reflex action.

Resuscitation

Reviving apparently lifeless puppies or ones in poor condition can be achieved in all manner of ways. Their condition is quite often owed to a lack of oxygen caused by a blockage in the mouth and nostrils; a prolonged birth, when the placenta has become detached prematurely; or by the effects of anaesthetic given to the bitch during a Caesarean operation. Firstly, make sure that the air passages are free from obstruction. Opening the mouth is sometimes enough to make the puppy gasp. Wipe away any fluid from the mouth and nostrils and watch for more fluid being discharged (the puppy may well have inhaled liquid during its birth). Stimulate the puppy by rubbing against the grain of the coat briskly but gently with a rough towel. A drop of brandy on the tongue may encourage the all-important first breath which, once achieved, usually results in normal respiration. In a short time, as oxygen enters the blood-stream the skin colour will turn a much more healthy pink and at this point the puppy can be returned to its mother who will carry on the stimulation with her licking. There are all kinds of ways that have achieved success and the end is far more important than the means. Dipping alternately in hot and cold water is one, and I know of another where the owner tried everything to no avail, so dropped the 'dead' puppy into an empty bucket only to hear cries a couple of minutes later. It seems the shock of the drop had 'bump-started' the puppy into life and it was returned to the mother, raised and subsequently became a champion.

Fading Puppy Syndrome

Fading Puppy Syndrome as it is now universally called, has been known for some time, but came to the fore a few years ago when a scourge of epidemic proportions affected many breeders.

A litter of apparently healthy puppies begin to cry incessantly, become cold, begin to dehydrate, stop or find difficulty in suckling, before gradually fading and dying. There are a number of known causes, some with suspected links, and others that are unknown. Many of the suspected causes are in themselves a danger to the newborn litter but they may be isolated problems unconnected with fading puppy syndrome. All you can do is treat each problem as and when it arises, but be vigilant for other tell-tale signs.

Of the suspected causes, I have already dealt with overheating and hypothermia (see pages 108–9). In addition, acid milk has been linked to the problem but all milk is slightly acidic. To ease your mind, you can give the mother milk of magnesia or some other anti-acid treatment. When puppies are suckling without making prog-ress it could be that the dam is overwrought or in mild shock for some reason, often after a Caesarean delivery, and is retaining the milk. A course of tranquillizers often remedies this problem.

Kennel cough, although rarely fatal, is highly infectious and the accompanying breathing problems are thought to have some con-nection with this syndrome (see Chapter 11, page 212). Certainly it can be dangerous to the unborn puppies, particularly during the last three weeks when they are developing rapidly. However, I know of a bitch who contracted kennel cough two days before whelping without any resulting ills to her litter. The veterinary comment was that the puppies were fully developed by that time, the crisis point being well past.

The importance of allowing blood to flow from the placenta to the newborn puppy for a few minutes after the birth has already been stated. It has been suggested that if severance of the cord is done too early, the puppy fails to receive enough protection by way of antibodies in its blood to fight infection.

Dehydration is often an accompanying symptom of Fading Puppy Syndrome and can be tested for by pinching the skin of the puppy. If the skin stays pinched or is slow to return to its normal state, the puppy is dehydrated. This can be quickly treated with a dropper or tubeful of cooled boiled water with two tablespoons of glucose and one teaspoon of salt added. Give freely (every half-hour) until recovered. Bad management, that is dirty housing, poor food and so on, will bring all kinds of ills to a kennel and whether there is a link with Fading Puppy Syndrome or not, it is to be deplored.

The fact that blood incompatibility can exist in humans is an established fact, and it is known to exist in certain blood groups of dogs. It has been suggested that this incompatibility may be a cause of Fading Puppy Syndrome. A course of antibiotic injections, tablets or preferably liquid (administered by tube) given to the puppies may help. I dislike newborn puppies having injections as in their weakened condition I fear the shock of the injection may do more harm than good. If blood incompatibility is feared, a different stud-dog should be used in future.

Certain infections are known to cause fading in puppies. *Beta haemolytic streptococcus*, otherwise known as BHS or 'strep', was the first to be investigated. It causes fading by leaving behind an infectious residue in the bitch's throat or vagina after an attack of tonsilitis or vaginitis, which is thought to infect the puppies after birth. They will die very quickly unless they receive treatment. Penicillin can have a dramatic effect if given early enough and should be given to both puppies and dam. Gamahtine serum is useful as it provides many of the protective antibodies found in blood. Infectious canine hepatitis also causes fading in puppies and should be treated in the same way as for BHS.

B- and E-coli bacteria live normally in the intestines, but for some reason they may multiply and become dangerous, often when the puppy is weak and susceptible. The advised procedure for this infection is to take the puppies away as soon as they begin to cry, feeding them on glucose and boiled water for three days or until they cease crying. Meantime, the bitch is treated with Penbritin injections. The puppies can be returned after three days when they will receive some of the antibiotics given to the bitch by injection through her milk as they suckle. The chances of there being any surviving puppies after three days, however, is very limited. My good friend Mrs Peggy Gamble who, together with husband Roy, owns the famous Blands Pembroke Welsh Corgi kennel went through two years of this scourge. During that time, much research was done with different serums being made up to counteract diffe-rent strains of infection. The Gambles overcame this problem by employing a strict regime which is still operated today.

All kennels, runs, etc., are disinfected twice daily with a proprie-tary canine disinfectant specifically formulated to kill infection. All bitches and prospective stud-dogs are treated for five days before the mating with Synulox. In-whelp bitches are treated again at five weeks' which is the optimum time that a bitch may absorb the litter, and again in the five days preceding the whelping. The Gambles even treat their pet goats as well! Any infected puppies are given children's liquid penicillin, and the bitch a course of Synulox. Peggy maintains that if the puppies are not treated as well, there is little chance of survival because the infection is so lethal that it will kill the puppies before they can be returned to the mother.

The use of Synulox is preferred as Peggy tells me that in her experience BHS and various forms of E-coli will build up immunity to other antibiotics, whereas Synulox contains a substance that 'eats through' the resistance in all infections before the antibiotic works.

It would seem, therefore, that the saying 'prevention is better than cure' is especially wise advice to follow. Should one of these infections be suspected, treat with the appropriate antibiotic before mating, during pregnancy (five weeks) and before whelping.

Having read about the problems and difficulties that can be encoun-tered you would be forgiven for having feelings of trepidation at the prospect of breeding a litter. I often feel the same way when I read about ailments and diseases. But let me reassure you and put the whole thing in perspective. Have you ever sat in the doctor's surgery and, to pass the time, read the posters about heart disease, muscular dystrophy and other equally serious afflictions? Before long the imagination starts to run away at full speed, until the ache in your arm after yesterday's gardening becomes a sign of imminent heart attack. A vivid imagination will frighten you out of your mind sometimes. The facts are that, yes, all these difficulties, problems, infections, ailments and diseases do exist and, given a long and involved association with dogs, you will come across some of them at some time, but the vast majority of litters born and dogs kept are raised with little or no troubles at all.

Aftercare from Birth to Weaning

Even when whelping is trouble-free, I always let the dam have a precautionary antibiotic injection within twenty-four hours of the whelping. Her temperature will usually rise to about 103 °F (39.4 °C) in the immediate forty-eight hours but should return to the normal 101.2 °F (38.3 °C) at the end of that time. She will have a uterine discharge of blood and mucus for ten to fourteen days which turns a greenish colour on contact with air. This is quite normal. Newborn puppies will often be smeared with this green uterine discharge, becoming whiter as she licks them clean. They look quite like wet hamsters until they have dried and filled out, after a few days they always remind me of miniature polar bears.

After a day or two, the rear end of the bitch can be cleaned, and I do this by standing her hind legs in a bucket of warm soapy water in order to wash the area. Be sure to rinse and dry thoroughly before returning her to the litter. If the temperature stays high or the discharge starts to smell offensive and, possibly, contain traces of pus, this is a sign of infection, possibly metritis, and veterinary assistance is required immediately.

For the first few days, her motions will be black and possibly loose; again, this is normal but should it persist consult your vet. Check that her milk is flowing, which will be stimulated by the puppies' attempts to suckle. I have already mentioned the importance of colostrum (first milk), and care should be taken to ensure that each puppy is suckling properly. Depending on the size of the litter, the bitch will often turn on just enough 'taps' to feed them or open and close teats at will.

The ideal size of litter for a West Highland White Terrier is between three and five, although litters of up to eight are quite frequent. More than six and you will probably have to supplement the feeding with the occasional hand-feed. Personally, I prefer quality to quantity, though it does not follow that a small litter in number will be of any better quality than a large one. However, more puppies inevitably need more nourishment to help them grow properly and large litters impose a great strain on the resources of the bitch. I once had a litter of one puppy, which would have been a disappointment to many. That one puppy subsequently became Ch. Rotella Mighty Miss, so I would not mind all my litters comprising only one puppy as long as it became a champion!

Diet and Exercise

The dam needs good nourishment not only to rebuild her own physical strength but to supply her litter too. A high-protein diet of meat, fish, milk and eggs with added supplements in the correct amounts will provide this. Keep her on a light diet for the first few days: milk, eggs, thin milky porridge, and so on, are suitable and will alleviate the risk of mammary abscesses. Fish, tripe and chicken can be given if the bitch will take them. After a few days, try feeding good-quality raw meat, possibly minced, which is high in protein and stimulates milk production. Four or five meals a day is not too much and should be given in amounts that the bitch will take. Two milk feeds fortified with cereal or egg and two or three meat feeds, all supplemented with calcium (for bones and teeth), and seaweed powder (for pigmentation) is a useful guide. Clean drinking water should be available at all times.

Examine the bitch every day during one of her regular periods of exercise and, in particular, check the teats for any signs of swelling or mastitis. Although she will be very reluctant to leave the litter at first, her exercise periods should be gradually extended as the puppies become older and larger. Gentle exercise helps maintain lactation, and will make weaning that much easier when the time comes.

Dew-Claws

The dew-claws should be removed at three days unless the puppies are weak or very small, in which case they can be left a further day or two as I feel that although it is a very minor operation causing the minimum of discomfort, it can put the puppies back a day. I strongly advise the removal of dew-claws as the few seconds of discomfort at this early age saves much pain and trouble later in life when the dog inevitably snags them in long grass or on wire mesh. If they are left on, they will need to be trimmed regularly because, as they make no contact with the ground, there is no natural filing down and they can quickly grow into the leg, causing great pain and probably lameness. If left unattended, the area may become infected.

The removal of dew-claws can be done by the experienced layman with a pair of sharp, sterilized scissors. Simply remove the dew-claw above the pad where it joins the leg making sure to take away the root of the claw otherwise it may regrow. Blood loss and pain can be greatly reduced by exerting pressure above the pad using the thumb and forefinger. Cotton wool soaked in permanganate of potash, iodine or another mild antiseptic, can be used to staunch the initial blood loss.

The puppies are best taken away into a different room to the dam, as she will naturally become upset if the puppy cries out. In point of fact, many puppies do not cry out at all and I have known some that have slept right through the procedure. Return the puppies to the dam as each is completed where they will quickly settle down to suckle as if nothing had happened. Minor as it is, the novice should have a vet or an experienced person to do the job, whilst watching carefully and noting its execution for future reference.

Eyes and Ears

The puppies' eyes will begin to open at about ten to fourteen days and the ears a day or two later. Do not subject the puppies to any bright light at this time and then only gradually during the following week.

Most pups are born with pink noses and pads, although some will have darker colouring at birth on occasion. The pigment will usually start to darken after a couple of days, gradualy deepening in colour until the nose and pads are black. It is no great fault if some of the pads remain pink or partly so, as the Breed Standard says 'preferably black', but the nose should be black. However, patience is a great virtue and sometimes there may be a spot of pink on the nose itself or more usually on the top where the nose joins the muzzle which stubbornly refuses to turn black for weeks and, more rarely, months. In the vast majority of cases these small areas of pink eventually change to the desired colour.

Sweet dreams. (Photo by Chris Kernick.)

General Health

Be watchful at all times for signs of any problem or illness and check each puppy daily to see that it is gaining weight. Do continue to give a couple of drops of children's vitamins to each puppy daily. Otherwise, given that the dam is doing her duty and there are no other difficulties, all that is required for the first few weeks is a clean dry bed, 75 °F (23.9 °C) of warmth, milk on tap as and when required, and a good mum to keep them clean.

6

Puppy Management

By far the most involved stage of management in a dog's life is the period from weaning to adolescence. Having successfully bred the litter and seen the puppies through the first three weeks, when the dam has more or less taken care of their every need, the time comes when they gradually start to become more independent of her. It is also a time when your workload will multiply appreciably as you begin to take over the responsibilities.

Weaning and Early Feeding

Generally, puppies will be ready for weaning around five weeks of age and should be fully weaned by eight weeks at the latest. Of

Mischief by the armful. A litter of puppies aged six weeks. (Photo by Chris Kernick.)

course, there are so many variables with some dipping into mum's bowl almost as soon as they can stand at about three weeks, and others quite happy to keep on feeding from the dam.

Several factors can necessitate the want to wean earlier than normal. The dam may be a show specimen and wanted for that purpose, or she may not have sufficient milk to feed her offspring, or perhaps the puppies are orphans. Whatever the reason, the job can be started as early as three weeks of age by first teaching them to lap. There are numerous milk-substitute products on the market, all scientifically produced to simulate as near as possible, the bitch's own milk, although it must be said that her milk is best. One of these brands should be used to start the weaning process. Cow's milk contains only a third and goat's milk about half of the protein found in the bitch's own milk, so if either of these are used they should be enriched by adding full-cream milk powder. Add one tablespoon of powder to half a pint of cow's milk, and pro rata for goat's milk or different amounts, and boil together while whisking to ensure even distribution.

A raised feeding bowl is best for small puppies because it stops them walking in the food and can be adjusted to the correct height, which will help them in learning to feed. You may need to help by lifting them to the edge of the bowl and introducing their mouths to the milk. At first, you will probably need to dip each puppy's muzzle into the milk, just enough for it to be able to get its first taste, and after a splutter or two it will usually lick the milk off. With a little patience, puppies soon get the idea and within a day or two will be awaiting the next bowlful. At four weeks, meat, eggs and cereal can be introduced. Supplement one of the early milk feeds with crushed wheat biscuits and raw egg yolk can be added to another of the milk feeds. Egg whites should be cooked before being fed as, if fed raw, they destroy one of the B vitamins called biotin. Raw meat (lean beef) should be finely scraped for the first couple of days and the scrapings introduced to each puppy in turn on the end of a finger. Once this is being taken readily it can then be fed finely minced. Red minced meat should be fed raw, but no foods should be given to any dog direct from the fridge (ice-box) and any frozen foods should be properly thawed before feeding. Cooked minced chicken or fish can be added to the diet thus building up the variety of foods now being taken. Other than for milk, I like to feed the puppies in separate bowls to ensure that each gets its share. But watch them, for even at this tender age there will be squabbles when the gluttonous ones finish first and then try to steal what is left in the other bowls.

If you have not already started the process of weaning, it will start automatically at about five weeks with the advent of the needle-sharp milk teeth, all twenty-eight of them. Owing to the obvious discomfort, the dam will become more reluctant to feed the pups and will be spending longer periods away. She will continue to want to visit them several times a day, when she will check them out and play with them, and possibly allowing them to feed but only for short periods. By the time they are seven weeks old, she will probably have no milk left but will still want to see them from time to time. At this stage, mother and puppies should be separated or the sleeping box should be partitioned so that she can visit them but not vice versa.

With the puppies growing rapidly, the amount of food should be gradually increased. By six weeks, they should be having five meals a day, three milk-based and two of meat. Supplements of calcium, bone meal, seaweed powder and so on, can be added to the food in the correct amounts throughout puppyhood, adolescence and during adult life. Continue to give a few drops of children's liquid vitamins per puppy, per day throughout puppyhood.

Puppies are full of energy!
(Photo by Chris Kernick.)

They will enjoy chewing on digestive wheat biscuits or baby rusks and these can be given from five weeks on and the variety and amounts of food increased. Puppies require a high protein diet and any good wholesome food, rich in protein, can be given in the correct form. Between six and eight weeks, fine terrier meal or complete diet meal can be fed, which can then be gradually built up so that eventually it becomes the staple diet of the adolescent. As with all dogs, fresh drinking water should always be available, but it is especially important for puppies as they are naturally very active and will drink a lot.

Puppies should not go to new homes before they are at least eight weeks old, by which time they should be fully weaned and have been wormed twice. All new owners should be provided with a diet sheet, transfer form and a pedigree of at least three generations. Typically, a diet sheet for an eight-week-old puppy would be:

8 a.m.   Crushed wheat biscuits in warm milk.
11 a.m.   Scrambled or boiled egg with a little fine terrier meal.
2 p.m.   Raw minced beef, cooked minced chicken or fish.
6 p.m.   As 11 a.m.
9 p.m.   As 2 p.m.
10 p.m.   Warm milk.

One very experienced breeder I know habitually feeds at least one meal of tinned dog food, the reasoning being that some of the pups will be going to pet homes and, no matter what the advice given on feeding, may be given tinned food. If this happens, at least their digestive system will have become accustomed to it. Any change of diet should be done gradually otherwise diarrhoea can result, which is especially dangerous in young pups and the reason for this breeder's practice.

It will pay dividends to socialize your puppies as much as possible, not only for the benefit of the new owners but also for yourself. Handle them regularly, if only in play, and from four weeks place each one on a table and give it a light brushing every day. Get them used to different sounds by having a radio or television in the same room. Eventually, they will go into the big wide world so it is as well if they have been given an insight into what to expect.

By ten weeks, the complete diet meal can be increased, but still feed plenty of raw minced beef or tripe. Eggs in every form will help satisfy the growing and voracious youngster. By now, many pups will be showing less enthusiasm for the milk substitute and the milk-based feeds, and some will have weaned themselves off these feeds altogether. Ordinary cow's milk can now be given instead, possibly just morning and night.

The number of feeds can be reduced to four a day at about twelve weeks and then down to three a day at four or five months. With milk foods gone completely, the amounts of each feed should be increased with the addition of more complete diet meal or dog biscuit and meat, tripe or fish.

Worming

Treating for worms is not the drawn out, sometimes painful practice it used to be. There is no scouring of the stomach and no undue stress involved. Today's treatments are safe to use, easily administered and quite painless. There is no need to fast the puppies beforehand, but as they will turn out the contents of the stomach, it is wise to give the treatment a few hours before feeding time.

Puppies should be treated for tapeworms and roundworms twice, usually at six weeks and then again at eight weeks. Your vet will supply both product and advice, or there are many early-wormer products available from pet shops and the like, which, as always, should be used according to the manufacturer's instructions. For the treatment of roundworm only, I prefer to use the cream wormer. The amount given is determined by the weight of the dog. I prefer it because it is easily administered on to the tongue, the pups seem to like it and, unlike tablets, it is not easily spat out.

The incubation period for worm eggs is ten days, hence the need for the repeat dosing after two weeks. The first dose will get rid of any worms present, the second deals with newly hatched worms before they are mature enough to lay eggs of their own. Once treated, the process should be repeated throughout life, the frequency depending on the treatment you have chosen to use. Follow your vet's advice.

Exercise

Up to about ten weeks, puppies alternate between periods of immense activity and sleep. Older puppies are just the same except they sleep less in between. With a litter, there is little you will need to do to encourage exercise except to provide new and interesting playthings. They will dash around together expending energy, but with a single puppy you will have to take the place of its litter-mates otherwise, apart from short bursts, it will have nothing to run around for and will become bored, introverted and shy. Playthings such as a ball, squeaky toys, old socks or slippers and, not forgetting every puppy's favourite the cardboard box, will allay boredom and stimulate activity. Up to twelve weeks of age this kind of exercise will be enough. Until they have had their inoculations at twelve weeks you cannot take them out for exercise anyway and are limited to letting them play in the garden, in a play-pen or in kennel runs.

Once the inoculations are completed, puppies can be taken out for walks but the exercise should be increased only in gradual stages. Exercise of different kinds and the amounts in which it is given can improve or impair the overall conformation, (this subject is dealt with more fully in the next chapter, *see* pages 135–6). No matter how sturdy a puppy, it does not do to overtire them when they are still very young. With a gradual increase, coupled with their increased strength and maturity, by the time puppies are six months old they will be capable of all the activity and exercise you could reasonably expect (and you should expect a lot).

Running On

For showing and breeding purposes, when keeping pups to run on a while longer, it is always better to keep at least two. If you have another litter of a similar age, one from each litter could be kept. A lone puppy is infinitely more problematic when very young, and the two will be company for each other. Even if they do become the terrible twins, they at least will be much happier with a pal to share the blame. No matter if you do not intend keeping the second puppy permanently, it is wise to run the two together until the selected one can safely join the rest of the kennel.

Teething

At about three weeks of age the first of two sets of teeth begin to appear. These are called the first, the deciduous or the milk teeth, and will be completely grown by the end of the fifth week. There are twenty-eight milk teeth in a full complement, and, because there are not so many teeth as in the second (permanent) set, they are more widely spaced. They are softer and sharper and, unlike permanent teeth, they have no roots. They loosen before beginning to fall out as the permanent teeth start to come through at about four months of age.

Permanent teeth number forty-two in a full complement, and usually the last of these to cut are the canines. During the cutting of the permanent teeth, the puppy may go off its food and be a little lacklustre, as the cutting of this second set can be painful. Should this be the case, give a quarter of an aspirin every six hours to ease the discomfort.

The milk teeth should all come out as the permanent teeth push through. However, some milk teeth, particularly the canines, can be very stubborn and there is always the danger of misalignment. You can help the loosening by gently pressing each tooth in alternately opposite directions. If any milk teeth remain and the permanent teeth are well through the gums, a visit to the vet may be necessary to remove the offenders.

Chewing

This period of changing teeth is the time when puppies are most likely to chew. Chewing is an instinctive reaction to loosen the milk teeth. To limit damage to kennels, furniture and so on, it is wise to give the puppy something specific to chew. Cow hoofs are excellent as are the chew sticks that are available. Knuckle bones can be given and are excellent, but change them regularly to save the puppy swallowing any splinters it might gnaw away. If you can manage the puppy through this period without its getting into the habit of chewing the kennels or furniture, it is unlikely to form any permanent chewing habit.

Housing

The question of kennel housing will be more fully explained later. The small breeder or exhibitor can continue the regime employed with the puppies in their present accommodation as the whelping room will double as a puppy room. Larger kennels will have a separate puppy kennel with similar arrangements. Thought should be given to the arrangements for pet or house puppies and it must be borne in mind that they have come from a warm, dry, secure place and will need to be accommodated in an equally caring and responsible fashion. A box or bed with a small pen around it will help in all manner of ways: the puppy will be happy and secure, soon accepting this place to be its home; it will be safe from heavy feet and slamming doors at times when you have other chores to do; and allow some freedom of movement at such times, which will help with house-training. Careful thought should be given to its siting. Dogs will not thrive in permanently damp or draughty conditions, so choose a corner of a room away from outside doors and windows. Nor will they thrive if kept permanently away from companionship and human activity. For sleeping, a box is preferable to a basket or cage, which offer no resistance to draughts. A box raised up on blocks about 2in (5cm) from the floor allows air to pass underneath. Travelling boxes, available in various materials and sizes at pet shops and dog shows, are ideal. Used primarily as a place of rest and sleep, they can be used as a safe and secure place in transit and on benches at dog shows later. The best bedding material is a proprietary brand of the soft washable fleece that is now available. It is expensive but well worth the investment. It is hard-wearing, easily washed and hygienic. Newspapers in the play-pen facilitate house-training, are easily available and disposable, absorbent and prevent smells. From weaning to the time when the puppy is either house-trained or joins the outside kennel, excreta will be produced in ever-increasing amounts. Several layers of newspapers will be needed and the popular practice is to remove the top layers as they become soiled and replace with fresh layers. Deep litter systems are used by some, whereby fresh layers of newspaper are placed on top of the soiled ones throughout the day. The whole lot is cleared away and the system started afresh, once or twice a day. Deep littering has its advantages, but should there be any signs of diarrhoea, all the papers should be removed to prevent the spread of infection.

Early Training

Being naturally intelligent and gregarious, West Highland White Terriers thrive on attention and are easily trained. It is generally a fault of the owner or trainer using confusing or conflicting methods of training and upbringing, that lead to an insubordinate dog. In almost every case, a bad dog is not born but made, by humans. Bad habits are easily formed but difficult to break in the minds of the young. Therefore, in all aspects of training, be clear in the methods you employ, use the same commands, in the same tone of voice every time, and most dogs will quickly learn.

Training starts as soon as the puppy can see and hear, as it realizes by your actions or voice that something is being requested or encouraged. For the most part, when they are very young, all the signs are of encouragement as you heap praise on the puppy for performing a simple task, for example starting to lap. However, although they will understand some of the signs you give, complete understanding takes some weeks or even months and is usually a gradual process. Until a puppy fully understands, it may be difficult to get the message through. This can be a frustrating period, but the pup should never be beaten or struck with any force as this will only frighten it. There always seems to be one in each litter that demands constant attention and barks for it at all hours of the day and night. No matter how forceful the language used, as soon as your back is turned it starts again, so what do you do? I have found that a swipe

Peek-a-boo. Puppies aged ten weeks. (Photo by Chris Kernick.)

with a folded newspaper (which is aimed to miss), or a spray with tepid water from an old spray-gel bottle does the trick. Of course, the mischief maker will soon get wise to that course of action and treat it as a game, so you will have to employ new, harmless, but equally effective deterrents, until finally the puppy either understands or grows out of what is one of many passing phases.

Training to stand on a table will be of great advantage not only for the show ring but for grooming and visits to the vet. Five minutes on the table for brushing, trimming or some attention to toilette should be part of every puppy's daily routine. Show puppies can be taught to stand properly on the table during this early training, but at this stage they should be made to feel that it is all a game.

Take the puppy out in the car with you as often as you can. Many puppies are car sick but quickly overcome this after a while, so the sooner you start the better. Puppies intended for the show ring in particular are best taken in a box or cage, as this will no doubt be the mode of transit later.

House-Training

When you begin house-training, bear in mind that young puppies regularly defecate and urinate at certain times: after sleeping and after a meal. The use of newspapers is invaluable for this training. If run on newspaper, puppies will naturally use this area to empty themselves. When you allow free use of the house, always place some sheets of newspaper near the door. Each time a puppy goes to use these sheets, pick him up and put him outside. Never leave a puppy alone outside, no matter how long you have to wait, but immediately he has relieved himself, take him back inside with words of high praise. As they become used to this practice, it is an easy step to reduce the sheets over a couple of weeks, until finally they simply go to the door when they want to go out.

Remember that no puppy can go for hours on end without relief and should never be locked away for long periods. A soiled bed or floor will be the result and may undo much of the training learned. No puppy has a perfect control over its bladder and accidents will happen occasionally, but should never be punished. Puppies have little control, especially when excited or frightened. There is nothing to worry about, for these accidents will become less frequent and gradually disappear with puppyhood.

Lead-Training

Lead-training can be started as early as six weeks by fitting a puppy collar for a few minutes. This gets the pup used to having something around its neck. The length of time the collar is left on can be gradually increased until it has been completely accepted. The next step is to attach a lead, letting the pup play with it for a few minutes at first, before picking up the lead and encouraging the puppy to follow you. Puppies do vary in their acceptance of a lead: some will offer little or no resistance, while others will fight frantically to free themselves before finally accepting it. As always, soothing words of encouragement will help, but never pull or drag a puppy against its will, as it will only be frightened and possibly more determined not to accept it.

Early Grooming and Handling

Nails are best kept short throughout a dog's life. If they are allowed to grow, the quick also lengthens making nail trimming painful for the dog. Long nails will also spoil the feet, giving rise to splaying and flat-footedness by inhibiting the ability of the pads to close properly.

The nails can be trimmed weekly from about two weeks of age, using nail clippers or a pair of sharp scissors. This will also save discomfort to the dam as the puppy suckles. After weaning, and later in life if the dog is exercised on concrete, there will be little if any trimming or filing required, as the nails will be filed down naturally. An eye kept on their condition during grooming sessions will reveal any such need. Keep the hair between the pads short as this can soon become matted and harbour small stones, thorns and the like resulting in lameness.

Other than shaping the tail and ears, and removing the long hair from around the anus a puppy up to about eight to ten weeks requires little trimming. Light trimming of show specimens, however, often starts as early as five or six weeks with the removal of the long hairs from the top coat and a little shaping here and there. These long hairs which can be likened to baby hair are obvious in appearance and should not be confused with the profuse fluff seen in a soft coat. As the puppy reaches five to eight weeks, the new, tight coat can be seen beneath the longer hairs which are best removed by pulling a few hairs at a time, rather like plucking a chicken. If done properly, there is no pain, just a little discomfort. The puppy will no doubt complain, mostly at having to keep reasonably still for a while, which is totally abhorrent to it, so this removal should be done in several, very short sessions until completed. It is a matter of opinion whether or not the puppy looks better for this. Certainly, I can understand the attraction for the fluffy puppy, and the change in appearance, even with this very light trim, is quite startling, but how smart the puppy looks. Of course it is not only correct for the breed, but keeping a good shape and coat is much easier when started early and practised regularly, rather than having to start from square one on a coat that is completely overgrown.

Finally there is a preferred way to lift and hold dogs of all ages, especially applicable to puppies.

Entering from the left side of the puppy, place the left hand, palm up, under the chest and behind the forelegs. Wrap the thumb around the left foreleg, the index and middle finger fit between the legs for support and the third and little finger wrap around the right leg (reverse the directions if you are right-handed). When lifting, place your spare hand on top of its back to prevent struggling. Once lifted, hold the puppy close to your body, under your arm, where it will feel very secure. This method of carriage is used universally for all suitably sized dogs. Not only is it comfortable for the dog, but it is safe for both carrier and carried and gives the carrier a good degree of control.

7

Adolescent and Adult Management

When do puppies become adolescents, and adolescents become adults? For the show ring, the definition of each is as follows: up to twelve months, dogs are puppies; from twelve to eighteen months, they are juniors (adolescents); and over eighteen months they are, presumably, adults. In the context of management, particularly feeding and exercise, these exact ages do not apply.

The transition from one stage to another will depend on the individual dog, the breed, its strain, type and physical well-being. The change from puppyhood to adolescence can be more easily determined to be generally between ten and twelve months. From adolescence to adulthood is far more variable. Stages of maturity vary enormously from breed to breed, and from dog to dog within a breed. In our breed, some puppies are more mature than other three-year-old dogs and so in terms of management there are really no hard and fast rules. You simply have to treat each dog individually, according to its particular stage of physical and mental development and not place too much importance on age. With this in mind, the specifications given in this section can be adjusted to suit.

Feeding

My advice has been to introduce one of the complete diet feeds available at six to eight weeks. These bags of complete diet meal come in a variety of mixes which look like muesli, with higher or lower protein content, and are to a great degree all variations on a theme. However, do steer away from the ones that have a lot of flaked maize in them, which overheats our breed and will give rise to itchiness and often loose motions or diarrhoea. Cost has never been a deciding factor in my choice of foodstuffs, the important considerations being that the dogs enjoy the food and thrive on it. It does not necessarily follow that the more expensive ones will be better. In fact, having over the years used many different complete diet foods at various prices, I now use one of the cheapest, not for that reason but that the dogs do well on it.

Some take the view that complete diet foods are for the lazy owner, having only to mix with water or stock before serving. However, having tried many different methods and mixtures, I have found that not only is it easily prepared, stored, available and affordable, but my dogs enjoy and thrive on it. That is not to say that it is better than other ways of feeding, not at all, but I have always maintained that while the dogs do well on something I see no reason to change. It must be remembered that dogs are creatures of habit and dislike a change to their routine. You will hear tell of the dog that will eat nothing but rump steak or braised lamb, and would rather starve than eat dog food. This is the fault of the owner in serving up these delicacies, which have become the routine food for the dog, the food that he habitually expects to be served.

There are always times when a dog will go off his food for one reason or another, and at such times other foods will have to be used to tempt the dog to eat again. But by and large, dogs will look forward to feeding time with relish.

At six months, the puppy should be having three meals a day and this can be continued up to about nine months, the only change being to gradually increase the complete diet and reduce the additional foods. At twelve months, reduce the number of feeds to two per day, perhaps given morning and night. Remember to add some calcium, seaweed powder or bone meal to the food. There are also other supplements which you may consider beneficial for a particular reason, and these can be given as required. Brewer's yeast tablets are good for dogs of all ages and will be considered a treat, rather like sweets to children.

From this point on, it is a matter of opinion or, more correctly, good judgement, whether or not you reduce the feeds down to one per day. Some dogs will tell you by simply refusing one of their feeds, while other more greedy ones will eat as many meals as you care to supply. It will also depend on how active the dog is or what sort of metabolism he has. Very active dogs or those with a high metabolic rate will use more energy and therefore require a higher rate of nutrition to maintain the same condition. Is the dog well-bodied up and physically mature or lacking body and physically immature? The answers to these and other questions need to be known before you are able to decide. It is not really as complicated as it may sound and, in the final analysis, common sense should prevail. If you do reduce the number, content or amounts of food at any time and the dog begins to lose condition, it goes without saying that the process can easily be reversed until such time in the future when the change can be tried again.

Weight

To be able to set about improving the condition of an over- or underweight dog, an understanding of foods and their uses is required.

The protein content of food is essential to building the growing body, and repairing and renewing its tissues throughout life. Large amounts of carbohydrate coexist with the protein in the form of starch, which produces energy, excesses of which put on flesh. Therefore, an inactive dog who expends less energy, or a dog with a low metabolic rate, who is fed excess carbohydrate will put on body weight by converting carbohydrate to flesh. First-class proteins are to be found in lean meat, fish, eggs and milk. Root vegetables, beans, peas and grain products are second-class proteins.

Opinions vary, and some believe that feeding extra fat is best for putting on body. Fat provides the body with heat and there is no doubt that the dog will use the fat within its body to keep warm, any excess fat being absorbed into the tissues and adding to the body of the dog.

Bad Doers

Normally most dogs will empty their food bowls in double-quick time, especially when fed with or close to their kennel-mates. The term bad or poor doers is applied to those dogs who create problems by not eating regularly.

There are rarely problems of consumption with puppies or youngstock but if one of these refuses all food and at the same time is off-colour or lacklustre, I should have no hesitation in consulting expert advice.

However, occasionally an older adolescent or adult dog may go off his food for a time and there are also those finnicky individuals who are reluctant to eat any more than a subsistence diet. Unless loss of appetite is due to illness, this is not in itself anything to worry about for a day or so and the refused food should be taken away and fresh food offered at the next feeding time.

The exception to this is with the show dog, when amounts of body can be an important requirement, and I have noticed that by far the most important thing is to try to get the dog eating regularly again. The exact nutritional make-up of the new diet, though still important, is in the short term at least, a secondary consideration. For once the dog has regained his appetite he will in most cases, return quite happily to his regular food. Any good wholesome food can be tried as a change of diet. I have found that sheeps' tongues, lightly boiled and chopped, are a very tasty delicacy and are readily taken either alone or with a little biscuit or meal. Tripe and biscuit are often used as a staple and regular diet and can be a welcome change.

Some dogs are by nature at one stage or, even always, either slow eaters, or prefer to eat in seclusion, often eating only part of the food. The solution to this 'problem' is to feed them alone and where only part of the food is taken, to either feed two or more smaller meals or leave the bowl with the dog overnight. Almost without exception, the dog will eat more, and latterly all, of the remainder during the course of the night.

Obesity

Obesity is a scourge in all breeds of dog, particularly in our breed, which by its very nature is supposed to be very active and agile. Obesity will lead to an unfit, unhealthy, unrepresentative figure and, without doubt, shorten the life expectancy. It is often quite difficult to make a dog lose weight and, for this reason, it is better that the condition should not be allowed to set in.

I have used a very successful method of fat reduction at times and passed it on to others with equally good results. It should be stressed that this method is never used on old, sick or very unfit dogs in the manner prescribed, and should be employed with care in variations relative to each individual. I do not believe in abrupt, continuous starvation diets, as I consider them to be unkind. In order to reduce excess fat without distress it is important that the dog should still feel satisfied. I do this by feeding brawn, which is available in sausage-shaped tubes. It has little nutritional value and has a high water content. The dog can be fed brawn in the amounts he is accustomed to receiving, perhaps mixed with a very small amount of meal or biscuit, as usual. In this way, the dog's appetite is satisfied while the body is being undernourished. The body will then use up any excess fat by converting it to energy or heat. In a very short time, all the excess fat will have disappeared and the dog can then be placed on a carefully balanced, nutritional diet. When feeding this fat-reducing diet, I give the necessary amounts of vitamins and minerals in powder or tablet form.

Exercise

It is not my intention to specify to every reader the exact way to exercise a dog. From adolescence through to old age, the happy, healthy, well-trained dog will provide enormous amounts of pleasure. Being your constant companion in the park, on walks in the country, on the beach and so on, it is down to the individual to determine the amount and form the exercise will take. I stated previously that one of the great traits of the West Highland White Terrier is his adaptability, and he will happily take part in all forms of exercise from the short walk to the ten-mile hike. Exercise is gradually built up to what the dog can reasonably expect to be his regular and normal quota. It is unfair to expect the dog who has been used to a limited, if healthy, amount of exercise, suddenly to run for hours in chase of the ball you keep throwing for him while you are at the beach on holiday. So let common sense prevail.

With particular reference to show dogs, different types of exercise can either improve or impair the condition of the dog as a whole. At the same time, those forms of exercise used to improve a specific part of the dog may at the same time have an adverse effect on some other, equally important part. For example, while road walking will undoubtedly strengthen and tone up the muscles generally, especially in the hindquarters, it may also build up too much muscle in the shoulders of the dog, making them bossy or loaded. With this example in mind, take care to choose the correct exercises, and in the right degree, to accomplish your aims.

Free access to a small slope is excellent for building muscle in the thigh and second thigh. Exercise on rough or semi-rough concrete will file down the nails and save you an arduous task. Rough concrete and, better still, cinder or stony paths will tighten the feet and strengthen the pasterns, preventing splayed feet and weak pasterns which are so evident these days. A good 'valve opening' run each day will improve circulation, encourage bowel movement and stimulate the internal organs, in particular the heart and lungs. The experienced eye will soon notice the levels and types of exercise that are benefiting their dogs and make the necessary adjustments.

My own dogs have free exercise in their kennel runs throughout the day, a 'valve opener' at least once a day and the occasional walk on a lead. They are kennelled in pairs, a dog and a bitch together but swapped around at intervals throughout the day, which has the effect of encouraging activity as each dog plays with his new partner. It also allays boredom and stimulates new interest, as dogs, like humans, are all different, so that you are not just swapping one dog for another, but one individual for a completely different individual. It must be understood that however well you feed and groom your dogs, there is a mental factor involved. More about this in Chapters 9 and 10, but do try to understand their psychological needs and their thoughts – it can make a lot of difference.

Having never been too concerned about amounts of body, believing, as I keep repeating, that 'a fit dog is not a fat dog', I would rather wait until they body up naturally, than induce this bodying up artificially. The strain that I have always kept and bred tend to body up with maturity, usually between three and five years of age, and once they are in their prime, they last and last. I mention all this only to make a point to beginners, newcomers and that section of more experienced fanciers who think all good West Highland White Terriers are mature at two years of age. Unfortunately, market forces have been instrumental in encouraging this line of thought, with the result that, apart from the strains that mature early naturally, some dogs are spending a great deal of time locked in boxes.

So take care, think about the exercise you give and do not be too impatient as you wait for your lovely duckling to become an even lovelier swan.

Grooming and Handling

Regular brushing will remove tangles which if left may develop into a matting or felting of the coat. It will also remove much of the dirt and grime the dog picks up into its coat during its normal daily rompings. Do stick to having the dog on a table or raised surface, because it makes life so much easier. Remember to provide a non-slip surface: if you do not have a proper grooming table, a piece of carpet or the rubber foot-mats out of your car placed on the table top will be equally effective.

During this routine grooming session, check the length of the nails. If they are overlong and beginning to curl under, they need trimming. It is a job few dogs like and most dogs hate, so be as quick and as kind as you can. If you do not feel absolutely confident of doing the job efficiently and painlessly, enlist the help or guidance of a more experienced person. I prefer to use the guillotine type of nail clippers. Examine the nails first to establish how much you can take off without cutting into the quick, which can be painful. The quick is easily seen in light-coloured nails, not so easily in darker ones; you may find it easier to find if you look at the underside of the nail. Holding the paw in your spare hand, place the first nail into the clippers, measure the length of nail to be removed and quickly cut it off. Provided you have not cut into the quick and have carried out the job with speed, the dog will feel no pain and will probably not realize what has been done. Carry on in this manner nail by nail and paw by paw until the job is complete. If the dog is being difficult, it will help if someone holds his head while you finish. In extreme cases, you may have to let the vet do the job, who may sedate the dog beforehand.

Good, strong, clean teeth are not only a boon to the show dog but a subject of general care in every dog. The teeth will become discoloured and build up deposits of tartar which will lead to tooth decay. This can be prevented or alleviated by regular dental care. If practised from puppyhood, dental care will be more readily accepted as part of the normal routine. Tartar should be removed using a dental descaler or the edge of a clean coin and the teeth cleaned using a small toothbrush or clean mascara brush dipped in 10 per cent hydrogen peroxide, 90 per cent water, or ordinary toothpaste. I have seen the use of tooth powder being advocated for cleaning but a dentist friend tells me this can be harmful to the teeth. The powder is very abrasive and will in time remove the enamel from teeth, leaving them weakened and more susceptible to decay. Gnawing on a bone will help to keep the teeth in good order; it also stimulates the appetite and strengthens the jaws. Chicken and rabbit bones should never be given as they easily splinter. Similarly, small bones are dangerous if swallowed and care should be taken when giving any bones. Large lamb bones are safer and will give much pleasure.

Unless you wish to become involved in exhibition, wish to learn to trim as an accomplishment, hobby or for some aesthetic reason and have plenty of time and patience, my advice to all is to leave trimming to the knowledgeable. If you contact one of the breed club secretaries, they will put you in touch with a breeder or exhibitor in your area who takes in dogs for trimming. For a relatively small sum, they will trim your dog properly, so that he actually looks like a West Highland White Terrier. Depending on the individual you are introduced to, you may also find the fee paid is worth it just for the entertainment value. Many breeders and exhibitors have a great sense of humour (you wouldn't last long in the dog game otherwise), and you will no doubt be treated to all the gossip, funny stories and advice that can be fitted into a couple of hours. Should you be really keen to learn the whole job yourself, follow the instructions for roughing out in Chapter 8 (*see* page 153) and take every opportunity to watch a knowledgeable groomer at work. Otherwise, if you can shape the ears and tail, and remove the long hair around the anus, that will keep the dog reasonably presentable between trims.

The biggest drawback of our breed (if I dare admit to any) could be that they are white, or supposed to be. Sometimes when they have been digging or rolling you would not think so. How quickly they become dirty will largely depend on the environment in which they live and the amount of mischief they are allowed to get into. However, much of the dirt and grime will come out with brushing when the coat is dry. Many people bathe dogs too often, which spoils the coat in our breed. It is much better to wash just the head, legs and undercarriage. Perhaps giving a complete bath two or three times a year, say, after a trim. Dry shampoo can be used to clean up the grubby dog and will do no great harm to the coat. If over-bathed the coat loses its natural oils and opens up, so that the weatherproof jacket is ruined and the coat affords no protection from wind and rain.

Housing

What starts with the breeding of an occasional litter can soon snowball into something much bigger, as you become more involved in exhibition and breeding show dogs. The provision of extra facilities needs to be planned to enable you to keep the dogs in the proper manner and to make the keeping of them easier for yourself. There are also laws covering the aspects of keeping and breeding dogs which need to be adhered to.

The Breeding of Dogs Act 1973 forbids the keeping of more than two bitches of breeding age without a breeder's licence, though oddly it makes no reference to the number of male dogs which can be kept, and those numbers remain unlimited. The Act itself was designed to prohibit the numbers of puppy farms and all the undesirable elements of dog breeding and management that go with them. Not surprisingly, it has failed miserably in that intent and has effectively penalized the ordinary, caring, responsible breeders which it should have sought to protect. Be that as it may, until there is a change in the legislation, you are obliged to hold a licence.

Consideration must be given to neighbours when planning your kennel. They have rights under the Law of Nuisance reasonably to enjoy their property and undue noise from barking dogs may well result in your being served with a Noise Abatement Notice. So take every care when planning your kennel and the numbers of dogs you keep, and make provision to limit the nuisance your hobby will cause to others.

Before embarking on any building project or cash outlay, take stock of your present needs and try to allow for future expansion. Not many kennels in our breed today keep more than twenty dogs permanently, and the average is between six and ten dogs. Dog showing and breeding has fast become an interest of the masses and is within the reach of all, unlike the days when it was a sport of the wealthy, with kennels of a hundred dogs and more on large estates with kennelmen to take care of them. But size, status and wealth does not guarantee quality or success. Far from it, much of the best stock and many top winners have been bred and raised in the backyards of terraced houses.

Ideally, the small kennel should have enough housing, with indoor and outdoor exercise areas (runs), to accommodate the present level of stock, and to allow for some expansion. In addition, a separate puppy kennel, a whelping room, an isolation kennel, a trimming room, a separate chalking room and a dog kitchen are desirable.

In all probability, not all of these facilities will be possible at once, so start with the essentials and make additions when you need or can afford them. Some of the places will have alternative uses, as and when the need arises, for example trimming and chalking areas can be combined, as can whelping and puppy rooms, and so on.

Planning and Erecting Kennels

The type and layout of your kennel as a whole will depend on the facilities already at your disposal, the space you have available and/ or the cash limitations.

Outbuildings and garages are excellent for conversion to kennel housing. Make sure they are dry and draughtproof and have plenty of light, with opening windows or extractor fans to provide fresh air. It does not do for any dog to be kept in a dark, dank, gloomy environment. Wherever possible, I try to run my dogs in pairs, a dog and a bitch together both for sleeping and exercise. When sectioning off areas within outbuildings, it is wise to adjoin sleeping and exercise areas, but to have the facility of closing off the sleeping area when the dogs are free. This stops them making any mess there and allows you to clean each part separately. When space is limited, I have found that long, narrow exercise runs are preferable and more enjoyable for the dogs than square ones. The longer runs allow more freedom for their exercise and play. Outside exercise runs can be easily added to outbuildings in the same fashion. If the outside runs have roofs on them, they can be used in all but the most inclement of weathers.

Should you need to erect entirely new facilities, there are many different types of kennelling available. Building your own in brick or stone is preferable, but there are slab concrete and wooden kennels which can be bought ready-made. The cost of kennelling can be anything from a £100 to £1,000s.

Plan carefully when siting the first kennel, for if you subsequently add more kennels without planning for them, the whole area may finish up looking like a shanty town.

South-facing kennels will protect the inmates from the cold winds in winter and should be erected on solid foundations, preferably close to the house. Being near to you will be of benefit to yourself and the dogs. It will avoid the need for treks up the garden in the middle of winter, and our breed likes to feel part of the action, thriving on interest and attention. So kennelling them at the furthermost point may not be such a good idea, even if it would be quieter.

Sectional wooden kennels are probably the most popular and have the advantage of being relatively cheap, easily erected and can be re-sited to suit any change of plan. The disadvantages are that they will require regular maintenance by treating with wood preservative, are not so easy to clean and, without care, are an undoubted fire hazard.

Exercise runs can be easily made by anyone with a modicum of practical know-how. The height of the runs really depends on your dogs, some will scale great heights whilst others will not attempt to escape no matter how easy, seeming to accept the fact that this is their realm and not beyond. A height of 4ft (1.2m) will generally contain a West Highland White Terrier. Using 3 × 2in (7.6 × 5cm) timber, I make the rectangular frame in 8ft (2.4m) lengths, with support pieces every 4ft (1.2m). Then I cover the frame with suitable wire mesh of not more than 1in (2.5cm) gauge. I make the width sections in the same way and screw all the sections together. These can then be attached to the kennels or outside walls and can be extended by adding further sections with bolts. I then fix small offcut blocks of wood every 2ft (60cm) under the bottom sections, thus lifting it off the ground. This allows ease of cleaning, hosing and drying, will not harbour debris easily and helps protect the sections from rot setting in.

Exercise runs are best made using smooth, or semi-rough concrete, sloped away from the kennels to provide good drainage. Not only does it provide a good foundation for the kennel and is easy to clean, requiring little if any maintenance, but it helps by keeping nails and feet in good order and assists muscle tone in the dogs. Smooth concrete makes shovelling and sweeping easier but is less effective with nail and feet maintenance. Rough concrete will file down the nails and encourage tighter feet, but harbour excreta and other debris in its roughness. Flagging can be used and has the advantage of being able to be re-sited, although the same problems of debris entrapment exist. Whether to have an area of grass within the confines of exercise runs is debatable. Grass can create problems of hygiene when excreta becomes entangled with it, and it will turn to mud in wet weather. I prefer to let my dogs on to outside grass when the conditions permit. Exercise areas can be made more interesting, if space allows, by featuring a tree or some other ornament. No doubt, empty runs can be places of boredom for the dogs and a feature of this kind will at least give them something to chase around.

141

Gates should open inward and, if possible, double gates should be installed for extra security. I am thinking more in terms of dogs escaping rather than being stolen. If the gates open inward, the dogs have to move backwards, away from the gate as you enter. Gates should have trap-catches for when you are busy working in and around the kennels and bolts for more permanent use. The addition of padlocks is advised, particularly if you live in a built-up area.

For resting and sleeping, raised benches should be used in summer and either full sleeping boxes or deep-sided, drawer-like boxes should be used in winter. I never use bedding in warm weather, although this is a matter of personal preference. In winter, the boxes can be filled with shredded newspaper or, better still, the shredded, white tissue-paper now available and topped with a piece of blanket or the fleecy, washable material that is widely available. The dogs soon snuggle down into their nests and will be untroubled by the cold outside. On the question of heat provision during winter, I never provide extra heat, except in unusually cold spells. If the housing and bedding are correct, a West Highland White Terrier with a correct double coat is naturally able not only to cope with, but to be unaffected by the cold. Exceptions to this are the very young, old or sick animals, who would either need extra provision outside or, more realistically, should be brought into the house. But the hardiness of the healthy West Highland Terrier has never ceased to amaze me on the days of heavy snowfalls, when I have had to dig my way into the kennels. Clearing the runs of drifts of snow, I have worried about how the dogs will be, only to find that when the doors are opened they come bouncing out as if it were just another spring morning.

Cleaning and Disinfection

Wash kennels, runs, boxes, benches and all other such areas or equipment, regularly, using a good household disinfectant or, if you prefer, one of the ones specifically made for dogs, which offer protection against all manner of disease and infection. However, I do not advocate overuse of disinfectants, because the dogs should meet up with some germs and bacteria in order to build up a degree of immunity against them. Disposable bedding should be changed regularly and blankets washed. It is a good idea, and part of good management, to spray all the dogs, kennels, boxes, benches and bedding with flea spray every now and again, whether you suspect infestation or not.

The Kennel Regime

The way individuals keep their dogs will differ and is to a great extent a personal thing. However, as I have said before, although our breed is adaptable, dogs in general are creatures of habit. Therefore, it is a great advantage to manage your dogs according to your own lifestyle, so that you can adhere to that routine as much as possible. Success in the show ring owes nearly as much to the way the dogs are managed as to any amount of trimming and presentation. How often is a good-quality dog downgraded because he shows no character or zest for life and all its interests? Careful management and study of the kennel as a whole, and its individual inmates with their particular needs and idiosyncrasies, will pay rich rewards to those who take the time and trouble to employ them.

The kennel dog can become quite bored if he is left out all day. It is better to have a routine consisting of time out and time in. In this way, the dog will look forward to his time out and fill that time with interest. Having a very small kennel, I usually keep my dogs in pairs of a dog and a bitch, or trios with one dog and two bitches. Swapping the partners a few times during the day always stimulates activity and alleviates boredom, and a few different playthings, even for older dogs, are appreciated. Most dogs love old socks, cardboard boxes, empty washing-up bottles, and that sort of thing, and will spend many a happy hour tearing them to pieces.

If you also feed your dogs in pairs or trios, there will be little trouble with appetite: each one will wolf down his food lest another should steal it. Some dogs have a fascination for water bowls and will toss them in the air in play, not a practice conducive to keeping either dogs or runs tidy. For this reason, I rarely leave water bowls in the runs all the time and prefer to give fresh drinks several times a day.

From six to eight weeks of age, I always run the dogs on sawdust. It is clean, easy to use, disposable, has a lovely fresh smell and is absorbent. However, be careful not to use sawdust derived from wood which has been chemically treated; in fact sterilized sawdust can now be bought cheaply. Also some dogs are allergic to sawdust and will scratch constantly inflaming the skin, which could lead to hair loss and skin trouble. This is a rare occurrence – I have had only two cases in twenty years – but if it happens the dog in question should be taken off sawdust completely to save any further damage or discomfort.

Happiness is a contented dog, and noticing the individual needs and preferences will make for a happy dog. If you see it, so will others and it goes a long way in the show ring, with other exhibitors, spectators and judges alike wondering how it's done. It is not done with happy pills; just good sense and management.

Old Age

Dogs age at the rate of about seven years to our one, so using the criteria we apply to ourselves, a dog would be in the prime of life between three and six years of age. Middle age would be the seventh and eighth years and old age from nine years on. These assumptions, based on the relative ages of the human race and the canine race would be about right. But that is as far as the comparisons will work. I suppose the average life expectancy of a West Highland White Terrier is between twelve and fifteen years, relatively few die before reaching double figures and many live well into their teens. Simple arithmetic will tell you that the average figure given is between eighty-four and 105 years old in our terms. However, the ageing process cannot be suitably compared to humans. Some dogs in our breed will live the same very active life as always until just before death. Most seem either untouched by middle age, or its relative effect comes much later in comparison. They tend to carry on in the same way until about ten years of age, before gradually slowing down. Even then they are just as keen, if more in mind than body and limb, should some new sport present itself.

So we tend not to think of a dog being old until he reaches his tenth year, and then he is still a youthful oldie. As dogs are individuals, there will always be variations. There are eight-year-olds that appear for all intents and purposes to be much older than some teenagers. Good health apart, to a great degree the secret is probably in the mentality of the individual; as they say, 'You're as old as you feel.' Some of my lot obviously do not know they are supposed just to lie by the fire; instead they carry on regardless.

However, at some point, age will start to take its toll, though it is hoped, nothing serious or painful. There will be a general slowing

Ch. Birkfell Student Prince (1991), holds the record for the oldest West Highland White Terrier to gain his title. (Photo by Chris Kernick.)

down and, just like ourselves, the older dog will probably have stiffness and those little aches and pains, where in more youthful times there were none.

The dog in old age will need that extra little bit of care and consideration. Warm, dry living conditions are a prerequisite to a healthy life for all dogs, but more so with the oldies when rheumatism or arthritis can easily set in. The amounts of food needed may not be as great when the dog is less active, but the nutritional value should be just as good if not more so. Obesity in the older dog is dangerous and will shorten life expectancy. Most old dogs will develop that extra ripple of fat around the shoulders, but the overall fitness and condition of the dog should not be allowed to deteriorate into gross obesity. However, it would probably be dangerous to embark on a starvation diet or too vigorous an increase in exercise to reverse the condition. Prevention is better than the cure, but if your oldie has got too fat, try to lose the weight very gradually. Oldies

145

Ch. Arctic Snowstorm of Makerch (1990). The former record holder and a mere lad at nine years, proving the longevity of the breed. (Photo by Chris Kernick.)

will slow themselves down and the amount and degree of exercise taken will be progressively less. Even so, they still enjoy a good walk, only now instead of sprinting out in front, darting this way and that, they will more likely amble along by your side taking stock of the world as it goes by.

Euthanasia

There may come a time when for reasons of ill health and suffering, you have to make a difficult decision. It is always a very sad and difficult time and it is easy to forget or push aside your moral responsibility. I remember quite vividly the day I had my first champion, Ch. Rotella Royal Penny, put to sleep. I sat on a wall in a busy street outside the vet's surgery with an empty lead in my hand, heartbroken. But the decision had been made to save her any further suffering, and it was the right decision. When the time comes, the only consideration should be what is best for the dog, and sentiment simply has to go out the window. At these times, I have found it comforting and more realistic after the initial sadness, to treasure the happier times and inwardly celebrate the life, rather than mourn the death.

8

Preparation for Exhibition

It seems to be a popular misconception that skilled presentation can make a poor dog into a good one. Of course, this notion is ridiculous, but good trimming and preparation, along with clever handling, will make any dog look better. Given that an animal has enough quality, the better the presentation the better the chances of success. Many is the time when a top-quality animal poorly trimmed has had little or no success, but in more knowledgeable hands has looked a different dog and quickly gained his title.

No one can teach the natural talent possessed by the top-flight groomers: the necessary information can be given, but having the information is no guarantee that it will be translated into skill. Six different people could be taught the same basic grooming techniques and a year later they would all present their dogs differently, because of their individuality. Knowledge, experience, dexterity, ingenuity, an 'eye for a dog' and much more, combine together to separate one individual's level of expertise from another's. I make these points so that it is understood that no matter how much

Ch. Flash Harry of Tapestries (1990).

information is given in this chapter, it is up to you as an individual to use and develop it, or some of it, to the best advantage. As with most things akin to dogs, there is no easy route to the top; dedication and attention to detail are never easy.

In bygone days, most of the trimming was done by hand using only the finger-and-thumb method of stripping, and even today there are those purists who will advocate only such methods. Amongst the best presenters of our breed, you will find some who trim by finger and thumb, and others, equally as good, who use other means or a combination of means. There are many techniques, different methods and various equipment at our disposal, and trimming by hand using the finger-and-thumb method is a good one, but not the only one. So long as the desired effect is achieved, the coat is in good order and there is no unnecessary suffering to the animal, any method is good. In fact, invention and innovation are two extra qualities possessed by the clever groomer.

That said, much of the trimming must be done either by hand, using finger and thumb, or with a stripping knife because the action of these two are the only ones that will give the desired effect without harming the coat.

Hand and Knife

By gripping between the finger and thumb or knife blade and thumb, a few hairs at a time are removed, either by taking out the whole hair from the root, or severing at a desired length along the hair shaft. The action is one of either plucking, pulling or breaking, not cutting. Hand or knife stripping will give the same effect and I would advocate the learning and use of both. When using a knife, there is a tendency to use only the first inch or so of the blade at its point. But by practice and experimentation by using each part of the blade on a particular area and for some specific purpose, all users will be able to develop their skills. The trimming knife in skilled hands can be an invaluable multi-purpose tool.

The point itself is extremely useful for picking out specific hairs and for the more delicate work needed in finishing. However, the shank (middle) and heel (nearest the handle) should also be used: the shank for reducing volume on the more accessible areas of the dog; the heel can be used likewise and also for specific areas which are more difficult to reach, especially around the tail.

My personal preference is to do most of the trimming with the knife and I find this tool to be very versatile. I then use finger and thumb to tidy up the dog's coat once it is in the peak of condition.

Scissors

Scissors should never be used on the main body of the coat. They create a clean, straight cut called blocking, which in all but the very professional of hands will leave steps or lines in the coat. Blocking also induces a tendency for the hair to curl, which is a fault mentioned in the Breed Standard. Regular or straight scissors are generally used only to shape the ears, feet, tail and to remove hairs from around the anus. All scissors should be held in the same way: on the end of the thumb, midway between the end of the thumb and the first joint, and the third finger, just above the first joint. This gives the best balance, keeps the main part of the hand away from the coat, and allows the user more flexibility and freedom of extension whilst still retaining control. The only blade to move should be the one controlled by the thumb, the other blade remains quite still, thus giving a straight cut.

Thinning Scissors

Thinning scissors are used more extensively these days, often for expediency, but used properly, they can be useful and are a boon to the clever groomer. The action again is one of cutting, but because they have at least one serrated blade they only cut part of the coat, thus thinning it rather than removing it.

They have various uses, mainly on the furnishings (head, legs and skirt) but are of particular advantage when trimming heads, because of the feathering effect given by thinning the hair, which in turn can soften the appearance. This allows the groomer to soften or harden the appearance as desired. They are favoured for shaping because, unless used very heavily, they leave no steps and since the thinning process means that the hair removal is gradual, they allow the groomer more latitude for error. They are also often used to remove or take away substantial parts of the growth from the more delicate areas of the dog, such as the chest, which can be painful, if plucked or stripped too vigorously, before finishing off by hand or knife. When using thinning scissors, particularly on the throat or

149

chest, it is better to hold them vertically so that the blades are in line with the hair growth, not across it. So, when thinning the throat or chest, the blades will point roughly from legs to head, and thus reduce the risk of leaving scissor marks.

Hair Facts

It will be useful if I give some simple explanations about a few of the popular misconceptions concerning hair and hair growth. Hair does not grow; it forms. Waste deposits from the blood and glands, mainly the sebaceous gland, collect at the base of the hair follicles. As these deposits mount, they are pushed upwards within the hair follicles until they meet the air. On meeting the air these deposits harden to form hair and the hair becomes longer as the deposits continue to mount. Therefore, hair is dead matter; it does not live, it has no roots; it contains no nervous system so cannot feel pain, and contains no blood so it cannot bleed. The terms we use, such as 'grow' and 'root', are in fact misnomers.

There is a belief that trimming done with scissors or clippers not only encourages skin problems but ruins the coat forever. On both counts, I disagree. Many thousands of dogs are trimmed in this way throughout their lives and, to date, there is no substantial evidence that these animals are more prone to skin disorders than others. There is no doubt that scissor or clipper trimming will ruin a good existing coat, but that will not affect the quality of coat that has yet to grow. This can be compared to human hair which has been permed.

Kennel Club Rules

In the UK, there is a rule devised and promulgated by the Kennel Club to which all exhibitors are supposed to adhere:

> No substance which alters the natural colour, texture or body of the coat may be used in the preparation of a dog for exhibition either before or at the Show. Any other substance which may be used in the preparation of a dog for exhibition must not be allowed to remain on a dog at the time of exhibition.

If I were to accept and advocate the complete adherence to this rule, the following pages would be blank. Simply shampooing your dog would alter the natural texture and body of the coat and it is an undisputed fact that rainwater does the same.

To the vast majority of the dog-showing fraternity, adhering to this rule to the letter imposes impossible restrictions upon them. Every breed has its own quirk of presentation which, under this rule, would be illegal. The idea behind the law itself is to stop some people cheating by, for example, using hair colour on a badly coloured dog, or bleaching a discoloured coat to make it whiter than white; it is not to stop the honest, responsible, stalwart supporters of a breed from making the most of their charges.

After much lobbying, it seems to have been generally accepted that chalk can be used as an aid to trimming and for cleaning our dogs outside the precincts of the showground. Although the rule itself has not changed, it would appear that common sense has prevailed and that only serious abuse of the rule in this regard will be penalized. The final judgement remains at the discretion of the Kennel Club. There remains the obstacle that if we use chalk to trim and clean, the rule states that this should all be removed before exhibition. It is an impossibility to remove every grain of chalk so, once again, as exhibitors, we must hope that our best efforts will be rewarded by understanding and discretion on the part of the governing body.

If you clean and prepare your dogs the night before the show, as most of us do, by the time you exhibit, the dog has shaken himself countless times, removing excess chalk every time. This process can be helped by patting the dog, and in the course of grooming before exhibition chalk is also removed. Given all this, any chalk left in the coat should not be considered an abuse of the rule if by your efforts, you have acted in good faith.

Procedure

What follows is an explanation of how I generally prepare dogs for exhibition and why, although, with all the differences between individual dogs, it is impossible to cover every eventuality. As I do most of the work with a stripping knife, those of you who wish to use finger and thumb should substitute this method wherever knife use is specified.

It is important to have the right equipment to hand and a routine

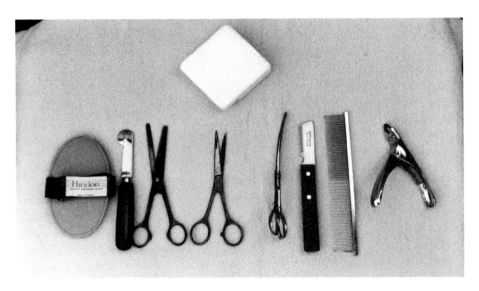

Tools from left to right: terrier pad, trimming knife, thinning scissors, regular scissors, curved-blade scissors, rough trimming knife, anti-static comb, nail clippers, and (above) chalk block. (Photo by Chris Kernick.)

designed to help rather than obstruct the work done. I always use a rubber-topped grooming table and a grooming stand, which is attached to the table by a clamp. This holds the dog, leaving the groomer both hands free. There is nothing more infuriating than a dog who continually sits down or moves around when you are trying to perfect some aspect of preparation, and all dogs should be trained to accept its use from an early age. I keep all the equipment that is likely to be needed within arm's reach. I must admit to being a great stickler for detail and tidiness, so a waste bin or cardboard box is kept next to the grooming table. Every few minutes throughout the session the loose hair is collected and deposited in the bin. It never ceases to amaze me how some trimmers can work on a dog surrounded by mounds of loose hair, which can be confusing to the eye. I suppose it is each to their own.

Before starting any trimming session, always brush the dog through to remove any tangles and apply chalk by using a chalk block. This will help in a manner of ways but is primarily to enable the groomer to obtain a better grip. Then brush the dog as you would for the show ring. This is very important because any trimming is done to make the dog look his best in the show ring, so you need to see what needs doing when the dog is brushed for show. If you trim and then brush, the effect will look completely different. On this same point, each time you do some work, stop, brush the area, and look to see whether it is right or requires further improvement. It is also a great advantage to view the dog from a distance, moving or standing naturally, so now and again brush the dog as for show and pop him in an exercise pen. Then you can observe the dog and make a further assessment of the work done or needing to be done. This helps in another way as it splits up the time the dog spends on the table. Sessions are best broken up because dogs get bored and start to move around, which is not conducive to good trimming.

Roughing Out

The object of roughing out is to remove the unwanted hair, giving the dog a foundation shape and outline. On this the groomer can build by working on the dog over a period of weeks or months, in order to obtain that mind's eye picture of the finished article. When trimming, I tend to move from one area of the dog to another, rather than working strictly to pattern (say, neck to tail), but I keep within the part, i.e. topline, forelegs, hind legs, etc. I also repeat the work over the whole dog part by part, taking off more coat as required, rather than trying to complete each area in one fell swoop.

Using the stripping knife, and starting behind the ears, always strip the hair in the direction you want it to lie. If you are right-handed, hold the knife firmly in your right hand, the blade between index finger and thumb. Trap the hair you wish to remove between your thumb and the blade and tug quickly in the direction the coat is growing. It is advisable to use your spare hand to keep the dog steady and to stretch the skin above, and in the opposite direction of, the area you are trimming. This helps to make the process easier for you, and more comfortable for the dog.

The hair behind the ears, where the lead will fit, can be trimmed quite short before gradually lengthening as you move down the neck to the shoulders. Continue all the way along the topline to the base of the tail. What you are trying to achieve is a continuus flow from the ears to the tail, which encompasses the neck, shoulder placement and back without the joining of these three areas being

153

apparent. So get down to topline level, with the dog stood in show position to check the shape and level, taking off more hair as required. Once the neck and topline are finished, start on the area around the tail which extends down the hindquarters. When trimming around the tail, care should be taken not to remove too much hair, which will make the tail look low set. In fact, if the coat is left thicker in the last inch of the tail-end of the topline, it will have the effect of making the back appear shorter.

When viewed in profile, the outer contour of the hindquarters directly behind the tail should be fashioned to have a rounded appearance, giving the dog 'something behind the tail'. Dogs who are overtrimmed here look chopped off behind the tail, creating the appearance of weakness in the hindquarters and of being low set. Care has to be taken when removing furnishings and leg hair because they are so slow growing that a slip now will mean a long wait for it to regrow to the correct length. However, continue carefully down the hind legs to the hock before scrubbing up (*see* page 168) the whole leg and smoothing into position.

All the trimming so far has been done with the knife. Now for the first time, the regular scissors can be used to trim around the feet and remove the hair from between the pads. (Curved-blade scissors are especially designed for uses of this kind, so that if the dog should move suddenly there is no risk of hurting him with the scissor points.) Do not pick up a foot in order to trim round it, but do this when the dog is standing on it. Many dogs are touchy about having their feet trimmed, so whichever foot you are trimming, fore or hind, pick up the other foot with your spare hand. This deters the dog from moving or fidgeting about.

Using the knife or thinning scissors, or a combination of both, trim the hair on the hock to blend in with the rest of the leg. The length of the hair at the front or stifle side of the hind leg can now be shortened and shaped. This is best done with the knife, perhaps just shaping the tips with thinning scissors, although I usually use a knife for the whole job. The front lengths of the hind legs from skirt to foot can be done by finger and thumb or, by reversing the knife in your hand and holding a few strands of hair by the tips. Unwanted hair can be taken away by backcombing it with the knife. This leaves the leg hair looking natural with no straight lines or blocked appearance. Always complete one leg before matching the other, brushing and observing the same area of each leg as you go along.

The sides and flanks of the dog are stripped with a knife bearing in mind the desired wedge shape, and blended into the skirt which can then be shortened, shaped and possibly thinned to match the hindquarters using the same technique as before.

Many dogs carry a profusion of skirt which seems to attract tangles particularly on the belly, and male dogs will often become heavily stained around the penis, which not only smells but is sometimes difficult to remove and therefore detracts from the presentation. I often cut a central channel underneath the dog about two inches wide, taking off all the hair from the naval to a point in line with the elbow. It does not detract from the show dog as it is not visible and, in the case of the male dog, is more hygienic.

There should be no obvious line of trimming along the flanks of the dog, if you have problems with the blending, try stripping this area in a more horizontal rather than vertical direction. This can be made easier by having the dog stand on his hind legs, while holding his forelegs and taking off the hair in a now vertical direction, foreleg to hind leg with the finger and thumb, or knife. It goes without saying that the dog should spend only very short periods in this position and that the work will have to be carried out in several sessions to complete.

The forequarters have now to be blended into several other areas, all requiring different lengths of coat. From ear to shoulder, the neck should gradually thicken towards its base. From ear to approximately 1in (2.5cm) above the elbow the coat should be taken quite close to give the desired champagne-bottle-neck look. Then, from ear to ear across the chest down to the breastbone, the coat should be taken close but also has to blend into the area from ear to shoulder.

All the chest area ought to be done by knife but many dogs object very strongly to this, so thinning scissors are often used instead. Although working out of turn, I find the best and easiest way is to take away the hair from ear to ear using the jawbone as a guide. Then take off the hair on the chest to the point of the breastbone and all across to each leg, at a length of about ½in (1.2cm). Although trimmed short, the coat length on the neck and chest area will depend largely on the overall shape and balance of the dog, and the trimming will, as always, be in keeping with that. Most West Highland White Terriers have a ruff down the sides of the neck and this can be used as a guiding line. Once this is done, the whole area can be skimmed over with a knife, blending each area together and giving a smoother finish.

Scrub up the forelegs and brush into place so you can see what needs to be done. Use the knife as much as possible to shape the leg. Short feathering should be left on the back of the leg, which can mostly be done with the knife, perhaps just tipping with thinning scissors. Remove the hair from between the pads in the same way as before. For shaping the front feet scrub up the whole leg and then carefully brush each overlapping section into place, shaping each section in turn, using regular or thinning scissors. Blend in and shorten the hair from the breastbone between the legs to match the front and the length of skirt, either by knife in the backcombing manner given or with thinning scissors. When viewed head on, there should be an even, vertical line from the sides of the shoulder to the feet. Many are left with an indentation where the body ends and the legs begin which detracts from the appearance. Remember the front legs are best described as looking like shirt sleeves.

To trim the tail in the desired carrot shape, the first thing to do is determine its length. Holding the tip of the tail between the thumb and index finger, remove any longer hair. I use regular scissors but thinning scissors or the knife can be used. Now you can set about shaping the tail with the knife, by stripping out the bulk all around, gradually tapering it to a point. Once the shape has been outlined it can be given more definition with either regular or thinning scissors.

Finally the crowning glory, the head, can be done. There is a tendency at present to overtrim heads in a very sharp and severe fashion, which is wholly untypical of the breed. The accepted description of the trimmed head is 'like a chrysanthemum'. I do not know which variety the inventor of this metaphor had in mind, but I am quite certain it was not some that we see in the show ring of late.

Brushing the untrimmed head as you would for the show ring is of paramount importance, because only then can you really picture the shape you want and decide what needs to be done to achieve that effect. Start by trimming the top inch (2.5cm) of the ears using regular scissors, making the sharp-pointed, inverted V-shape. Then take off all the hair from the front and back of this last inch of the ear in the same way. Never cut across the ear, but point the scissors downwards, towards the base of the ear. Done carefully this will leave no lines and the finish will be quite startling as you compare the size and thickness of the trimmed ear to the untrimmed one. Most dogs develop a few strands of discoloured hair on either side of the bottom jaw, which is caused by the acidity of the gastric juices in saliva. This hair can be taken away with either pair of scissors. This is only a small point but it could be the deciding one to a judge.

After brushing the head, the frame can be shaped. Using the knife, start by removing some bulk and shaping the area between the ears, regularly stopping to brush and reappraise the effect from all angles. Continue in the same fashion, just tipping the hair on the skull with thinning scissors until the correct shape is found. Now make the desired frame from the outside of one ear, around to the outside of the other. This is best done with the thinning scissors held at a right angle to the hair which is being cut, with the points of the scissors facing toward you, not at right angles, with the points following the contour of the cut. The reason for this, is that the former, although taking more time, gives a more natural finish and allows more latitude for error. After rebrushing, finish off the head by removing hair from the muzzle to match the frame and skull. The hair on the muzzle, if left untrimmed, will eventually become heavy and lie flat as it extends to the frame. This gives rise to a long, weak and snipey appearance, and the removal of some of the bulk will stop this happening.

Finishing

Finishing is the term I use for all work from the roughing out stage onwards. All that needs to be done now is to carry on in the same fashion regularly. Maybe twice a week, go over the dog, making improvements by taking off a few hairs here and there, which over a period of time will result in the dog being ready for exhibition. The only real difference in procedure is that almost all the work done in the roughing out stage with thinning scissors can now be done by knife as the coat is now much more manageable.

Even when a dog is being shown and is in great coat and condition, improvements can still be made and maintenance work must be done. If you continue the routine of work every week, you can keep the dog in good coat indefinitely. This is called a 'rolling coat'. Because the coat is being removed a few hairs at a time on a regular basis, all the hairs will be at various stages of growth and therefore different lengths, so that there is always enough good coat to maintain show condition. If this method is used, there is rarely a need to take a dog out of the ring, possibly at a very important time, to grow a new coat.

The untrimmed dog. (Photo by Chris Kernick.)

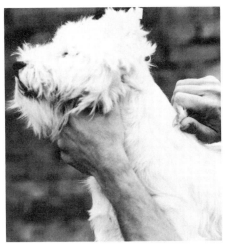

Stripping the coat with a trimming knife. Note the method, action, and how the free hand is used to help. (Photo by Chris Kernick.)

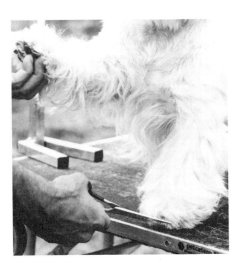

Shape the feet while holding the opposite leg up, so that the dog remains still. (Photo by Chris Kernick).

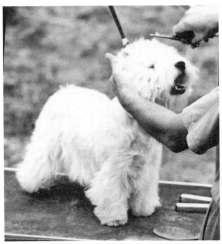

Tipping the head hair. (Photo by Chris Kernick.)

Brushing can make a big difference. Note the way the leg hair is brushed (scrubbed) before being smoothed into place. (Photo by Chris Kernick.)

The end product, ready for the show ring. (Photo by Chris Kernick.)

Disguising Faults

All dogs have faults. It is for the groomer to try to hide them and the judges to find them. Good judges will not be fooled by clever trimming and presentation on a really poor-quality specimen and these dogs should not be in the show ring. But it has always been the case that all dogs of good quality benefit from the use of clever trimming and presentation. The only change through time has been in the progression and degree of expertise. With better knowledge, tuition, equipment and grooming products, a fair degree of expertise is practised by all, and the groomers at the very highest level have to be applauded for their excellence, innovation and dexterity no matter what.

Most faults can be disguised. Some problems are not faults in the dog at all, but faults in handling, and some faults can be helped by a combination of trimming, presentation and handling. The aspects of handling will be fully discussed in Chapter 9 (*see* pages 177–89). Outlined below are some of the faults you may encounter and wish to disguise by trimming, along with some suggestions for dealing with them. It is hoped that you are not trying to disguise all these faults in the same dog; if you are, start again with a new dog!

Ears Too Big   Trim the top inch (25mm) of the ears, as close as possible. Leave slightly more hair on top of the skull and around the ears.

Weak Foreface   Thin the hair on the muzzle and foreface so that more volume can be attained when the head is scrubbed up.

Long Foreface   The remedy for a weak foreface should be applied, but also trim around the nose where it joins the muzzle. The skin colour on the muzzle is almost always black and a little hair off here will make the nose just slightly bigger, but at the same time the foreface shorter.

Light Eyes   I have only ever seen one case of very light, yellow eyes but to disguise this, leave the eyebrows longer so that the eye is difficult to see without a close inspection.

Neck Too Short   Trim the front neck area of the dog very close and similarly as close as you dare behind the ears. For extra length, the close trimming on the back of the neck can be extended to encroach slightly on to the back of the skull.

Neck Too Long   Reverse the above.

Upright But Close-Fitting Shoulders   Trim the neck and shoulder areas so that the shoulder placement looks to be laid further back, by building up the coat from the actual placement towards the small of the back.

Bossy or Loaded Shoulders   Leave more coat on the sides of the neck from ear to shoulder, but trim close on the sides of the shoulder to just above the elbow.

Forelegs Not Straight   Redesign the leg to look straight by trimming and brushing.

Forefeet Turn Out   Redesign shape of foot by trimming closely on the outside edge and leaving more hair on the inside edge.

Forefeet Turn In   Redesign following the reverse of above.

Dipped Back or Uneven Topline   Level the topline by building up the coat in the area where it dips and trimming slightly shorter where it rises.

Rising Loin   Trim the loin area and possibly the top part of hindquarters shorter.

Long Back   Leave more coat from neck to back and build up the coat on the topline just before the root of the tail.

Low-Set Tail   Build up the hair on the topline around the tail and on the hindquarters behind it, giving the rear end a more rounded look in profile.

Long Tail   Follow procedure for disguising a low-set tail.

Gay or Curved Tail   As much as possible, fill the arc created by the curve in the tail by building up the hair within it.

161

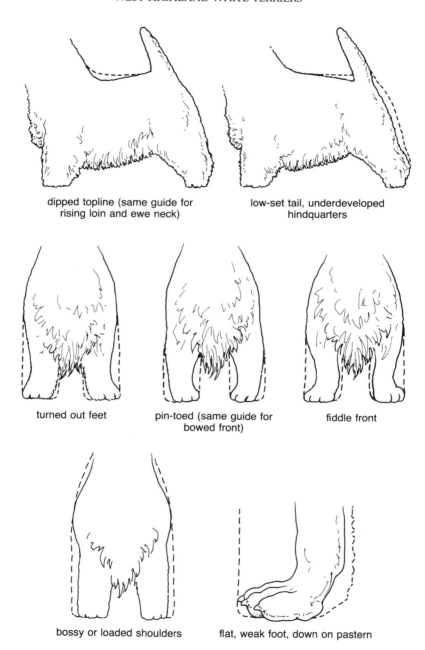

dipped topline (same guide for
rising loin and ewe neck)

low-set tail, underdeveloped
hindquarters

turned out feet

pin-toed (same guide for
bowed front)

fiddle front

bossy or loaded shoulders

flat, weak foot, down on pastern

*The broken line is the guide to the trimmer on how to disguise the
fault.*

162

Hocks Turn In   Take off more hair on the inside of the hocks and add more volume to the lower outside of the leg by brushing.

Hocks Turn Out   Reverse the above procedure.

Close Moving   Fore or aft, the remedy is the same. Take off more hair from the inside of the leg and add more volume to the outside by brushing. For close-moving fronts, the hair on the chest and between the legs can also be reduced to good effect.

Long on the Leg   Keep the topline trimmed as short as is acceptable and brush it flat. Leave a longer skirt and do not trim to define the leg so much.

Short on the Leg   Build up the topline with slightly longer coat, mainly by brushing, and shorten the skirt, but only to a length that is still acceptable to the eye.

Soft Coat   I have no experience of dealing with this problem, but I understand that if the coat is habitually pulled by finger and thumb, there can be a marked improvement in its texture.

I have dealt with what at first I believed to be a soft coat, but what I then found to be an overgrown, profuse undercoat. The undercoat had outgrown the outer coat and had stifled the growth of the harder hair, rather like weeds taking a hold in a lawn. I found this was remedied by raking most of the undercoat out, using a medium or rough blade stripping knife, which allowed the outer coat to establish itself. From that point on, the undercoat was raked every now and again to keep it in check, and the dog has to this day the very best of coats.

Wavy Coat   The really hard, wiry coats are the worst to deal with and are best managed by keeping them short. The waves in the coat can be reduced and made easier to manage if they are thinned with a knife and trimmed as normal on the crest of the waves.

Lumpy Coat   This is not a fault in itself, but often thick lumps of coat develop which are difficult to handle. Reduce their size by first thinning them using a knife. This is best done by picking up the lump of coat in question and spreading it in your fingers. Start by taking a few hairs out from the bottom of the lump (nearest the skin) and then work through the rest of it as evenly as possible. On rare occasions, thinning scissors can be used initially, before finishing with a knife.

Coat Discoloration   This can be an inherited problem, or a result of diet, but more often than not it is caused by over-zealous or incorrect trimming. If the problem is inherited, it may be difficult to improve, but if the diet is suspected to be the cause, it can easily be changed. Rice and white meat are best given as they are recommended for convalescence and are therefore mild to the constitution. If trimming is the cause, the discoloration has to be removed over a period of time, with very light trimming sessions. Using the knife held flat to the coat, skim over it, taking off just a few hairs from the top layer of coat at a time. Sometimes the discoloration is patchy, so using the same method concentrate on the affected areas.

Bathing

Unless a dog has become excessively dirty or, for some other reason, has to have a complete wash, I would never bath a dog for the show ring. A really thorough, all-over bath takes away all the natural oils, which are essential in holding the coat together, and causes the coat to blow about loosely until the natural oils re-establish themselves. I tell a lie, it can be done, but only with a hair-drier to blow-wave the topcoat back into position. Even then, it does not knit together as it should, so all-over bathing should be avoided if at all possible. It should not be necessary anyway, because when a dog has been prepared once and is shown regularly, provided he is kept in a suitable manner, he will not become so dirty.

I always clean the dogs the night before a show. I do this a couple of hours after they have been fed so that they have exercised and relieved themselves and, after preparation, can be put into boxes or clean kennels with little chance of their getting dirty again.

Washing the legs, tail, skirt and head in that order is done on the grooming table with a sponge. Start by making the preparations. A towel or clean newspaper should be placed on top of the table to absorb any dripping water. For each dog, have two towels available at arm's reach, a bowl of warm, soapy water and a sponge. The dog's head should be held by the grooming stand as it would be for a trimming session, so that you have both hands free to work.

Brush the dog through first. This is important because tangles are made worse when washed. The show dog undergoing regular preparation should require only the soiled areas to be rubbed with a damp, soapy sponge. To wash out stubborn or heavier soiled areas, the legs and tail can be held over the bowl, and the head and skirt can be done with the bowl placed underneath. Either way, most of the water used for this more thorough cleaning will be caught in the bowl. Wash one leg at a time holding the leg in one hand whilst sponging with the other, which stops the dog moving about. The tail and skirt are easily done and need no further explanation. Great care needs to be taken when washing the head. If only a damp sponge is being used, there is no problem, but when giving a thorough wash you must take every precaution to keep water out of the ears and eyes. For extra safety you may prefer to plug the ears with cotton wool. I find it best to wash the head in two separate halves, using an imaginary line down the centre from occiput to nose. The head can then be tilted so that any surplus water runs away from the ears and eyes. Also the eye on whichever side you are operating can be covered with the thumb of the hand holding the head.

Once the washing is complete, rinse before towel-drying, starting with the head and working backwards. Then remove the towel or newspapers from the table top.

Chalking

Rub hair cream or petroleum jelly into every part of the coat, both with and against the grain. This is used because in the first instance it collects and holds the dirt and grime in the coat before holding chalk in the same way. The cleaning process is completed when the newly applied chalk absorbs the hair cream together with the dirt and then leaves the coat as the dog shakes or is patted or brushed.

Of late, the practice of using various mousses and gels, instead of hair cream or petroleum jelly, to help support and control the coat, has become popular. The arguments may rage both for and against each substance and every argument carries a certain amount of logic and conviction. It would be worrying if something of this nature were used on the jacket of the dog, altering the colour, texture or body of it, since this is the area that a judge feels to ascertain the texture of the coat. Like many, I keep an open mind, in the

165

knowledge that eventually the serious fanciers of the breed will come to the right conclusion and, in the meantime, the choice is left to the individual.

There are various types of whitener, available in powder, block and spray form. The common practice is to use a powder form of calcium carbonate or magnesium carbonate. I use light magnesium carbonate which, because it is very light, is possibly more difficult to use, but it is very white. Calcium carbonate is much heavier and easier to use but is off-white in colour. Sprays can be handy for tidying up after a long journey, just before you enter the show-ground.

Using a terrier pad, chalk the whole dog by lifting the coat and applying the chalk to the bottom section first before working on each overlapping section in turn. In this way, you will clean all the coat and not just the surface. Starting with the topline at the base of the tail, work towards the head until this area is completed. Then do each hind leg in turn, working up the leg from toe to tail (do not forget to do inside each leg too). The tail can be done in the same fashion by first brushing the hair against the grain. Apply to each side of skirt in turn, working up to meet the already completed topline area. Cover the forelegs in the same way as the hind legs and finish the main body of the dog by whitening the remaining neck and chest areas.

The head is more difficult as most dogs dislike having this part done. So the same care of ears and more especially eyes, nostrils and mouth need to be taken. The nose can be smeared with petroleum jelly, which is wiped away leaving a clean, shiny nose once the job is done. In fairness to the dog, and with safety in mind, it is best to apply the chalk to the underside of the frame first and then to each overlapping section of the head and muzzle, working away from the eyes, nose and mouth as you go. The eyes can be protected by the thumb in the same way as for washing. Once completed, allow the dog to shake on the table, before putting him into a dry exercise pen. Most dogs will relieve and empty themselves after this grooming and it is good to know that this is done before putting the dog away into his box or kennel until tomorrow's big day.

The dog will need to be exercised before setting off to the show, and probably at the show or even *en route* if the journey is a long one. Often the feet, skirt and muzzle become soiled and bearing in mind the rules on preparation, you virtually take your dog-showing life in your hands if you decide to clean the dog up. But who wants to take a half-clean dog into the ring? No one, because it defeats the whole object of the exercise and negates all the hard work, time, effort and expense. So when you, like many others in most breeds, do your tidying, do so as discreetly as possible. There are many aids to quick preparation available, and dry shampoo and a little block chalk are probably all you will need.

Brushing

The importance of brushing is often underestimated. The way a dog is brushed has a great role to play in the trimming and presentation of a dog for the show ring. The difference that brushing can make to the overall appearance can be quite startling, so it is advisable to practise different methods, note the effects each have and then use the most effective one.

Once you decide on a way of brushing, use that method habitually, so that it becomes an almost subconscious action. There will be variations from dog to dog because of their differences and, over the years, changes can be made which are thought to be beneficial, but until you make the considered decision to change, use the same method and technique. This is not only good for you but also for the dogs, who are happier with a routine and soon come to know what is expected of them.

Trimming a dog properly and to the best effect is virtually impossible unless the dog is brushed during the trimming sessions in the same way as he will be to enter the show ring. Hence the advice in the section on trimming (*see* pages 152–3), to brush each individual part before trimming and as the trimming progresses, checking your work and assessing it, why, how or where more work is needed.

Over-grooming, particularly with brushes that have extra-long metal spikes or with a comb, can have a very detrimental effect on the coat. The undercoat will be raked out so that the outer, tight-fitting jacket has little or nothing to bind with, giving rise to open-coatedness. Our breed should be double-coated, and single coats, whether under or outer, will be heavily penalized, so care must be taken.

For thorough grooming before a trimming session, I mainly use a terrier pad and an anti-static comb, although I do use other brushes as and when required. But with rare exceptions, all the grooming done at a show before entering the ring is done with just a terrier pad. Opinions, methods, techniques and use of equipment vary, so I can only explain my own way.

Scrubbing Up

This is a method of brushing various parts of a dog to obtain more fullness, which then enables the groomer to smooth the coat into a chosen shape or direction to give the best effect. By giving the coat more body, this method also lends support so that the coat will hold its new shape better and therefore gives the groomer a greater element of control.

To do this, work to a set routine of completing (scrubbing and finishing) each part or area of the dog before moving on to the next. Using a terrier pad, scrubbing is a forwards and backwards movement rather like scratching an itch.

Head   After brushing the frame of the head into position, scrub the hair from the occiput to the eyes horizontally, from side to side across the skull. Then each side of the head in turn can be done, scrubbing vertically from mouth to ear.

Forelegs   The movement is vertical all around each leg from toe to elbow.

Chest   Scrub horizontally between the legs.

Hindquarters and Legs   Taken as a whole, this area is done vertically from toe to tail. Separate or special attention can be given to the area from toe to hock.

Skirt   This is groomed to match by scrubbing horizontally from foreleg to hind leg.

To finish off, simply smooth the coat into its final position.

In conclusion, a West Highland White Terrier in the peak of coat and condition is always a source of admiration, whether at home for your own eyes, or in the show ring for everyone to see. For this to be the result of your own efforts, leaves the individual with a great feeling of pride, accomplishment and self-satisfaction, and rightly so.

9

Showing

The Show Scene

Dog showing can be one of the most enjoyable and fascinating pastimes of all. I use the word 'pastime' reservedly because once you are 'bitten by the show-bug', dog showing and breeding often consumes your whole life, so much so that you will find yourself living, eating and breathing dogs.

As with every other form of competition and keen involvement, there is a credit side and a debit side, though most of what is written leaves the reader with the impression that dog showing is all sweetness and light. In fairness, the newcomer needs to be aware that although the credits far outweigh the debits, there is a darker side: prejudice, jealousy, bitterness and bad sportsmanship, which appears to a greater or lesser degree throughout the world of dogs. But this should not be confused with the general tongue in cheek banter, the conversational post-mortem or inquisition which is part and parcel of the dog game and, I might add, half the fun. It is only natural that fanciers will get together, whether socially or during the course of the day at a show, and discuss the various decisions or events of recent times. Opinions vary, debate and discussion are not only interesting and entertaining but often educational.

The darker or more unsavoury side, although thankfully still not prominent, is no new phenomenon and was clearly illustrated in 1952 by the highly esteemed author Thomas Corbett in his excellent work *The Dog Breeders Text Book*:

> The show-ring can provide a tremendous activity and joy . . . It is here where the dog breeder becomes an exhibitor, and a new experience opens. It is here, indeed, where he promptly discovers a new world. A world of excitement, delight, friendliness on the one side, and sometimes bitterness, frustration and even suspicion on the other. . . . Human nature being what it is, it is obvious that in show

169

Miss Grieve judging a typical line-up. (Photo by Chris Kernick.)

circles will be found a variety of 'mental make-ups' which of necessity produces a whole variety of attitudes, in and out, of the show-ring. Some – the vast majority in fact – approach the show-ring in that spirit of sportsmanship that in reality is the backbone of the colossal success attained by dog shows. Others – and a small section can easily bring shadow upon the brightest scene – will be discovered of a different type, who approach the show-ring with the sole intention of winning, honestly if they can, but winning. Oft-times it is due to that curious outlook, which so readily occupies the mind, that the dogs they own must of necessity be far better than any others shown. Even if they are not, they cannot help but feel aggrieved that there should be others present better than their own, and they reveal their feelings in a variety of ways, usually by subtle innuendos as to the capabilities or honesty of the judge; sometimes by wholesale criticism of the dog or dogs which beat their own exhibit; sometimes by means of a tirade amongst ringsiders upon the judge, the management and the Fancy in general.

. . . In another respect, too, the newcomer must be prepared to meet criticism. If so be that he makes the mistake of so many, and becomes an exhibitor without first becoming acquainted with the requirements in a dog in order to win prizes, he will usually discover that his exhibit does not appear in the prize list. If that be so, and with that feeling of admitted inferiority upon him he is often forlorn, he will discover plenty of fellow exhibitors ready to breathe encouragement upon him. Advice, pleadings will be showered willingly. Let him commence to win, however, and the story will become of an entirely different pattern. Criticism is loudest upon the winners. It can be likened to the statement of a most successful friend of mine, who says, 'Take a dog to a dog show and just win a "codding" card (that is a reserve or V.H.C.) and you are an Angel to be loved. Start to win a few firsts and you are a villain.' That is exaggerated of course, but there is the element of truth in it. The reason! That same small body of 'shadow' raisers. The small people with the big voice; though even that voice is loudest in effect when used in 'whispers'.

. . . What I have written I have penned advisedly . . . it is only right that the light and shade be revealed without bias or favour. With full knowledge of the pitfalls, the less favourable sidelights as well as the joys, the interest and the intriguing fascination of dog breeding and showing the newcomer will enter dogdom well armed.

Popularity, though having nothing to do with the quality of the dogs shown or the relative capabilities of the individual, will inevitably play a part in the degree of success attained and progression made. That is to say that human nature being what it is, some judges will be more inclined toward an exhibit belonging to someone they like, than to someone they dislike, or inevitably votes will be cast or support given not solely on the suitability and qualifications of the nominee. In the perfect world, personalities should not be a consideration, but it does happen. This concept can be applied in every aspect of life and the human factor cannot be dismissed, however small a part it plays.

How any person becomes popular and retains that popularity could be the subject of a quite complex study. The necessary ingredients seem to be a combination of being Mr Nice Guy and having intense training as a career diplomat. That is perhaps an exaggeration, but many a true word is spoken in jest. It is nevertheless true to say that outspokenness, being open with opinions and becoming embroiled in the 'political' side of the dog game will not, by and large, endear the individual to all, or assist in the progress of one's career in dogs.

There is so much to enjoy within the world of show dogs, that what has been said on the debit side will, it is hoped, pale into insignificance when compared with the credit side. But at least the newcomer is now aware of some of the idiosyncrasies akin to the dog game, so let us move on.

Dog shows come in various shapes and sizes. Newcomers, as it has been previously advised, would do well to use the smaller shows as a training ground for their ultimate aspirations, before entering the heady world of Championship Shows.

It may also be useful at this point to mention some general items, which ought to be carefully considered. Dog showing, particularly at Championship Show level, involves a great deal of time, effort and expense. Following the fancy may often stretch the endurance and pocket of the average individual to its furthest limits. If the interest lies with only one partner in a relationship, the relationship itself may be severely tested. So it is wise to keep your feet firmly on the ground and try to keep your hobby within sensible and afford-able confines.

It has often been wondered by many, including myself, what sort of people would want to spend 365 days a year, every year, pandering to the needs of show dogs? Who would really want to go outside in the depths of winter to tend to their animals, when they could be stretched out warm and snug by a blazing fire? Chasing

There are no age barriers at dog shows, as this young lady proves showing Eng. and Am. Ch. Ashgate Lochinvar (1976). (Don Petrulis photography.)

around the country, doling out money and missing out on the 'island in the sun' holidays and so on, for the apparent sake of winnings that, on a good day, amount to a couple of pieces of cardboard. Are we all mad? We are certainly not normal. I have no answer. Maybe it is an obsession, maybe dedication, whatever the reason it becomes an all-consuming way of life.

Types of Show

In the UK, all dog shows have to be licensed by the Kennel Club, except Exemption Shows, which, as implied by their name, are exempt. Exemption Shows are often organized to raise funds for some charity or other and are more fun shows, with such classes as 'The Dog with the Waggiest Tail', 'The Dog with the Brightest Eyes' or 'The Dog in Best Condition', and so on. They often have classes for pedigree dogs and can be very enjoyable if not taken too seriously.

To exhibit at a licensed show, the exhibit must be registered at the Kennel Club and be at least six months of age. Details of dog shows and how to enter can be found in the weekly dog press. There are four types of licensed show, which are simply defined.

Sanction Shows

These shows are confined to members of the society that organizes it. No class higher than Post Graduate may be offered at a Sanction Show.

Limited Shows

These shows are also confined to society members. No dog is eligible for exhibition at a Limited or Sanction Show if he has won a Challenge Certificate or obtained any show award that counts towards the title of Champion under the rules of any governing body recognized by the Kennel Club.

Open Shows

These shows are open to all pedigree dogs, including champions. No Challenge Certificates are offered at Open Shows.

Championship Shows

Championship Shows are open to all pedigree dogs, including champions, and are the only shows where Challenge Certificates are on offer.

Of these, Sanction Shows are fast dying out to the point where, at the time of writing, they are virtually extinct. This is a pity because, along with Match Meetings (local training classes) and Limited Shows, they serve a very useful purpose in giving novice handlers and dogs the opportunity to learn and become accustomed to dog shows and showing, at the grassroots level. Where they are scheduled, Sanction, Limited and, to a lesser degree, Open Shows, should be used as training grounds in preparation for either dog, handler or both, before moving up to Championship Shows.

These types of show can be further divided into All-Breed Shows, which are for any breed of dog, Breed Shows, which are for one particular breed only and, in our case, Terrier Shows, which are for any terrier breed.

Qualifying for Titles

There are two titles of major importance: Champion and, to a lesser degree, Junior Warrant.

Junior Warrants are an achievement for the younger dog, and are meant to be an indication of merit in a young dog, before the dog is quite ready and mature enough to win Challenge Certificates (often abbreviated to CCs or colloquially called 'tickets'). However, this is contradicted by the fact that many dogs win CCs and the title of Champion while still classed as juniors. Quite rightly, no dog who is considered to be of sufficient merit, is debarred from winning Challenge Certificates.

To qualify for a Junior Warrant, the exhibit has to amass at least twenty-five points, between the ages of twelve and eighteen months. First prizes in the breed at Open Shows are worth one point each and first prizes at Championship Shows are worth three points each. It is no easy target to reach and enables the owner to place the letters J.W. after the dog's name in recognition of the achievement.

Winning Challenge Certificates and making up champions is a

little more complicated and needs a fuller explanation. Challenge Certificates are only available at shows with championship status, whether All-Breed, Terrier or Breed Club Shows. To qualify for the title of Champion a dog has to win three CCs under three separate judges and at least one CC when over twelve months of age.

There are all kinds of classes that may be scheduled at Championship Shows. Sometimes the classes are mixed, that is to say for both sexes, but this is a very rare occurrence in our breed, except in the Veteran class. The classification will usually be the same for both sexes, but dogs and bitches will be judged separately. All classes are defined by sex, age and the amount of winning attained. As an example, I shall give the definitions of classes that are usually scheduled for our breed at All-Breed Championship Shows.

Minor Puppy

For dogs of six and not exceeding nine calendar months of age on the first day of the show.

Puppy

For dogs of six and not exceeding twelve calendar months of age on the first day of the show.

Junior

For dogs of six and not exceeding eighteen calendar months of age on the first day of the show.

Novice

For dogs who have not won a Challenge Certificate or three or more first prizes at Open and Championship Shows. (Puppy, Special Puppy, Minor Puppy and Special Minor Puppy classes excepted whether restricted or not.)

Post Graduate

For dogs who have not won a Challenge Certificate or five or more first prizes at Championship Shows in Post Graduate, Minor Limit, Mid-Limit, Limit and Open classes, whether restricted or not.

Limit

For dogs who have not won three Challenge Certificates under three different judges or seven or more first prizes in all at Championship Shows in Limit and Open classes, confined to the breed, whether restricted or not, at shows where Challenge Certificates were offered for the breed.

Open

For all dogs of the breeds for which the class was provided and eligible for entry at the show.

Using these seven classes as an example of a show's schedule, the judge will take the seven dog classes first and then the seven bitch classes. When the dog classes have finished, and assuming that a different dog wins each of the dog classes, the steward will ask for 'all unbeaten dogs to come to the ring'. The judge then decides which one of these unbeaten dogs is the best and which one is second best. To the best dog, he awards a CC; to the second best, he awards a Reserve CC (RCC). On very rare occasions, the judge may decide that there is insufficient merit in any of the dogs for him to award the certificate. The judge may wish to award the RCC to the dog who was second in the class to the CC winner. This is quite acceptable and is often the case. RCCs do not count towards the title of Champion no matter how many are won. The award is made in case the CC winner is subsequently disqualified for some reason, in which case the CC is then awarded to the RCC winner. Although they do not count towards attaining a title, RCCs are still a very high award to win.

The procedure is exactly the same for the bitches, until after all the classes have been judged and the CCs and RCCs awarded there remains the job of choosing the Best of Breed. The best dog and the best bitch are called into the ring. The judge then chooses the one he considers to be the best: the Best of Breed. At an All-Breed Show, the Best of Breed then becomes the representative of his breed in the next stage of competition, in our case the Terrier Group.

As you can see, to win a CC, which means that in the judge's opinion your dog or bitch was the best of its sex on the day, is quite an achievement. Now all you have to do is repeat the process twice more under two different judges and you have a Champion!

176

To finish this explanation of Championship Shows, I shall explain how Groups and Best in Shows are won. All dogs of whatever breed are classified into a group. There are six different groups of pedigree dogs, namely: terriers, toys, hounds, gundogs, utility and working. Each Best of Breed goes forward with all the others to compete in his breed's group. The Best of Breeds are judged again, usually by a different judge entirely, who chooses the Group Winner and the Reserve Group Winner. When each group has been judged, we are left with just six unbeaten dogs, out of perhaps many thousands who started. At the end of the show, these six are then judged again. The judge chooses a winner and a runner-up: The Best in Show and the Reserve Best in Show.

Ringcraft

Having a dog of show quality and being able to present him in good order for the show ring are two parts of the requirement. All this can and often is ruined by less than capable handling, a lack of ringcraft and a proper understanding of the dog, both specifically and as a breed. Over the years, many exhibitors improve their stock by breeding, presentation and handling, not only by practice and experience but also by the accumulation of knowledge which gives them an almost innate understanding of what is required. The ones that fall into this category can truly be described as 'dog men'. Unfortunately, at the present time, it is an oft-misplaced description, but it was brought into perspective by the overheard words of some wag who commented, 'There are a lot of men with dogs, but not many dog men.'

When watching experienced exhibitors from the ringside, you could be forgiven for thinking how easy it all is. In fact it is a testament to the skill and knowledge of the exhibitor that this appears to be the case. There is much to learn of basic and more advanced techniques than meets the eye. In this respect, it is the job of the clever handler to enhance the appearance and chances of the dog they are handling, by highlighting the dog's strong points and disguising his weaknesses with skilful use of brushing and handling techniques, to create optical illusions. There is of course a line dividing what is acceptable and what is not. The latter would be regarded as cheating and there can be little satisfaction in that, no matter what the success.

Once the basics have been learnt, everything is a progression from there onwards, and it is up to the individual to watch and listen, and to learn from their own perceptions and from others', often without the donor of the information being aware.

Handling dogs can be divided into two main parts: standing in show position (stacking) and moving. These are each made up of many component parts, some of which are used regularly on every dog, others that are used only to overcome a problem on a particular dog. The whole job can be made easier by having a dog who is a natural showman, but even the naturals need to be assisted. The foundation stone for any improvements made by the handler, is an in-depth knowledge of the dog himself, both physical and mental, which includes temperament.

I am often asked how to get a dog to show. The answer could be a variety of ways, but some years ago I coined a saying when asked this question, which seems to me to encompass the whole: 'Every dog is like a locked door, each with a different key. Find the right key and you can unlock the door to the dog.' There are many different 'keys' and sometimes several of them have to be used together to obtain a result.

It is very much a trial-and-error situation and finding the right key will depend as much on your own observation of the dog as on anything else. Squeaky toys, balls, liver, biscuits, simple words of encouragement are all known to be advantageous in your search. Occasionally the key will be found completely by accident, as once when I simply pointed a finger at a bitch, and to my amazement she stood, rock steady, in precise show position with ears and tail up. I used the pointed finger at the very next show and won the CC! At that time, I was handling five of these dogs, who were all related, coming from the same kennel, and they all did the same thing – showed for a pointed finger. I thought they must have been trained this way by their owner, but no, she was just as amazed as I.

So observing each dog and noting his response to certain methods of handling or objects is of prime importance. With a dog in regular exhibition, once the key is found, say, for example, it is a ball, the dog should be starved of that particular thing from show to show. Allow him to see it again for only a minute or two the night before the show and just before you enter the show ring. There will be no need to worry whether he will wag his tail, move smartly around the ring and, most of all be happy – he knows he is going to have his favourite ball to play with. In the ring, let him have a few moments of enjoyment when the judge is otherwise occupied and then, after it's all over, give him the toy to play with for a while. He deserves it.

There is no better start for the potential show dog than to be trained from puppyhood. All the training at this time should be made into a game, but in such a way that the puppy understands what is required of him. This applies to all dogs, for most are only too willing to please provided they are sure of what is expected. That is why it is so important to have a basic method in all you do that can be adjusted to suit the individual.

A good temperament is invaluable. The dog who is naturally happy, quick to learn and willing to please, is infinitely better suited to showing than the snappy, shy, or dull animal. I think that happiness is really the important factor here, and much of that happiness comes from the regime under which the dog is kept.

When showing puppies or youngstock, the most important consideration should be whether they enjoy it. The winning or achievement should be very much a secondary consideration, because now is the time when the dog will decide whether this is a worthwhile exercise or not. It matters not that they fidget, hop, skip, lick the judge's face or whatever else, so long as the lasting impression in the dog's mind is that it is fun. For this same reason, it is a mistake to over-show dogs, particularly young ones, no matter how good they are or how many prizes they win. Many a potential champion has been ruined by being over-shown.

Ring shyness, poor showmanship and over-aggression could be temperamental faults and are difficult to deal with. Early and continued training, with general socialization, will eliminate ring shyness in almost every case. If a dog continues to be frightened or dull in the show ring, you must accept that he is unsuitable as a show specimen. Poor showmanship can be habitual or can happen with a normally good showman. One of the many solutions to this problem is in the feeding, and this often succeeds when all else fails. Complete abstinence from food for up to twenty-four hours before a show, and then baiting in the ring with chicken or some other food, has proved to be highly successful, and is a method favoured particularly on the continent. While some may feel that such a method is cruel, it should be pointed out that many kennels practise a day of abstinence per week as part of their regime of management. In bygone days, this practice was the norm. On the odd occasions I have used hunger as a means of animating a show dog, I have compromised: the normal feeding time for my dogs is in the early evening, so rather than completely starve the dog I feed at lunch-time the day before the show, and not again until the normal evening feed after the show. This compromise has had the same effect of encouraging the dog to show for bait, without any undue abstinence that could possibly be construed as cruelty.

With large classes, or at the height of the season with many shows, dogs often lose their edge. Often, dogs who are good natural showmen, will not show as well in the latter part of the class, than they did at first. The same applies to dogs who are really over-keen in the show ring: they expend so much nervous energy, tire themselves out or get themselves into such a state that they do not stand or move as well as they can. In many cases, more thoughtful handling could have helped. The trick, as practised by all the top handlers, is to be able to switch the dog off and on, take his mind away from dog shows and conserve the sparkle that may help the dog win the class. When the judge's attention is elsewhere, there is no need for your dog to show himself off, except for the ringsiders. There are various ways to 'switch off' the dog and the method chosen will again depend on your observation of the parti-cular animal. Loosening your hold on the lead and allowing the dog to relax is one way. Bending down and holding the dog's head, perhaps doing a little brushing, will stop him seeing all the other dogs, which, being a show dog, he may want to spar up to. And there are others. Again, it is a trial-and-error situation. The same applies for 'switching on', and if you can find a way of doing this, the dog is less likely to tire or become overexcited and ruin his own chances.

Over-aggression is a temperamental fault. This should not be confused with a good terrier temperament or high spirits. The bad-tempered, over-aggressive dog that snaps and lunges at every other animal around, often with tail down and ears pinned back, is abhorrent and should find no favour. Male animals in particular will often be seen to spar up to other dogs and are a pleasure to see. In this natural position the true shape and style can be seen, as each dog pulls himself together, lengthens his neck and shows himself off. My definition of a good 'Highlander' temperament, is shown by a dog who can stand face to face with another showing himself off, never backing down, but not snapping or lunging either. Good showmen with high spirits and excitement for the occasion can be a handful, but need only correct handling to make full use of this natural, if lately undervalued quality.

Just a few more general tips before we cover stacking and moving in depth.

To you, your dog is more than just a subject of the idealists' whims, which is what he is if you consider the very nature of judging dogs at a dog show. To you he is a friend, a companion and a source of endless joy and amusement, with his own character and personality. It is very easy to fall into the trap of overestimating your own stock and it is with different eyes and a different attitude of mind that one has to make any evaluation. For this reason, it is better to be hypercritical of your own stock. You will be better prepared for any disappointments which come your way. Much of the disenchantment with the dog-showing world is caused by the individual's inability to see or admit to their dogs' faults. It is called 'kennel blindness', and being kennel blind is the surest way to lure yourself into a true sense of obscurity!

Choose your clothing and footwear for dog shows carefully. Besides thinking of the weather and the aspects of decency, (remember all the bending), you should ensure that you have enough pockets for your brush, comb, ball, liver or whatever else. Footwear is very important as you will be on your feet for a long time, so comfort must be a priority. In a nutshell, your attire should be smart, comfortable and serviceable. It is not a fashion show, and all that you do during a day at a show can be the ruin of good clothes. It may be as well to have a couple of outfits specifically reserved for the job and footwear that is broken in for comfort.

You are not supposed to talk to the judge in the ring, except in special circumstances. If you have a problem or a question, it should be directed through one of the stewards. However, if the judge says something which begs a reply, such as 'What age is your dog', answer politely but briefly. Do not try to engage the judge in a full-length conversation, informing him of your dog's recent wins, or break into a diatribe about another dog. It is not the done thing and will do no good anyway.

There are two other very important points to remember when in the ring. Firstly, try to keep an eye on all that is happening and particularly on the judge when moving and stacking your dog. First impressions are often lasting ones, so it is important that when the judge is casting an eye in your direction your charge is seen in the best light. Secondly, and equally importantly, practise self-control. You may be bursting inside, with your heart seemingly pounding in your throat, but it must not show, no matter what. I do not know how, but it is accepted that emotions transmit themselves down the lead to the dog, who seems to be able to sense excitement. So if you allow your emotions to get the better of you, it may affect him as well as you. It will impair your judgement and awareness and you will find yourself making the most elementary mistakes, which could be very costly. I can think of two personal examples that illustrate the difficultes that can be caused by your state of mind. In my case, emotion tends to show itself five minutes after leaving the ring, which can give the impression of disinterest or ungratefulness, even after just winning Best of Breed, when in fact there is an explosion of emotion going on inside. The second example is how a loss of self-control can be costly: I had the good fortune to win the Terrier Group with a dog I was handling, and was into the last six challenging for Best in Show at a major Championship Show. This was a new experience to me and of course I was very excited. On the way through from the collecting ring to the Best in Show ring, my dog was attacked by a spectator's dog. From that point on, I did just about everything wrong. I moved the dog too fast; I did not stand him in profile for the judge; I talked to the dog, which I knew had an adverse effect; all in all, I forgot about my own self-control, and it cost us dear. On reading the Best in Show judge's critique, it was quite apparent that had the dog (and handler) performed correctly, the dog was favourite to win Best in Show. So no matter how good the dog you are showing, there is in many ways a great onus of responsibility on the handler.

Stacking

Stacking is the setting up of a dog in a standing position, on the ground or on a table, and its purpose is to show the dog to his best advantage.

This involves placing the dog so that all the component parts are in the correct, symmetrical positions, offering to the eye the correct head carriage, level topline, straight front, and so on. He should stand as if on the tiptoe of expectation, that some sport is just visible on the horizon. There is ample photographic material within these pages in illustration of this, which can be used as reference.

A major priority for the handler is to become ambidextrous, in order to be able to cope with any situation.

Most dogs are easily stacked up and leave little more for the handler to do than to check that the feet are in line before holding up the tail. Others, whether by training, lack of training, general high spirits or because of faults need to be coerced and placed in all particulars. Most handlers will in fact pay more attention to detail than is strictly necessary. I, for one, do, often repeating the actions several times. This is as much to relieve tension as to make any further improvement.

It is impossible to predict every situation or offer remedies for every eventuality, but I hope the following pointers may be of use.

Always place the front feet first, this is the foundation for all subsequent placings. The feet should be placed so that they are straight and vertical (or appear so) and slightly under the body. Wide or narrow fronts can be assisted by placing closer or wider and disguising that fact by careful brushing. Care should be taken not to place a wide front too close, for this will seriously alter the line of the leg and give rise to a pin-toed look.

The head should be carried at a right angle or less to the axis of the neck. Some dogs either toss their heads back, stretch out their necks with their noses in the air, like a pointer, or lean into the lead pulling their whole body forward on to it, and choke themselves. To remedy the first two, simply press down on the muzzle of the dog until the correct or more nearly correct position is obtained. This

Have your dog well turned out and standing correctly to catch the judge's eye. In this instance, the author has the puppy Rotella Knight of the Realm on the judging table, awaiting inspection. (Photo by Chris Kernick.)

183

should be practised at home until the dog understands. The third of the problems can be countered by leaving the head placement until last. Once the rest of the dog is in position, with loose lead, place the head in the correct position before taking up the slackness in the lead to support the carriage. It may also help to alter the angle of support by moving the lead-holding hand slightly towards the tail. But it is so important to have the head in position first, so that the lead is only giving support, and not to try to alter the head carriage by pulling back with the lead, which will only result in the dog pushing against the force and choking himself even more.

The topline should be level. If your dog has a good topline but, on checking this in the ring, it is less than true, the fault is either yours or the uneven ground's. It may be that the forelegs are placed too far forward and/or the hind legs too far back. This over-extension can be used to straighten an uneven topline but gives a rocking-horse effect, it is really a matter of deciding between the two evils.

Do take notice of the ground. Most summer shows are held outdoors, and ground conditions vary. If your dog has his front feet in a depression or his hind feet on a rise, it will detract from the appearance. Look for the nearest piece of level ground, which often is only a few inches either side, and move there. If there is no even ground near you, do not be afraid to move to a different place entirely, usually at the end of the line, to find one. This is rarely necessary but I am sure would meet with understanding.

The hind legs are placed in a slightly extended position, but do not over-extend, as this will detract from the whole balance of the dog. In placing the hind legs correctly, we are also seeking to highlight the flexion of the hock and, to a lesser degree, the turn of stifle. Incorrect placement of the hind legs, head, neck and tail, or a combination of these, can give the unwanted illusion of extra length in the back, by extending the continuous, horizontal line of these combining features.

The tail should be held erect or just slightly inclining towards the ears. It is good to see a dog, even one who has been placed in every other point, holding his own tail erect with no help from the handler, bar the occasional stroke with the hand. However, it is usual that tails are held and this should be done by supporting the back of the tail from root to point with open fingers. Inclining the tail slightly towards the ears not only looks better but has the effect of shortening the back, this can be further aided with correct brushing of the topline.

Finally ear carriage can be a problem, with dogs 'flying' their ears, that is holding them back and not erectly. Simple stroking with the open hand from behind the ears down the neck will often encourage the dog to use them. Opening the slip-lead and placing three or four fingers in the collar part will widen the lead, thus supporting each ear from behind. Placing the favourite ball or squeaky toy under your foot just in front of the dog often brings the ears up, as well as extending the neck as he reaches to have a closer look.

Does your position in the line make a difference? Yes it does. If you have a dog who is either on the large or small side, you should stand next to or preferably between two other dogs of similar size. Standing next to or between dogs at the opposite end of the size scale to your own will only highlight the disparity, which may not be in your favour. If there is no such choice available, stand either at the head or end of the line, leaving a space between your dog and the next one in the line so that it is more difficult to see the disparity.

Do not get stuck in a corner; the judge will probably not be able to see you. In large classes the line of dogs may extend along two sides of the ring, so if you find yourself in the corner position it is perfectly acceptable to stand your dog across the angle of the corner, turning the angle of the two lines into one arched line.

If you have a dog who will free-show, that is show himself naturally, albeit with encouragement and baiting from you, fine. It looks good and is infinitely preferable to stacking. There are not many dogs who will show themselves when standing and because of the large classes and their duration, it may not be possible to keep the dog going all the time, and in the end you may have to stack-up like everyone else. If you are to free-show even partly, it is probably better that you stand either at the head of the line or at the end of it, so that your dog's movements and your encouragements will disturb no one.

Finally, and this always applies but is of particular note when in the show ring, protect your dog. Keeping him away from known aggressive dogs in case he gets bitten or frightened is a consideration, but not the one I had in mind. I was thinking about weather. If it is very hot or comes on to rain during your class, stoop over your dog to stop him getting wet or stand between the dog and the sun to give him some shade at the very least. In hot conditions, it is acceptable to drape a cold, damp towel over the dog when the judge is busy with the others. If a shower starts, hope that someone offers you an umbrella and if they do willingly accept.

Movement

A dog will not move well unless he has had time to loosen up after the journey to the show. Nor will he move well if he needs to relieve himself. It is very important that each dog is allowed some exercise before exhibition to satisfy both these needs. For several reasons, I find the use of an exercise pen much better than lead-walking each dog. With white dogs, such as ours, it is so easy for them to become grubby after all the preparation to get them clean, particularly at an outdoor show if the ground is wet. Many dogs can be lead-walked for ages without emptying themselves (time which could be better employed in some form of preparation), only to empty himself in the show ring during the class or, heaven forbid, during the individual movement. An exercise pen can be set up in a clean corner of the showground and any mess cleared up immediately. Dogs seem to relieve themselves more readily in a pen when they have relative freedom of movement. They also settle into the surroundings, turning to look this way and that, as other dogs pass by.

There are really three phases of movement in the show ring, although the actual movement of the dog will no doubt be the same in all three. The first phase is when the dogs enter the ring and find a place in the line. Judges often watch and gain a first impression of the dogs as they come in. First impressions are very important. The judge with an eye for a dog, will, in small classes at least, have spotted the likely challengers for first place, unless something untoward is found with them, either on the table or in movement. The second phase is when the dogs are asked to move around the ring together. The judge will view them from the centre of the ring, so that each dog is seen in profile, showing his general appearance, carriage and traction. The final phase is the movement of individual dogs after they have been examined on the table. The judge will ask the exhibitor to move his dog in a triangle, and then straight up and down. The triangular movement is actually an inverted triangle, whereby the judge can view the dog's hind and front action in a direct line with the dog, and the shape and traction of the dog in profile. The straight up and down movement is for the judge to double-check that the dog is sound fore and aft. Sometimes they are moved again, as individuals or, less often, in pairs. This is done from the line, when judges are formulating their final decisions. The movement is usually straight up and down.

In the first phase it is enough to be aware that eyes are watching and have the dog immaculate and raring to go, before you make your entrance.

In the second phase, most dogs will move better than at any other time, because they are in company. West Highland White Terriers are gregarious creatures and are happier when striding out with others. This collective movement also allows the dogs to loosen up and settle into a pattern, possibly weighing up the opposition! This may sound incredible but, once they have been to a few shows, many dogs know the procedure and on entering a show ring will pull themselves together, with head carried high and tail up, almost inviting the audience to admire them.

If you have a dog who really strides out and covers the ground, it will be an advantage to stand first in line, so that when the judge asks for 'once around the ring, please', he can push off into his natural stride pattern, bringing his excellent movement to the notice of all, including the judge. Should you choose a position between other dogs, it may not be possible to highlight this point because of the encumbrance of a less athletic dog in front of you. However, the drawback of standing first in line is that you will also be first to be examined on the table, which means that you will have little time to prepare your dog by brushing and standing correctly, before the judge's eyes turn in your direction.

The third phase is probably the most important and more often than not results in a higher or lower placing. After placing your dog back on the ground, spend a few seconds making sure that the lead is in the right place, the dog is ready to go, the judge is in position and that you have decided just where you are going, before striking off into the triangle. Try to move the dog at an even pace from the start, keeping an eye and your mind on your pre-decided line of travel. Watch the action of the dog so that adjustment can be made where necessary, and glance once or twice at the judge to ascertain his position – if he has moved you will need to alter your proposed line of return. Always keep the movement flowing by rounding off the corners of the triangle and making the transition from triangle to straight up and down in a small semicircle, rather than stopping to turn around. This keeps the dog flowing at the given pace and is more likely to produce an impressive result than stopping and starting. All your concentration at this time should be on the showing of the dog. Often one sees someone moving a dog without taking any notice of him at all, sauntering along as if tomorrow will do or strutting around obviously more concerned about whether their own appearance is right. At this point, it is too late to worry about that, just do the best job you can with the dog.

Similarly, if the dogs are being asked to move again after table examination, do not wait until you are asked before standing up from the stacking position. Carefully time that point so that when your turn comes all the small acts of preparation have been done and the dog is already moving, if only around your body. The judge may be moving along the line asking each exhibitor in turn, to move again, but sometimes the judge will stand in the centre of the ring requesting each dog to move again straight up and down, starting from where the judge is standing. If this is the case, carefully time your approach to the 'starting line' from behind the judge, so that when your dog comes into the judge's view, he is already in full flow.

Whether to move your dog on a loose or tight lead is a decision only you should make. One or two judges insist on loose leads and although the exhibitor cannot really refuse, I think it is wrong for the judge to insist. The dog may have been trained to walk on a tighter lead and to believe that once the lead is slackened, it is time to relax, drop his head, sniff the grass, and so on; others are so eager and full of themselves that they require firmer handling. By all means, if the movement is unsatisfactory on the tighter lead, the judge ought to advise the exhibitor of this and suggest trying a loose lead. That is helpful. But insistence on matters of this kind gives the dog who is normally moved on a loose lead an unfair advantage.

The whole point of using a lead is so the handler has a degree of control. Moving in the show ring is quite different from taking a dog for a walk in the fields. Having the right pace for the dog is very important. A free-moving dog is a pleasure to have and, as with most dogs, can be allowed to move at a fairly brisk pace. The only danger is that the faster a dog moves, the more inclined the legs become towards the centre of the dog, and if a dog moves too fast he can quite easily single track. Adjustment of a free-moving dog's pace is easily done by simple checking on the lead.

The easiest way to explain the degree of control used by the handler, is by use of a horse-riding metaphor. Imagine that the lead around the dog's neck is the bit in a horse's mouth. By taking up the slackness in the lead, the dog is then 'on the bit'. Once on the bit, the dog is in control without being strung up or dragged about and can be directed, adjusted and effectively controlled by the very slightest of movement from the handler.

Sometimes a dog will stop when moving in the show ring, digging in his feet and refusing to go any further. It is a difficult problem but I have found it often to be the fault of the handler taking off into the stride and leaving the dog behind. The dog is then effectively being pulled along and the more the handler pulls, the less willing the dog becomes. Before moving off, stand with the dog in line with your hip, then give the command to move. Maybe you say 'Come on boy', or whatever, and at the same time give a light, almost imperceptible tug on the lead. The dog will almost certainly strike off leaving the handler half a pace behind. That, it seems, is often what the problem is: the dog wants to be the leader.

Being gregarious animals, many dogs do not move quite so well on their own. To help this, and it is of particular help when showing a male dog, try to have one of the sides of your triangle parallel to the line of the standing dogs. Most male dogs will spark up in the presence of others and moving along this line at least should present no problem. Once he has got his tail up and pulled himself together for the other dogs, he may well hold that physical position for the remainder of the movement.

When a dog lacks sparkle or is prone to losing it after a while, it is as well to keep the movement as short as possible. Therefore make the triangle a small one, and the straight up and down a moderate length. There is a practice of optical illusion used in which the handler shortens his own stride, so as to make it appear that he is having to walk faster in order to keep up with the dog. I have not used it myself, but I suppose it may fool some judges, although I have noticed that more and more are becoming wise to its use of late. Conversely, with the outstanding, free-moving dog, use the full limits of the show ring to highlight the point.

On completing the movements off the table, as you approach the judge again, he will no doubt want to see a good expression before moving on to the next exhibit. Judges employ various means to try to conjure up an alert expression, ranging from flailing their hands and arms about to making silly noises at the dog. A lot of dogs are quite unmoved by all this and you should have your own solution, whether it be a titbit in your hand, the favourite toy or simply throwing your terrier pad a yard or so beyond the dog. Whatever your solution, use it, because you know that it works.

After all this, if you are lucky enough to be pulled out in the final line-up, carry on showing your dog as you have been doing until the awards are announced and the prize cards handed out. It does not happen often, but there have been occasions when the judge has altered the placements right at the very end of the class. Should you be a winner and required to challenge for the CC later, put the dog away in his box for a rest until the time comes. Dog showing is tiring and stressful to dogs as well as to exhibitors, and you will do yourself and your dog no favours by hanging around the show ring with your dog between classes. This time of relaxation cannot of course be given to the first- and second-prize winners in the Open Class as the challenge will take place almost immediately. However, it is advisable, whenever possible, to pick the dog up and take him to a table just outside the ring, if only for a minute. It may just be the breathing space that makes the difference between winning the CC and not. The same element of self-control should be exerted even if you do win the CC, for there is still Best of Breed to challenge for. But once it is all over let the dog have a well-earned rest, while you enjoy your achievement.

Whatever objection you may have to the judging, it does not do any good to confront the judge in an angry fashion at a show. Try to take the decisions philosophically or wait to cool off for a while when, probably, with the benefit of hindsight, you will think better of it. However, it is interesting to find out the judge's views, maybe at a later show. Good judges know exactly why the placings were made the way they were.

But for the newcomer in particular, discretion is often the better part of valour and by inexperience you may say the wrong things. That is why it is so important for the newcomer to learn the mechanics of the dog game before entering its world.

Two stories spring to mind, which are both true. The first is a graphic illustration of the misunderstanding of a newcomer; the second a lesson to all in the art of repartee. An exhibitor went to the secretaries' tent before judging and explained, 'My little bitch is entered in Maiden today, but I mated her last week. Does she still qualify?' The second story concerns that great old terrier man and Cairn specialist, the late Walter Bradshaw, who, after judging Cairns at a show, was accosted by an irate lady exhibitor, who said, 'I don't know why you placed me fourth. My dog has a lovely head, a beautiful coat and a perfect tail!' Mr Bradshaw, being a true 'dyed-in-the-wool' dog man replied, with typical brevity, 'Well madam, you should have shown just the tail!'

The moral of the stories is clear; if in doubt, keep quiet, but enjoy your showing and good luck!

10

Judging

What sort of person makes a good judge? What qualities and abilities are required? What are the responsibilities involved? These seem to me to be the questions that each aspiring judge should ask themselves. The powers that be are forever telling us about the shortage of quality judges at all levels, an assertion which I do not share. There are many good and competent prospective judges awaiting the call to the next level. Unfortunately, the system of selection, particularly at the highest level, is not geared to accept the information and knowledge necessary for seeking out these people, and remains distant from the grass-roots opinion. At the same time, great care is required in choosing judges, for there are always those who aspire to the dizzy heights and often reach them, not solely on the merits of knowledge and capability.

Honesty, integrity, knowledge, understanding, and the ability to use that knowledge and understanding when judging, are to me the most important of the many requirements of a good judge. There are some who never want to judge, feeling that they lack the necessary confidence or ability to translate their knowledge in practice, or more often in the knowledge that it can be a thankless task. I know of one very highly esteemed breeder and exhibitor in our breed who hates judging but feels that it is her duty to 'put her head on the chopping block' every few years for two reasons: first, so that the present condition of the breed can be appraised; and, second, she considers that unless you are prepared to do the job yourself, you can hardly justify your criticisms of others. I agree with those sentiments, although I really enjoy my days of judging.

There is no doubt that friendships have been lost or impaired through judging decisions. If, for example, you have ten classes to judge and each class is won by a different dog, you have ten reasonably happy exhibitors and others whose dogs were placed lower or not at all, with varying degrees of disappointment. The good, honest judge who has made his decisions purely on the merits and failings of the dogs before him on the day has nothing to fear. There will always be criticisms no matter what the decisions are; the important point is that the judge knows exactly why those decisions were made.

To judge the breed at the highest level (awarding Challenge Certificates) is one of the highest accolades bestowed upon a dedicated fancier, and to carry out this task to the best of one's ability, without fear or favour, gives a great feeling of satisfaction. Even though I had awarded CCs several times before and was retrospectively happy with my decisions, I remember, after the fourth time I judged at this level, having such a feeling of satisfaction in the knowledge that I had done exactly as I wanted and knew why. Throughout the whole day, in every aspect of judging and organization, I felt completely in control, and the resulting feeling of satisfaction bordered on elation for weeks afterwards, as if I had just won Best in Show!

Besides the important requirements already outlined, there is one more thing of equal and possibly greater importance, that is required of a judge, but which is, I suspect, rarely taken into account. It is the one thing that applies to judges at all levels and in all breeds to a greater or lesser degree, and that is a duty of care. Everyone involved in the breeding, exhibition or judging of a breed of dog is to some extent a guardian of that breed, and therefore has a responsibility for its present and future well-being. By his actions, each judge is pointing the direction of the breed by stating that one dog is better than another for whatever reason; by giving these assessments over a period of time, and collectively with other judges, he is saying 'this is right' or 'this is wrong' or more right or wrong, thus determining the ideas and thoughts of what are deemed to be the rights and wrongs in the breeding programmes of tomorrow. In conclusion, judges have a great responsibility to the breeds they judge and must be clear in mind of what the breed should be and the effect their decisions may have in the future.

How and When to Start Judging

Learning to judge starts immediately one becomes interested in the breed as something more than just a pet. The knowledge required is built up over a long period by examining dogs (in the first instance your own), watching judging at dog shows and listening to the comments of the experienced. It is a long but fascinating process of knowledge accumulation, which goes inadvertently hand in hand with the learning done in order to breed and exhibit dogs. Eventually using that knowledge to judge the breed is a natural extension of that learning.

By judging your own dogs or arranging matches with your friends and their dogs in the garden, you can practise copying the procedure used by experienced judges you have watched. This will give valuable experience and a better understanding of what is involved. After a short while, you may be asked to judge at a match meeting or training class. Unless this is a breed club match, you will be judging all breeds, but not to worry, the secretary will have noticed you over a period of time and will ask you only when he feels you are capable. It really does not matter whether you know much about the breeds you have to judge, it is after all a training class and that training is for dogs, handlers and judges. It will teach you to handle the dogs properly and make you think, which is vitally important. You may amaze yourself, you know the best judges have an eye for a good dog even when they do not know why and, with notable breed exceptions, soundness, good movement and showmanship in a dog are not too difficult to recognize even for the novice.

For a time, remembering all the other things besides 'running the rule' over the dogs will seem almost impossible. How many times around the ring? Where should the dogs stand? Which way should the placements be started? And so on. It's very like learning to drive a car: in one breath, the instructor says 'left foot up, right foot down, check the mirror, indicate left, don't forget to look behind', and you wonder how you are supposed to remember all this and still avoid the other traffic. Just as co-ordination in driving comes with experience, so does co-ordination in the show ring: the ancillaries are done automatically leaving your mind free to concentrate on the important business of judging dogs.

Stewarding is a worthwhile exercise and show secretaries are always in need of more helpers. While you are doing this valuable work you will also be getting an insight into the way experienced judges go about their business, which will stand you in good stead when the time comes for you to take on the responsibility of judging.

Breed clubs have a number of judging lists, with clear definitions of the requirements a person needs to qualify for a particular list, for example the 'A' list is for persons who have already awarded Challenge Certificates in the breed, the 'B' list is for those the club would support to give Challenge Certificates but have not already done so, and the 'C' list is for those the club would support to judge the breed without awarding Challenge Certificates.

The clubs operate different modes of selection for these lists, some opting for a ballot of all the members, others by committee approval. By the time you are thought to be qualified for inclusion on a club judging list you will probably have judged some classes for the breed at an All Breed Show or Terrier Show.

When you are asked to judge for the first time, think carefully before accepting. Do not be put off by feelings of trepidation, for they are only natural and do not disqualify you. But do be honest with yourself and only accept the invitation when you feel that you have enough knowledge and experience to carry out the task properly and do justice to the exhibits and exhibitors. This important point should be borne in mind each time you climb another rung of the judging ladder.

One of the main causes of consternation these days is that lots of people take on judging appointments before they are ready, and they lack the degree of experience, knowledge and understanding required. With notable exceptions, it is simply not good enough just to be the spouse or partner of a successful breeder, exhibitor or judge. To be an experienced steward is not in itself enough qualification. Service on some committee, no matter how high the office or expertise required, is a job apart, and is certainly no credential for judging dogs at any level. Unless you have taken a very active part, especially with the preparation and exhibition of show dogs, then almost without exception there will be some aspect of judging which you are unable to comprehend.

Lots of newcomers are in too much of a hurry to 'get to the top'. Few people achieve massive success in the show ring until they have learned 'the basics' which usually takes several years. There are notable exceptions, often when a newcomer is lucky enough to purchase a top-class exhibit as their first show dog, but this is more by luck than judgement, and initial success is usually followed by a period of less success as they then serve their apprenticeship of learning. Judging appointments at the present time, however, are relatively easy to come by and the impatient, self-deluded and/or highly motivated newcomer can find openings here.

One of the criteria necessary in qualifying to award Challenge

Certificates is to have judged at least twenty-five classes in the breed. When I started in the 1970s, and up to seven or eight years ago, twenty-five breed classes were not so easy to come by, so therefore, by the time those classes were amassed, several years had elapsed. It was hoped that during these years, the individual would have gained considerable knowledge and experience, so that when the Championship Show invitation fell through the letter box the recipient was ready and qualified to accept. These days, because it is so popular, many more shows are scheduling our breed and are having to scrape around for someone to judge the classes, resulting in the flimsiest of connections with the breed being accepted as a qualification to judge. It is not all the fault of the newcomer: show secretaries and their committees should seek the advice of the breed clubs for suitable officials, but the onus of responsibility must still fall at the feet of the ill-prepared individual, who in his hurry to reach the top takes on a judging appointment, when a modicum of soul-searching would tell him to wait a little while longer. There is no better qualification to judge than the practical experience and knowledge gained by having a first-hand involvement with show dogs.

Trying to run before you can walk could be detrimental to the furtherance of a judging career. Exhibitors are no fools, and they will watch the way you conduct yourself. If you make a mess of things, the news will travel very quickly.

However, having done all your soul-searching and having come to the conclusion that you are ready, willing and able, you will find judging to be at the very least fascinating and often exhilarating.

A judge should carry out the job in hand with the correct attitude and a completely open mind. To be able to appraise each dog on its merits and failings on the day, with no regard for reputations, past success, friendships, personality likes and dislikes, grievances, rumours or anything else, is one of the greatest virtues a judge can hold. It is not always as evident as one would hope these days, but will always be admired and appreciated by all good dog people and will lead to the building of a first-class reputation.

Understanding, or at least trying to understand, the mentality of dogs is something that seems to receive little consideration from many judges. Puppies and young and inexperienced stock in particular, should be given extra consideration and more leeway than perhaps the seasoned campaigners. Try to be aware of what is going on in and around the ring and be prepared to give a little. West

Highland White Terriers are a very intelligent breed and soon become accustomed to new sights and sounds, so waving your hands around or making noises in order to see his expression is likely to meet with little response; he sees and hears those things every day. But throw something a yard in front of him or squeeze the squeaky toy you have behind your back and then you will no doubt see the sharp, piercing, intelligent expression you were looking for. In a nutshell, besides judging for breed type, conformation, movement, and so on, be aware that each dog is a thinking individual, not a robot, and that each will react differently to the world it perceives.

There are important practical aspects besides basic judging procedure. Be clear in your mind what you want, not only from the dogs in the ring, but from the exhibitors and your stewards. A few moments spent with your stewards before the judging will help the smooth running of the day. Good stewards will go about their jobs unobtrusively and are aware that their service is one of assistance and not instruction either to you or the exhibitors. If you do get an over-enthusiastic steward who perhaps, only through his keenness, is too intrusive, loud or regimental, do have a quiet word before the day is ruined for everyone.

When handling a dog on the table or floor, good judges will be noticed by how and where they feel a dog and exhibitors will know just what they are feeling for. It is quite unnecessary to squeeze, push, press or prod dogs, as is sometimes seen. This heavy-handedness is usually a smokescreen to hide the judge's own failings of breed knowledge and understanding. Do not make impulsive, unheralded movements towards a dog, but make your intention clear. Never approach or touch a dog from behind: you are asking for trouble and it is unfair to expect the dog not to flinch as if he should telepathically understand your intentions.

Take into account the condition of the ring surface and, if the ground is rough or uneven, find the most level piece you can to move the dogs, and then allow some latitude in the movement of the exhibits. Our breed should be able to cope with rough terrain but the eye can sometimes deceive, so a bit more concentration might be required.

Do take note of the weather, particularly hot weather, when judging. It is very inconsiderate for a judge to keep dogs waiting or to deliberate for too long when temperatures are high.

It is the practice of some judges to use first names when addressing exhibitors in the ring. I feel this is wrong no matter how well you know each other, because it is not fair to the odd newcomer whose name you do not know and leaves him with the impression that this is an old pals act, which is not necessarily true.

Assuming you have practical experience of show preparation and in exhibiting dogs yourself, you will be able to appreciate the degree of trimming excellence and handling of each exhibit. This also should be taken into account in your final decisions. Remember that it is the exhibitor's prerogative to make the best of his dog's appearance, using skilful presentation and handling, both to disguise faults and highlight virtues. The task of the judge is to find or notice these things, not just to find fault, but to give credit where it is due. It may be that you have two exhibits of equal merit in every other department and the selection of one in preference to the other could then depend on presentation and handling.

Try to be consistent in the type and conformation of the dogs you choose in each class and throughout the classes you judge. This may be difficult in some classes when types can vary from one extreme to another. But flitting about from one type to another, when there are positive choices of consistency, shows a lack of understanding, indecision or bias, and you may hear some wag whistling Elgar's *Enigma Variations* at the ringside.

Using your experience and knowledge, make your decisions by weighing up all the faults *and* virtues of each exhibit when compared with those of the other exhibits. Do not fall into the trap of fault-judging, which is to discard the dog without further deliberation after finding one fault.

In terms of Championship or Breed Club Shows, which draw large entries, although you will find it difficult to assess, the speed at which you judge is an important factor. Too fast and you will possibly not be paying enough attention to detail or giving the matter your full consideration. Exhibitors want to feel that they are being given value for money and that their dog has been properly and equally considered. It is important, therefore, that each exhibit, even the absolute no-hopers, receive the same amount of time and deliberation, at least until you have seen all the dogs on the table and in movement. Judging too slowly can be almost as bad in that exhibitors and spectators become bored, and dogs jaded. Exceptions, within limits, may be made where a judge is awarding Challenge Certificates for the first time. As a rough guide, three to four hours to judge 100–150 dogs would be acceptable.

Finally, when the time comes to make your final choice, be decisive. To exhibitors, there is nothing worse than a judge who places the dogs and then starts to fiddle about, swapping dogs around. If you have a large class, it is always better to select a number of dogs for further consideration and dispense with the rest, but do make it plain and audible to all that at this stage you are not placing the ones you have picked out.

Judging Attire

Judges of both sexes should look smart without being overdressed. The clothes and shoes should be chosen carefully according to the time of year, prevailing weather conditions and whether the show is indoors or outdoors. There can be a fine line drawn between well dressed and overdressed, and practicality is another consideration. Remember you are about to judge dogs, so what may be regarded as appropriate attire for a wedding is not necessarily suitable for a dog show, even though you may look and feel a million dollars.

Footwear is very important. You will be on your feet for several hours, often walking on uneven ground at outdoor shows, so new shoes, however expensive, are out. Instead, choose the ones you know to be comfortable for, believe me, there is nothing worse than having to stand for hours in chafing or pinching shoes; it will spoil your day, making it an endurance test rather than an enjoyable experience.

Awarding Challenge Certificates

To all but the capable few who go on to judge Groups and Best in Show, awarding Challenge Certificates in your breed or breeds is the pinnacle of judging attainment. There are set criteria laid down by the Kennel Club for qualification for this status. Once you have been invited to give these awards, the Kennel Club will send you a questionnaire to complete, which will then be studied by the appropriate committee who will decide whether or not, in their opinion, you are sufficiently qualified. This application must be made at least six months before the proposed date of judging. The criteria state that you must have been judging the breed for at least five years, judged at least twenty-five breed classes including a club show and will ask for and take into account your involvement and experience in this breed, i.e. number of litters bred, champions made up, and other successes. It will also ask for and take into account other information such as involvement and successes in other breeds and judging experience in general. Provided you can satisfy all these requirements, it is unusual for acceptance not to be given.

Judging Procedure

Having arrived in good time, collected your judging book from the show secretary and met with your stewards, you must find your ring and make the necessary arrangements before you start. These will include positioning the judging table to your satisfaction and checking that you have a rubber mat or carpet for the dogs to stand on (you will need a bucket and shovel, too). Most of these jobs will be done by your stewards but it is your ring so do make sure you are satisfied with it before you start. You have to sign the judging book on each page and I like to do this and any other little bits of organization before starting with the first class.

When everything is in order, let your steward call in the dogs. He will check for absentees and inform you of these, which you will note in your judging book. He will then arrange the exhibits as you have decided. Take a stroll along the line of dogs for an initial appraisal, then ask them to move together once or, better still, twice anticlockwise around the ring. This movement will give you a chance to see the action of each dog and also allow the dogs to loosen up and settle. Most dogs enjoy walking in the company of others and seem to do so with more freedom. The first exhibitor will then place his dog on the judging table. Approach from the front and offer the dog the back of a hand to smell before starting your examination. Now, bringing all your knowledge to bear, run your hands over the dog making a mental note of the salient points, good and not so good, at the same time using your eyes to discover likewise. It helps if you assess the dog's points in a set order. This will help to ensure that you do not miss anything out. That done, ask the exhibitor to move the dog firstly in a triangular fashion and then straight up and down. In the triangular movement, you can see the dog moving away, in profile and moving towards you. Straight up and down lets you concentrate on the line of movement.

During this moving section, you will be noting not just the movement, carriage and conformation but also the showmanship, personality and character of each dog.

Repeat this process until you have seen all the dogs, then stand back to make your final appraisal of the dogs in line before you. If you feel it necessary, you can move some or all of them again before making your selection. As a general rule of thumb, if you pick the dog you would most like to take home as your winner and then likewise in descending order, you will not be far away. Be quite definite when placing dogs, either by pointing to or touching the hand of the exhibitor at the same time saying first, second, third, fourth and fifth. Once selected, mark the full results and a brief critique of first- and second-placed dogs into your judging book. Continue in this fashion until all the classes and awards have been decided.

The Judge's Critique

After each judging engagement, you will be invited, and expected, to send your comments in the form of a written critique to the dog press and, if it is a Championship Show, to the breed clubs for publication. For Championship Shows, you make comment on the first and second in each class and give just the name of the third-placed dog. For any other type of show, your comments are restricted to the first in each class with only the names of the second and third. The people who exhibited dogs under you will look forward to this critique. They and other interested parties will note what you say and analyse your comments in respect of their own dogs in particular, and the other dogs for future reference. Therefore, great care must be taken when writing critiques that you are sure of the comments you are making. Many of the comments you make, of course, will be your own interpretation, but if, as an extreme example, you say 'has a bad mouth' and it becomes clear that the dog has a good mouth and you were mistaken, who looks the fool? So do be sure of what you say.

11

Ailments and Diseases

The canine species, as a whole, just like ourselves, are not immune to common ailments and, less frequently, more serious diseases. However, each breed seems to be more prone to a particular ill than others, particularly hereditary disease. West Highland White Terriers are fortunate in being hardy, tough individuals by nature, and in general rarely suffer from anything much, barring the most common of troubles. The more serious problems that have affected our breed are Perthes disease, craniomandibular osteoarthropathy (CMO), and to a lesser degree Keratoconjunctivitis sicca (KCS) or Dry Eye Syndrome. Though these diseases are not prevalent, they are well known.

Accidents

In cases of serious accident, there is the risk of internal bleeding, so veterinary attention should always be sought, regardless of the apparent symptoms.

Shock

A traumatic experience, such as poisoning, burns, or a road accident will result in shock. The symptoms are shaking and weakness, pale gums and inner eyelids, a drop in blood pressure, and rapid, shallow breathing. The dog's extremities will feel cold to the touch, and consciousness may be lost. Professional assistance should always be sought.

Treatment While waiting for assistance to arrive, the patient should be kept still and quiet, and covered with a coat or blanket, or anything to keep him warm. Avoid alcoholic drinks which tend to prolong any possible internal bleeding. The common practice for cases of shock is to give warm, sweet milk or tea. Opinions vary: some advocate that nothing should be given orally. Keep the dog on his side, with his head lower than his tail to assist the flow of blood to the brain.

Burns and Scalds

Whenever possible immerse the area in cold water or pour cold water on to the area. Minor cases, when the skin is unbroken and only affecting a small area, can be dressed with a bicarbonate of soda compress and bandaged. When the skin is broken, treat with a soothing ointment that is especially for burns or scalds. The application of wet, warm tea-leaves or linseed oil are also known to assist. Treat for shock and, in serious cases, call in professional assistance.

Stings

When dogs are stung, it is often the case that they caught the bee or wasp first. Young dogs, puppies in particular, will try to catch every fly, moth or butterfly, that comes within reach. Not surprisingly, the occasional bee or wasp is caught in the heat of the chase. Stings are not dangerous unless they are in the throat, or unless the dog is allergic to stings.

Treatment For allergic cases, have a supply of antihistamine tablets to hand. These can be obtained from your vet.

Bee stings should be taken out carefully and an alkaline solution such as washing soda applied. With wasp stings there is no sting to remove, but they should be treated with an application of diluted acid – vinegar or lemon juice are suitable.

If the dog has been stung in the throat, take him to a vet immediately as the consequent swelling will impair breathing.

Allergies

Allergies can be caused by virtually anything and everything but, more commonly, the source will be found in food, medicine, bedding or an insect sting. Occasionally, a dog will come out in a rash after being trimmed; some dogs' skin will redden after each trimming session and others will show this trait rarely. The cause is often over-vigorous or close stripping. A rash of this kind should not be confused with one caused by an allergy.

Treatment   An antihistamine injection given by the vet will give relief in the short term. For long-term cures, the course of the problem has to be isolated. If the cause is something that is easily remedied, such as food or bedding, this should be changed.

Anal Glands

The anal glands are located on either side of the anus. They are scent glands which were used by the domestic dog's wild ancestors for marking territory. They should express themselves naturally every time the dog defecates, but sometimes they become impacted with smelly, waste matter of a beige/light-brown colour. This causes inflammation and irritation which makes the dog drag his rear along the ground. If left unattended, this may develop into an abscess.

Treatment   Impaction is relieved by squeezing the glands with gauze, cotton wool or tissue-paper to empty them. In order to do this painlessly, practice is necessary. If in doubt, consult your vet for guidance. Regular attention in this way will prevent any further problems.

Arthritis

Arthritis is inflammation of the joints, which may have been caused by previous injury or more probably by effects of advancing years.

Treatment   Keep the dog in warm, dry conditions with a raised bed or sleeping area. Daily doses of cod-liver oil can be beneficial. If severe and painful, give the correct dosage of aspirin. Exercise should be limited and careful handling is a must.

Bad Breath (Halitosis)

The common cause of bad breath is gastric trouble, often caused by incorrect diet and/or gum disorders and tooth decay.

Treatment Change the diet. Practise regular dental care (descaling and brushing). Charcoal tablets will also help.

Balanitis

Balanitis is the infection of the membranes of the penis sheath (prepuce) of a male dog, which may be caused simply by laying on dirty ground. It is not dangerous but the symptomatic discharge, which may become reddish, soils carpets.

Treatment Internal flushing of the prepuce by syringe with a mild antiseptic. Serious cases will need a course of antibiotics.

Canker

This term covers a whole range of conditions resulting in a coloured, often yellowish, discharge from the ear.

Treatment Carefully clean the ear with cotton wool using a proprietary brand of ear cleaner or canker lotion. Cleaning can also be done by pouring warm olive oil into the ear, which will loosen the more solid wax which collects other waste and debris causing irritation and infection. Regular attention to cleanliness will reduce the risk of problems. If the condition persists it may be that the cause is more serious and professional assistance is necessary.

Car Sickness

Car sickness is more common in puppies and youngstock. The sickness usually starts with the animal drooling streams of saliva before actually vomiting. It can be a great problem, especially with the show dog and, in particular, our breed, taking into consideration the rules on preparation at a show.

Treatment Once dogs become used to travelling, they will not suffer from car sickness, so start early by taking the dog out in the car, on short journeys at first. By the time the dog is ready to be shown, with any luck he will have already overcome or grown out of the problem. Car sickness tablets for dogs can be given two hours before the journey or according to manufacturer's instructions; herbal tablets are preferred. The disadvantage of tablets is that they can cause drowsiness, which is not desirable in the active, sparkling show dog. It will help if the dog is not fed before the journey; if the food he last ate has been digested, the mess at least will be kept to a minimum. This will not, however, stop the dog from suffering car sickness.

Constipation

Constipation is caused by the accumulation of faeces in the rectum, seen as difficulty in defecating. It is usually caused by incorrect diet, lack of exercise or too little drinking water, or a combination of these.

Treatment The safest laxative is olive oil, given orally a teaspoon-ful at a time. A change of diet may be necessary and, until the condition is relieved and the cause known, advisable. Clean, fresh drinking water should be readily available.

Craniomandibular Osteoarthropathy (CMO)

CMO is a non-cancerous growth of bone on the lower jawbone or over the angle of the mandible and tympanic bulla. It is usually, but not always, bilateral (affecting both sides of the jaw). As there is early inflammation and pain, it can be detected as early as three to four weeks after its appearance, but more often between three and six months, or more rarely, later. The puppy will be dull, lethargic and unhappy. It will be unwilling to eat because of the pain and have a high temperature. Unlike the normal puppy that wriggles about when being handled simply because it is against its will, the CMO puppy will cry out in pain particularly when its mouth is opened. The effect of CMO often gives pain to the whole head and even the forelegs. The diagnosis can be confirmed by X-ray of the area and treatment can then begin.

CMO is inherited via a simple autosomal recessive gene, which means that *both* parents must have at least one CMO gene, and therefore are both definite carriers.

Treatment   Anti-inflammatory drugs (steroids) must be administered by a veterinary surgeon. The initial treatment is usually by steroid injection, followed by a course of steroid tablets. These will effect a full recovery, so that by the time the dog is two to three years old, it may be impossible to tell that the dog ever had the disease.

Testing and Eradication   Details of how widespread or prevalent the disease is in the UK are sketchy, although it would appear to be more widespread than the popular consensus would have us believe. This is because breeders and exhibitors are loath to divulge such information for fear of being blacklisted for potential sales, studs and also in the show ring, which in itself is not surprising. However, if we are ever to eradicate this and other diseases, in particular Perthes Disease, more openness will have to prevail. The difficulty with this disease is that there is no test for CMO, save that of test mating. So, unless the parents have been proved clear by testing, breeders cannot be certain of their own stock. It is possible to line-breed or even inbreed without producing CMO, even though some of the dogs are carriers, because if you never breed two carriers together, CMO cannot be produced. However, in mating one carrier to one clear parent, you would have to be incredibly fortunate and then keep one of the 50 per cent of the puppies who are clear (the other 50 per cent of course being carriers, and so on). With this in mind, I can quite openly and honestly state that no dogs of my breeding have ever had CMO. But I do not rule out the possibility for the future, but then I have never been one to hide my head in the sand, so I hope I have not just tempted providence.

What follows is a guide for those conscientious breeders who wish to help themselves and the breed. For there may come a time when proven clear stock, in particular stud-dogs, will be of more value than at present.

1.   To test unknown bitches, mate to a known carrier stud-dog and vice versa with a known carrier bitch to an unknown stud-dog.
2.   X-ray all puppies from test matings at four months of age to determine whether they show signs of CMO or not.
3.   Any puppies from test matings which are rehomed after their X-rays should carry endorsements so that they cannot be bred from.
4.   In this way, the probability of the unknown parent not being a

carrier is related by the number of clear puppies, i.e. eight puppies = 90 per cent, and sixteen = 99 per cent.

5.   Test breed any animals kept from a test mating to a known carrier in the same way as before.

6.   Only mate carrier bitches to clear studs unless testing the stud, and test mate anything you keep.

7.   Always mate clear bitches to clear studs. These matings cannot produce CMO, and you are on your way to eradicating CMO from your lines.

8.   Do not change your bloodlines. Work on the eradication, because you may be exchanging your own known problems, for someone else's unknown ones.

(I am indebted to Barbara Stoll, who gave much of this information in her excellent article published in The WHWT Club of England newsletter 1984.)

Cystitis

Cystitis is caused by an infection of the urinary organs, and often imposes pain and great irritation on the sufferer. Symptoms are the frequent passing of urine or the attempt to do so; the urine may contain traces of blood.

Treatment   Consult your veterinary surgeon.

Diarrhoea

Diarrhoea is one of the most common conditions and particularly serious in puppies. It is the excessive looseness of the stools caused by incorrect diet, stress, infection from B-coli, gastro-enteritis or canine parvovirus, or infestation of worms. It can be easily brought on by a change of diet or part of a diet. This is especially so in puppies when they go to their new homes. Always give a diet sheet to the new owners, and instructions of when next to treat the puppy for worms.

Treatment   Give a mixture of kaolin three times a day at the onset of the condition. If it continues, starve for at least twelve and, better still, twenty-four hours, except for water and arrowroot. (In new-born pups this can be given by tube.) Give two teaspoonsful of white kaolin mixture four times a day for three days. Continue the arrowroot throughout until the condition is relieved. It is extremely important to encourage the intake of water as this will help to prevent dehydration.

Begin feeding again on the third day by giving small amounts of boiled rice together with a little chicken, rabbit or fish. Increase the amount of food gradually and stay with the light diet of rice and chicken, rabbit or fish.

Should the diarrhoea persist or recur, the cause may be an infection, needing antibiotic treatment. Stop all food and seek veterinary assistance.

Even when the diarrhoea stops, finish the treatment or course of tablets and continue with the light diet for two days more. Once the dog is back to normal, bolster up the normal diet with extra protein and vitamins for a few days to offset the days of abstention.

Distemper and Infectious Hepatitis

These diseases used to be the scourge of the dog world, wiping out whole kennels, until vaccines were found. The immediate symptoms are a cough, high temperature and discharge from the eyes and nose. In itself, the disease is not usually fatal, but fatalities are common from the secondary infection which starts almost immediately with diarrhoea, liver problems and pneumonia. After treatment, many dogs seem to recover only to be ravaged further by the virus as it destroys parts of the central nervous system. The brain can be damaged resulting in fits which, depending on their severity, may cause permanent damage or death. Often dogs are left with chorea (permanently twitching limbs) which may improve with time.

Treatment Always have your puppies inoculated against this and other diseases and have regular booster injections. Should distemper be suspected, telephone your vet for him to make a house call. The disease is highly infectious so you should never take a dog suffering from suspected distemper to the surgery. Your kennels and/or house should be thoroughly disinfected and all the bedding, toys and clothing used in connection with the dogs burnt. Note:

Humans, cats, rabbits, guinea pigs and rats are not susceptible to canine distemper. Those which are include ferrets, mink, weasels, foxes, wolves, wild dogs, lynx and racoons.

Eczema

This condition is seen in various forms in patches of skin inflammation, some red and oozing, others dry and scaling. Often there is a loss of hair and it is accompanied by itchiness and irritation which will cause the dog to scratch and bite himself. The causes can be many: allergies to food or bedding, poor management and dirty housing, parasitic infestation, incorrect diet, overheating, and can even be started by over-zealous trimming, when it is known as 'trimming rash'. The veterinary profession expound the belief that our breed are very prone to skin problems, almost to the point of obsession, calling any and all skin ailments 'Westie skin'. I cannot go along with this argument and have seen no appreciable evidence in my own or many other kennels that this is the case.

Treatment This can be, and often is, very much a trial-and-error situation with some animals responding immediately to a simple cure, while it may take time to find the appropriate remedy for others. My own vet made a point which I think may be worth repeating: that dermatologists will never be out of work because their patients rarely die of their problems but they do not recover completely either. It really depends on the cause of the problem in the dog. Most dogs who suffer from a skin disorder are found a remedy to which they respond and never suffer from the same trouble again. It is a peculiarity that one puppy in a litter or one dog from a kennel can be affected, while the others are completely undisturbed. Even in the cases of parasitic infestation, this can be the case, but if parasites are found to be the cause, it is wise to treat all dogs, kennels and bedding as a safeguard. (*See* page 216.)

Any bald, inflamed or oozing areas should be treated with a suitable cream, powder or lotion obtained, ideally, from your veterinary surgeon. There are many such preparations available, most containing zinc oxide, although calamine, if present, acts as a soothing agent and can be used on its own to relieve the irritation and therefore stop the dog from scratching, which only makes the condition worse. Cortisone tablets or injections, given by the vet, will stop the irritation but these treatments can be given only on a short-term basis as continued use of Cortisone will cause internal damage, particularly to the liver. Occasionally, a dog will continue to scratch, even when the original cause of the problem has been remedied, thereby inflaming areas again. This is more often habitual rather than a resurgence of the problem. In these cases, soothing preparations and/or Cortisone should be applied, and an Elizabethan collar fitted until the whole area has healed. If the diet is suspected, feed boiled rice and white meat or fish until the problem is resolved. Too much protein and, in particular, too much maize will overheat a dog, causing irritation. A carefully chosen, balanced diet, suitable for the dog and the amount of work he does or energy he expends, will reduce this risk. Attention to detail and good management is always the watchword; poor hygiene, dirty living conditions, poor food or unsuitable diets are an invitation to all kinds of trouble.

Fits

These are seen as convulsions which resemble epileptic fits. There are many causes, some of which may be difficult to diagnose. The more common causes are: internal damage to the brain by some deformity at birth, or a blow to the head; viral infections, such as distemper, which cause damage to the central nervous system, spinal cord and brain; or infestation of worms. Fortunately, when a blow to the head is the cause, it is often the case that the patient will show no ill effects and the fits may never recur.

The signs of a fit are the dog not knowing where he is, staring vacantly, gnashing or grinding the teeth, possibly frothing at the mouth, shivering and convulsions. Often the dog goes through paddling motions and loses consciousness.

Treatment   In cases of deformity, or severe, prolonged fits caused by brain damage, it may be kinder to have the dog put to sleep. It all depends on the degree of the condition and veterinary advice should be taken.

Worm all dogs regularly and, in particular, take this step if a young puppy suffers a fit.

Watching and coping with a dog who is having a fit can be a harrowing experience. Most importantly, try to move the dog to a

210

restricted area, such as an enclosed box padded with towels or blankets, away from any hazards. In this way, as the dog strikes out involuntarily, he can do no harm to himself. Great care should be taken when handling a dog in a fit, as he will be unaware of what is happening and may bite even his beloved owner. After the seizure, the dog will slowly regain consciousness, although he may be unsteady and a little confused for a while. Keep him in a quiet place away from other dogs. Seek professional advice to try to determine the cause and, in the meantime (for the first twenty-four hours at least), feed a light diet.

Often a fit is an isolated incident, showing no serious or lasting effects. This is particularly true of puppies, but keep a careful eye on the subject until you are satisfied that the fit will not recur.

Flatulence

This is the evil-smelling gas coming from the alimentary canal. Quite often, it is caused by something in the diet.

Treatment Watch to see if any particular food is the cause, then remove it from the diet. Serious cases can be quickly offset by giving an enema. However, there may be other more serious causes for which veterinary advice should be taken.

Hernia

A hernia is the displacement of an organ or part of an organ in part of the bowel or uterus. There are three types: congenital, inguinal and umbilical. Bitches with congenital hernias should never be bred from, as there is a very strong possibility that she will die during pregnancy.

Treatment If a lump is noticed after a bitch has been mated it is very important to lay the bitch on her back and push the lump up into the abdomen. Do this every day for three weeks while the whelps are developing in the abdomen. If left unattended, a whelp may develop in the inguinal sack, eventually growing too large and bursting the sack and killing the bitch. Some puppies may have umbilical hernias, often caused by the cord being pulled during birth. These rarely present a problem and the bitch will whelp normally. Puppies sometimes develop inguinal hernias which are seen as a lump in the groin. There may be just one on one side, or one on each side and they vary in size. These should be pushed up from whence they came as often as possible. As the puppy grows these often stay pushed up and no further problems are experienced. In difficult or more serious cases the puppy can have a simple operation, whereby the lump is pushed back and the aperture is stitched.

It is important to consult your vet about any lumps that develop.

Hysteria

The dog gives all the outward appearances of being terrified, barking furiously at nothing in particular and, if free, running madly.

Treatment   Follow the treatment for fits (*see* page 210).

Interdigital Cysts

These eruptions between the toes can be likened to boils in the human. The cause is probably obesity and/or diet, although the possibility of bacterial and viral infection cannot be ignored.

Treatment   Change to a light diet and reduce the weight of obese animals. Bathe the swellings with warm salt water until the swelling becomes ripe and bursts. Keep the area clean, using a mild antiseptic solution. The dog will lick the area, keeping it free from dirt.

Kennel Cough

The canine parainfluenza virus and the *Bordetella bronchiseptica* bacterium are thought to be the most significant of the bacteria and viruses that can cause this disease. Kennel cough is contagious and is spread by airborne droplets, so that even dogs who have not been away from home can be infected, although the close proximity of other dogs at dog shows or in the park will undoubtedly increase the risk manifold.

It is characterized by a harsh, dry cough which may last several weeks but more usually five to ten days.

Treatment   There is no cure for kennel cough, although there is a vaccination to help prevention which, after an initial double dose, can be given as an annual booster (*see also* pages 112–13).

Keratoconjunctivitis Sicca (Dry Eye Syndrome)

This condition usually affects both eyes and is caused by the decrease in tear production, which is thought to be caused by an abnormality in the immune system. It affects dogs usually between the ages of two and seven years and, for some curious reason, middle-aged and spayed bitches in particular. The first signs are a discharge from the eyes which sticks the eyelids together. There is a loss of shine to the cornea and ulcers start to form. Each ulcer will cause damage to the eye resulting in a degree of transparency being lost where each ulcer has been. Over a period of time, as new ulcers form, the eye or that part of the eye, will become more and more opaque. The degree of this opaqueness is an indication of the relative amount of lost vision. Needless to say, the condition, if allowed to deteriorate, will eventually result in complete blindness.

Treatment   This can take two forms. The first is the cleaning of the eyes and the administering of false tears, using suitable eye drops on the recommendation of your vet. Your vet may well advise the use of drugs, too. Cleaning and application of eye-drops must be done several times a day and be continued for the rest of the dog's life. It is no great task and takes only a couple of minutes and personally I prefer this treatment to the second option of surgery. An operation can be performed which transplants the parotid duct, which is a salivary gland, thus lubricating the eye with saliva. Having seen cases where this operation has been done, and having spoken to the owners, I am told that although the problem of dryness in the eyes is solved, a further problem can be found when the saliva runs from the eyes down the muzzle and foreface of the patient. This burns channels through to the skin of the patient, causing a new discomfort. It seems that the operation is, for some, the greater of two evils. Once again, professional advice and opinion will be invaluable.

Mange

This skin disease comes in two forms: sarcoptic or common mange and demodectic or follicular mange.

Sarcoptic or Common Mange

This is one of the most common skin diseases in dogs and is highly contagious in both dogs and humans. It is caused by the spread of the sarcoptic parasite (mange mite), which burrows into the skin, primarily around the eyes, the edge of the ears, the groin and on the inside of the elbow. It will affect the whole of the dog if untreated or if it is unresponsive to treatment. It causes intense irritation, resulting in the dog continually scratching or biting at the troublesome areas, with the consequent soreness and loss of hair.

Treatment   The object is to kill the parasite and break its breeding cycle, thus ridding the dog of the problem. Dusting with Gammexane powder will accomplish this aim. Repeat the dustings at weekly intervals for four weeks just to be safe. All kennels, sleeping boxes, and so on, should also be dusted and the bedding burnt. The affected dog should be completely isolated until cured. Veterinary consultation is advised and the advice should be followed.

Demodectic or Follicular Mange

The demodex mite is the culprit here and is present in most canine follicles. Dogs carry this mite without any problems, but occasionally and for reasons unknown, they suddenly multiply giving the dog a mousy smell and causing irritation which the dog scratches and bites, again resulting in hair loss, inflamed skin and a thoroughly unhappy dog. Veterinary opinion is that it is due to a breakdown in immunity inherited from the mother, though it may not affect the whole litter and may not become apparent until much later on when the puppies are in new homes. The presence of the mite can be revealed by taking skin scrapings.

Treatment Demodectic mange is notoriously difficult to cure. However, there are many powders, creams, lotions and washes available. Treatment with mange wash and the application of mange lotion is sometimes successful. A diet of boiled rice and chicken or fish will reduce the risk of overheating which may increase the irritation and the want to scratch. However, although it is not contagious, it is still advisable to seek veterinary assistance. Follow veterinary advice, which will probably involve applying a prescribed medication several times a day.

Parasites

Mention is made here of only the most common parasites to affect dogs.

Worms

There are seven different kinds of worm, but the two most common are roundworm and tapeworm.

Roundworm (Toxocara canis)

The tabloid press has made much of the danger of *Toxocara canis* to children, in whom it can cause blindness. The danger does exist and blindness has been known to be caused, but there has to be a quite extraordinary sequence of events for that to happen. Therefore, the likelihood of its happening is very limited.

The roundworm is the most common parasite and can be found in most puppies. The long, thin, milky white worms are often seen in the stools and are occasionally vomited up. Adult dogs carry larvae, which in the male remain dormant and may never leave the carrier. In the female, however, they activate during pregnancy and some will be passed on to the foetuses, while others are retained in the bitch. More larvae will be passed on to the puppies through the dam's milk, and these will continue to grow inside the puppies. Worm eggs can be passed by the carrier on to grass and other areas. Worms do not breed or develop inside humans, but if a child should eat worm eggs there is a remote possibility that the eggs will pass around the body and affect the retina of the eye.

The symptoms of worm infestation are a pot-bellied appearance, thinness, dry scurfy skin and/or diarrhoea.

Treatment Worm all puppies at five weeks of age and again two weeks later. It will do no harm to worm them every two weeks until twelve weeks of age, then every six months throughout their lives.

Tapeworm

Tapeworms are not common, especially in puppies. The worms consist of small segments, which look like rice, although some segments can be much larger. Every segment contains thousands of eggs, and can be seen around the anus of infested animals. They are easily spread over wide areas by the wind. The principal carriers of these worms are fleas, rats, hedgehogs and farm animals, hence the importance of keeping dogs free of fleas.

Treatment Easily cured by use of a suitable vermifuge. Note: The excreta of an infested animal contains thousands of eggs within the small segments, so all excreta should be removed quickly from kennels, exercise areas and gardens.

Fleas

Although the flea is almost transparent, it is usually seen as a reddish-brown colour. This is because the flea sucks the blood of its host. Left untreated, dog fleas multiply at an alarming rate and will be passed on to others in the kennel. The first sign that a dog is harbouring fleas may be incessant scratching, but this is by no means universal. Some dogs tolerate large numbers of fleas without any apparent discomfort. The presence of fleas is often first detected when small black specks of flea dirt in the dog's coat are noticed.

Treatment Use a good flea powder or spray over the whole dog, and repeat once a week until the infestation has gone. Treat all bedding, kennelling, boxes and so on, in the same way. Fleas also live in other warm places such as around radiators, hot-water cylinders and fireplaces, which should all be treated. Bathing with insecticidal shampoo is effective and the immersion in a solution of concentrated insecticide will give immunity for up to three months. Note: Since fleas play an important role in the lifecycle of tapeworms, it is extremely important that fleas are eradicated.

Lice

The louse is seen as an off-white, greyish speck often around the ears and mouth. The eggs or nits can be seen with the naked eye when the dog's coat is examined. They are easily passed from dog to dog, but unlike fleas they do not jump.

Treatment   As for fleas, although lice spend their entire life cycle on their host, so treatment of the environment is not so necessary.

Ticks

Ticks are more commonly a parasite of the countryside and rural areas, than of urban areas. Their usual hosts are sheep but they will climb on to a dog. They bury their heads beneath the dog's skin to suck their blood. Once gorged, they will fall off, only to be picked up again later. Never try to remove ticks by instrument as the body will come away leaving the head buried, which can develop into a festering sore.

Treatment   Dab the ticks with methylated or surgical spirit to make it release its grip, before removing the tick intact with forceps or tweezers.

Harvest Mites

These small red mites, barely visible to the naked eye, usually affect the paws causing maddening irritation. They are, as the name suggests, a seasonal problem from mid- to late summer.

Treatment   For these and other mites picked up from the meadows and countryside, dust the area thoroughly or wash with an insecticidal shampoo, repeating the treatment regularly throughout the seasonal period. Benzyl benzonate gives good relief from the irritation that makes a dog bite his paws.

Parvovirus

This viral infection swept the UK in the 1970s and simultaneously seemed to scourge other countries too. Many dogs were lost as the virus spread rapidly.

The secondary form of this infection attacks the heart muscles of puppies between four and ten weeks of age. The incubation period is roughly five days. It is highly infectious and can be carried on clothing and equipment. It can be active for a long time.

The first signs are loss of appetite, followed by severe enteritis causing the patient to arch his back with pain. Vomiting and severe diarrhoea follow, both often carrying blood. Dehydration sets in, as it is virtually impossible for the dog to keep down any liquid and, in a very short time, the dog will succumb and die.

Treatment Treatment is administered by intravenous drip applied by your vet. If the dog pulls through the first few days, it may be possible for him to take liquids. The treatment for severe diarrhoea should then be given. In all cases, follow veterinary advice.

Vaccination is now, very fortunately, available and should be given as soon as possible and boosters given every year. The best way to protect a litter of puppies is for the mother to have a booster as soon as she comes in season.

Where an animal is diagnosed as having parvovirus, he should be kept in complete isolation. If possible, any person in contact with this animal should not be in contact with other dogs. Kennels, beds and all equipment should be scrubbed at least twice using a parvocide or strong household bleach. Puppies should not be reared in these kennels for at least six months.

Perthes Disease

This disease is also known as Leg Perthes. It is the disintegration of the whole or part of the femoral head, which can affect either or both hind legs. Typically, it affects puppies between three and ten months of age, when the first signs will often be lameness or the favouring of one hind leg whilst carrying the other. In all cases, there will be a degree of pain, often quite severe, as the disintegration of the femoral head progresses. Muscle waste will occur because the leg is little used or unused, and great care should be taken when handling suspected cases.

Treatment Confirmation of Perthes disease by X-ray is the first step. Professional advice should be followed thereafter. Less serious cases may be treated by giving a suitable drug to relieve the pain, and restricting movement, until the disintegration is complete. In most cases, an operation is advisable to remove the diseased femoral head which is the cause of the pain. Most dogs make a good recovery and live a fairly normal life afterwards. Note: After extensive study in Sweden and elsewhere, it has been concluded that this anomaly is the result of genetic inheritance, either recessive or polygenic. No animal that has had Perthes disease, even if it has been rectified by surgery, should be bred from.

Ravenous Appetite

This may be caused by a deficiency in the diet, glandular trouble, worms or it may just be habit or greed.

Treatment   If you are worried seek veterinary advice.

Ringworm

Ringworm is a fungoid infection of the skin, and not, as the name suggests, a worm. It often affects puppies, and it usually starts around the mouth and on the head. There is a loss of hair and crusts form on the affected areas. Ringworm can be transmitted to humans coming into contact with infected animals and, in particular, by practising the obnoxious habit of kissing the dog or allowing the dog to lick the face.

Treatment   Fungicides and tablets can be obtained from the vet.

Rheumatism

Rheumatism generally affects the older dog and may be chronic or acute.

Treatment   *See under* Arthritis, page 203.

Sterility

Dogs of both sexes become less fertile with age. One hears of many different 'cures' for sterility, low sex drive, and so on: some advocate the use of seaweed powder, others vitamin E, but by and large none of these remedies can be said to be successful. Bitches who have not had a season by the age of eighteen months may benefit from hormone injections.

12

Show Kennels of the Modern Era

The West Highland White Terrier, being such a popular breed, has attracted many followers and fanciers. What follows is a résumé of those kennels with a record of consistent success, some established for many years, some establishing themselves more recently.

ARNHOLME Ch. Purston Petite, handled by Fred Sills, became the first champion of Mr and Mrs Parr's Arnholme kennel in 1973, but the first half of the 1980s were extra special. Ch. Arnholme Ad Lib (1980), owned by Mr and Mrs Gordon, and Ch. Arnholme A-Cinch (1984) owned jointly by the Gordons and the Parrs, both handled by the Gordons' son, Angus, Ch. Half Moon of Olac (1980) and Ch. Arnholme Aphrodite, owned and handled by Mr D. Tattersall and Mrs J. Bowden respectively, and Ch. Arnholme April Jester (1981) handled by the late Mr Parr, were all bred at the Arnholme kennels. Mrs Parr has awarded CCs in the breed and although she is now wheelchair-bound, she is still an avid exhibitor and fancier of the breed.

ASHGATE Starting at the turn of the decade 1969/70 Andrew and Mrs Sue Thomson have met with great success. Stock from many of the top kennels of the day were brought into the Ashgate fold, and from these beginnings a definite strain has been established. All the preparation and exhibition is done by Sue, while Andrew no doubt casts a discerning eye over the kennel in general. To date, sixteen English champions carry the Ashgate name, with over a hundred gaining their titles in other countries. Both award CCs in the breed, Andrew being one of the top all-rounders in the world and in constant demand. Now retired from active committee service, Andrew is a former chairman and now life member of the Southern West Highland White Terrier Club, while Sue continues to serve on The West Highland White Terrier Club of England committee.

Ch. Ashgate Connel (1990).

BALLACOAR   Since she qualified Ch. Ballacoar Musetta of Cedar-fell for her title in 1971, Mrs Sheila Morgan has bred Ch. Ballacoar Samantha (1975), owned by Mrs Graham, Ch. Ballacoar Miss Muslin of Clanestar (1989), owned by Mrs Lancaster, and litter-sisters Ch. Ballacoar Josey is Justrite (1985) and Ch. Ballacoar Jinny is Justrite (1986), both owned by Mr and Mrs Armstrong.

Ch. Ballacoar Josey is Justrite (1985). (Photo by Diane Pearce.)

221

Ch. Brierlow Beezneez (1986). (Photo by David Dalton.)

BIRKFELL To date, seventeen English champions have been bred by Miss Sheila Cleland. This kennel is renowned throughout the world for its quality and breed type, as much today as ever. Miss Cleland has a passionate belief in what is the correct type and throughout the years has concentrated unfailingly on those beliefs. This can be seen by the limited outside stud-dog use, mainly from just three kennels, Famecheck, Pillerton and Quakertown. The year 1962 saw her first two champions in Ch. Birkfell Solitaire and Ch. Birkfell Sea Shanty, both sired by Ch. Famecheck Jolly Roger. All but two of the champions have been bitches, making the Birkfell strain into probably the strongest and most successful bitch line in the world. The two male champions also have a special place in the history books, the first Ch. Birkfell Sea Squall (1972) apart from being a prolific and influential sire, also holds the breed record as the youngest CC winner. Ch. Birkfell Student Prince (1991) has just overtaken Ch. Arctic Snowstorm of Makerch for the record of oldest champion, qualifying for his title at eleven years and three months of age. Miss Cleland is one of the most respected judges of the breed throughout the world and judged the breed at Cruft's in 1985.

BRIERLOW Mrs Janet Bowden started her kennel in 1978 and spent the first three years 'learning the trade' before venturing into the world of Championship Shows in 1981. Ch. Arnholme Aphrodite, bred by Mrs Parr, was the first champion in 1983 and was followed by Ch. Brierlow Beezneez who qualified for her title in

Doreen Lancaster with Ch. Ballacoar Miss Muslin of Clanestar, and Mary Torbet with Ch. Corrielaw at Newtonglen in 1989. (Photo by Chris Kernick.)

style by winning the bitch CC at Cruft's in 1986. Not to be outdone, the next champion, Ch. Brierlow Blazing Sensation, owned in partnership with Angus Gordon and capably handled by him, was Best of Breed at Cruft's in 1988 and top-winning bitch in the breed the same year. A Ch. Blazing Sensation litter-brother was sent to Penny-Belle Scorer in Canada at five months of age, and became Can. Am. and BDA Ch. Brierlow Blaze-a-Trail, the top-winning West Highland White Terrier in Canada for three consecutive years from 1986. Not bad for a lassie from Lancashire!

CLANESTAR Almost ever present around the ringside, Mrs Doreen Lancaster has made up two champions of her own: Ch. Birkfell Silver Thistle of Clanestar and Ch. Ballacoar Miss Muslin of Clanestar; and bred two others, Ch. Count of Kristajen and Ch. Kwickstep of Kristajen, both owned by her friend and constant companion Mrs Jean Abbey. Other successes, CCs and Best Puppy awards, and so on, have been picked up over the years. Mrs

223

Ch. Domaroy Erisort Serenade (1977).

Lancaster is a very accomplished presenter of her charges and an ardent supporter of the breed in general.

CRINAN All the present-day Crinans, owned by Mrs Barbara Hands, are of a very definite type and strain. The first champion was Ch. Candida of Crinan (1975) and has since been followed by six more champions, five of these home bred. The most notable of these is Ch. Clan of Crinan, who won seventeen CCs including Best of Breed at Cruft's in 1985. Lanny as he is known to his friends, was Top Stud-Dog in the breed in both 1989 and 1990. Well known on the show circuit, Barbara awards CCs in the breed and is an author, accomplished canine artist and sculptor.

DOMAROY Originally from Lancashire, Roy Wilshaw and his wife Dorothy now live in the south of England, along with the inmates of their highly successful kennel, started in the early 1970s. Unarguably 1977 must have been a dream year: not satisfied with having one champion to start the list, they made up a pair, Ch. Domaroy Last Pennyworth and Ch. Domaroy Erisort Serenade. These were the first of seven champions. Two others made up in the following year were the litter-brothers Ch. Domaroy Saracen and Ch. Domaroy Saraband of Whitebriar, the latter being owned by Miss M. Murphy and Mrs J.E. Beer, and handled by Miss Murphy.

Ch. Domaroy Saracen was the top dog in the breed that year and has since been top stud-dog in the breed, being a prolific and influential sire. Ch. Domaroy Erisort Serenade came out of retirement to win Best Veteran in Show at Richmond in 1987 looking absolutely superb, surely a true test of quality.

FAMECHECK Since collecting her first West Highland White Terrier on her bicycle, Miss F.M.C. Cook has made up thirty-seven English champions. This is by far the most post-war champions from the same kennel. They are all home bred, along with countless overseas champions. In the years that have passed since then, 'Cookie' as she is known to all, was until recently ever present at Championship Shows. So keen an exhibitor was she, that her van became a home for herself and her dogs, while she travelled the length and breadth of the country from show to show. Miss Cook has awarded CCs in the breed for many years and is known throughout the dog world not only for her renowned Famechecks, but also for her colourful character and keen journalistic wit.

FURZELEIGH This kennel is owned by John Hodsoll who has employed the expertise of professional handlers to take care of his charges, with great effect. Ch. Whitebriar Jonfair did a lot of winning in the early 1970s with Francis Rundle at the helm. Since then Geoff Corish has piloted several other Furzeleighs to their titles,

Famecheck Speciality, circa *1980. (Photo by Anne Roslin-Williams.)*

with Ch. Furzeleigh Star Trek taking Best in Show at Paignton in 1980. Mr Hodsoll awards CCs in the breed and also judges extensively abroad.

GILBRI The Broom family, that is Gill and Brian, together with offspring Tracy and Andrew, all show a great interest in the breed. Starting with lines based on Ashgate breeding, they made up their first champion, Ch. Tammy of Gilbri in 1983 and followed that up with Ch. Gilbri Pippins Pride, a favourite of mine, in 1986. Mrs Broom is a long-serving (or should that be long-suffering) member of the Southern West Highland White Terrier Club committee.

GLENVEAGH Mrs Modwena Johnston regularly makes the long trip across the Irish Sea to exhibit her dogs on the mainland. Her efforts have not been in vain, having made up Ch. Glenveagh Giselle in 1987, Ch. Glenveagh Tamara in 1989 and Ch. Glenveagh Gabriella in 1990. After winning her first CC and Best of Breed, Ch. Glenveagh Gabriella went on to win Best in Show at the Scottish Breeds Championship Show in 1990. Amongst other things, Mrs Johnston also finds time to be the secretary of The Northern Ireland West Highland White Terrier Club.

Ch. Furzeleigh Regal Lad (1989), handled by Geoff Corish. (Photo by Chris Kernick.)

HAWESWALTON Since making up their first champion, Ch. Haweswalton Houdini in 1981, Mr and Mrs Hawes have been responsible for a further thirteen English champions, mostly owner-bred and handled. Champions Haweswalton Houdini, Haweswalton Sportsman, Midshipman of Haweswalton and Haweswalton Ryan were all top dogs in the breed; Ch. Haweswalton Houdini was Best of Breed at Cruft's in 1983 and a subsequent Top Stud-Dog winner. Not to be outdone, Ch. Haweswalton Merry-Go-Round was Best Bitch at Cruft's in 1989, only to go one better and win Best of Breed at Cruft's in 1990, with Ch. Haweswalton Ryan taking the dog CC at the same show to give Mr and Mrs Hawes a memorable double. Mrs Hawes has awarded CCs in the breed since 1989.

INCHERIL Another family affair, the Incheril kennel belongs to Charles and Mrs Ela Berry, along with son Douglas, who have been keen fanciers of the breed for many years. The year 1966 saw the first Incheril champion in Ch. Incheril Amaarylis. Six others have followed, the most recent being Ch. Incheril And You're Mine in 1991; all are home bred. Mr Berry is a past president of The West Highland White Terrier Club, and Mrs Berry and Douglas presently serve on that committee where Mrs Berry is vice-president. Mrs Berry was the breed judge at Cruft's in 1982.

JUSTRITE Ron and Betty Armstrong started up their kennel in the 1960s, and purchased their first champion, Ch. Medallist of Cedarfell (1972), from Mrs Coy at the age of eight weeks. Mr and Mrs Armstrong have since been responsible, either as breeders, owners or exhibitors, for a further thirteen English champions, spanning each decade until the most recent one Ch. Arnaval Jill is Justrite (1991). Amongst these, Ch. Jaimont of Whitebriar won Best of Breed at Cruft's in 1984, going on to win the Terrier Group and challenge in the last six for Best in Show. Ch. Ballacoar Jinny is Justrite won Best in Show at The National Terrier Show in 1986 and was the top winner in the breed that same year. Highly successful, their charges are always presented to the minute by Mrs Armstrong and exhibited by both. Mr Armstrong has been awarding CCs in the breed for some time now and is judge elect for Cruft's 1995.

KRISTAJEN Five champions have come from this kennel since it was started by Mrs Jean Abbey along with her husband, the late Ken Abbey, in the mid-1960s. The first of these, Ch. Kristajen

Copyright, gained her title in 1978 and was owner-bred and hand-led. Four further champions have been qualified, one of which, Ch. Kristajen Charterman, was home bred. Of the others, Ch. Birkfell Sunrise, bred by Miss Cleland, was the breed's top-winning bitch in 1979, Count of Kristajen and Kwickstep of Kristajen, were bred by Mrs Lancaster, the latter being the breed's top-winning bitch 1990. Mrs Abbey, who is currently the secretary of The West Highland White Terrier Club of England, awarded CCs in the breed at Cruft's in 1986.

LASARA   Mrs Barbara Graham owned the Lasara kennel in partnership with her mother Mrs Hazel. The first Lasara champion was Ch. Lasara Lee (1962). In the years that followed, the Lasaras were to remain the same obvious type with successive champions until the late 1970s, early 1980s, when the type was changed, but still very much based on the earlier Lasara foundation. Then, in partnership with Miss Jane Kabel, the Lasaras continued their successes until Jane returned to her native Holland. Since then Mrs Graham has carried on campaigning more dogs to their titles. In all, there have been sixteen champions in the breed, mostly owner-bred and handled, with innumerable overseas champions. Mrs Graham has awarded CCs in the breed for many years, both at home and around the world, and has judged the breed at Cruft's.

Mrs Betty Armstrong with Ch. Jaimont of Whitebriar (1983), who won the Terrier Group at Cruft's in 1984.

NEWTONGLEN   Always a strong contender for the top prizes, the Newtonglen kennel was founded by Adair and Mrs Mary Torbet in the early 1970s. Though settling in Bedfordshire, both hail from north of the border. Their kennel is now the home of nine English champions. The first, who was purchased in 1974 from breeder Miss Cook with one CC, was Ch. Famecheck Silver Charm. Cruft's seems to be the second home of their charges: Ch. Glengordon Hannah who was bred by the late Mrs Budden, won thirteen CCs in all, and took the CC at Cruft's in 1977, only to go one better and take Best of Breed in 1978. Newtonglen Harriett won one of her two CCs and Best of Breed at Cruft's in 1980, but sadly she died soon after whelping her first litter. Another Best of Breed at Cruft's was won with Ch. Newtonglen Macintosh in 1982. Full brother to this dog was Ch. Newtonglen Footprint, who was Best in Show at the Scottish Club Show in 1982, before being exported across the big lake, where he quickly gained his American and Canadian titles. Champions Newtonglen Miss Muffet (1984), Newtonglen Louise (1985), Newtonglen Scotsman (1986), Newtonglen Mame and Corrielaw at Newtonglen (1989) make up the nine to date, with several more CC and RCC winners in this country, plus many overseas champions. All the exhibiting is done by Mrs Torbet with support

Ch. Lasara Lookatim (1984) shown by Mrs Barbara Graham. (Photo by Chris Kernick.)

Eng. and Am. Ch. Newtonglen Footprint (1981).

A happy Mary Torbet with Ch. Newtonglen Miss Muffet (1984). (Photo by David J. Lindsay.)

and a critical eye from Mr Torbet, who is the president of the Southern West Highland White Terrier Club and made his Championship Show judging début in 1989. Mrs Torbet has awarded CCs in the breed since 1983 and also judges abroad.

OLAC The name of Olac now seems to be synonymous with winning in the show ring. Mr and Mrs Tattersall, known worldwide in doggy circles as Derek and Joan, have had immense successes with their seven English champions. Ch. Olac Moonraker was the first, in 1974, winning ten CCs. He sired Ch. Olac Moonbeam, who was the first West Highland White Terrier to qualify for the Pup of the Year finals and was the top-winning bitch in the breed in 1976. Ch. Olac Moondrift won twelve CCs, was the top winner in the breed in 1979, and Best of Opposite Sex at Cruft's in 1980. He sired Ch. Halfmoon of Olac (bred by Mrs Parr) who gained her title in 1980 along with another bitch Ch. Olac Moondream. Ch. Halfmoon of Olac had a tremendous career winning the coveted title of Pup of the Year 1980, then going on to collect a total of fifteen CCs (a breed

Ch. Olac Moonpilot (1987).
(Photo Chris Kernick.)

231

Ch. Pepabby Poacher (1986).

record in bitches), one of which was gained at Cruft's in 1982. Ch. Olac Moonpoppy (1983) also collected a CC at Cruft's, this time in 1984. Then in 1987, along came the one that everyone will remember: Ch. Olac Moonpilot. Compared to some of the other Olacs he had to struggle a bit in his youth, but once he got going there was hardly any stopping him for three years. He was top winner in the breed in 1987, 1988 and 1989. Top Dog All Breeds 1988 and runner up to Top Dog All Breeds in 1989. Finally he was Best in Show at Cruft's in 1990. In all, he won forty-eight CCs (which overtook the previous best of thirty-three CCs set by Ch. Glenalwyne Sonny Boy), ten Best in Shows, six Reserve Best in Shows, eighteen Terrier Groups, eight Reserve Terrier Groups and Best in Show at six Club Shows.

All these dogs were trimmed and presented and handled by Derek Tattersall, the sheer artistry of whose trimming and presentation is second to none, and can only be admired for the attention to detail in the finished article. He is a former treasurer and now committee member of The West Highland White Terrier Club of England and both he and his wife Joan are Championship Show judges of the breed.

Pepabby Promise.

PEPABBY   This is a real family affair for Mr and Mrs Edmondson, and daughter Julie Farmer. Mrs Pat Edmondson takes care of the day-to-day running and breeding programme of the kennel, and husband Joe does all the trimming, leaving Julie the simple job of showing their charges and making champions!

The year 1985 was the start of it all when Pepabby Poacher won two CCs and Pepabby Promise joined in the act at Leeds Championship Show. After seeing litter-brother Pepabby Poacher win the dog CC, she won the bitch CC and Best of Breed and was in the last three in the Group; quite a day for all concerned. Ch. Pepabby Poacher won his crown at Cruft's the following year, also taking Best of Breed and later going Reserve Best in Show at the Scottish Breeds Championship Show in 1986. Ch. Pepabby Petite started on the trail in 1986 and gained her title the following year. Ch. Pepabby Poppet makes up the trio of champions to date, qualifying for her title in 1990. Mrs Edmondson is a serving member of The West Highland White Terrier Club of England.

Eng. Nord. and Tri. Int. Ch. Rotella Royal Fortune (1980), at nine years of age.

ROTELLA Starting my kennel in 1972 with a bitch of Birkfell bloodlines, I spent the next four years around the smaller shows until I began showing at Championship Shows in 1976. My first two 'big league' contenders were Rotella Ringmaster and Rotella Royal Penny (1978) was my first champion, winning a total of five CCs. She was the dam of Eng., Nord. and Tri. Int. Ch. Rotella Royal Fortune, who won six CCs and, along with her son Eng. and Nor. Ch. Rotella Mighty Mike, became a champion in 1980, completing a memorable double at SKC that year. Ch. Rotella Royal Fortune became an international champion in Scandinavia and at the age of seven years, was Reserve Best in Show at the Swedish Club Show. She gained her Nordic title when over nine years old. Ch. Rotella Mighty Mike went to Norway and was Best in Show at the Swedish Club Show the year after his mother, but sadly he died aged eight. His full sister from a later litter was Ch. Rotella Mighty Miss (1984), who was very unlucky, winning twelve Open Bitch classes but only three CCs. The last of my five champions was a Mighty Mike son,

Ch. Cregneash Candytuft of Rotella, bred by Stuart and Denise Limb, who gained his title in 1986. Since then, there have been four more champions, whom I have made up for their owners, during a two-year stint of professional handling.

SARMAC Audrey and Ray Millen's kennel has housed or bred eleven English champions. First in the line was Ch. Lindenhall Drambui, who was Best Dog at Cruft's in 1968 and made up the following year. Freddie Sills handled Ch. Sarmac Heathstream Drummer Boy, who won ten CCs and was Best Terrier at Chester in 1972. With Ch. Ardenrun Merryman of Sarmac (1980), the home-bred Ch. Sarmac Big Snob (1982), Ch. Sarmac Silver Secret of Lusundy (1986) owned by Mrs Helen Dangerfield, and Ch. Sarmac Drummers Boy (1987) all following, professional handlers have been employed to good effect since. Geoff Corish handled both Ch. Sarmac First Lady (1988) and Ch. Sarmac Merry Monarch (1991), whilst Ch. Hazlan Silver Knight of Sarmac and Ch. Silver Lady of Sarmac were handled by me. Mrs Millen awards CCs in the breed.

Ch. Sarmac First Impression of Kingsview (1991) owned by Mrs Julie Coley. (Photo by David Bull.)

TASMAN In 1972, Alan and Lotte Bonas had a flying start to their show career with two of their four home-bred champions gaining their titles. Ch. Tasman Adoration was all their own work, both sire and dam being Tasmans, too. But it is the second of the two, Ch. Tasman March of Time, who has left his mark, being the sire of champions and many good winners. Ch. Tasman Elation, owned by Sue Thomson, came next in 1976 and after a lull Mr and Mrs Bonas bounced back in style in 1988 with Ch. Tasman Admired.

TIELLOS Previously in partnership with his late father, now with his mother, Angus Gordon has handled four champions to their titles. The first two, Ch. Arnholme Ad Lib (1980) and Ch. Arnholme A-Cinch (1984) were bred by Mrs Parr. The home-bred Ch. Tiellos Toby Jugge clinched his title in 1988, as did Ch. Brierlow Blazing Sensation, owned in partnership with Mrs Janet Bowden, who was Best of Breed at Cruft's in 1988. Starting as a young lad, Angus is one of those very capable handlers, quick to learn and innovative. The combination of having quality dogs, together with slick handling and excellent presentation has paid rich dividends. Both he and his mother Anice are keen fanciers and Angus awarded CCs in the breed for the first time in 1990.

Mrs M. Duell's Lorell kennel has housed Ch. Lorell Last Legacy and Ch. Cabon Capella at Lorell. Mrs M. Dickenson has bred two Kirkgordon champions: Ch. Kirkgordon Musical Cowboy and Ch. Kirkgordon Morning Song. Mrs C. Hartmann, a regular exhibitor for many years, has just added the first home-bred champion, in Ch. Fritsilver Wish Me Luck after thirty-two years of dedication, to go with her other champion bitch Ch. Lasara Lend A Hand. Likewise Mrs Nellie Wright has two in Ch. Drummersdale Oops a Daisy, owned by Mrs J. Lea, and Ch. Gyllie of Drummersdale. Stuart and Denise Limb, although exhibiting very sparingly, have bred two champions: Ch. Cregneash Candytuft of Rotella and Ch. Cregneash Crusader. Mrs Lester's Leastar kennel has been prominent, and Mrs Helen Dangerfield's Lusundy kennel, with Ch. Sarmac Silver Secret of Lusundy and recently Lusundy Sally-Anne, has been 'knocking at the door' with two CCs and several reserves.

Of the newer exhibitors to come to the fore, Mr and Mrs Fox have Ch. Hillstead Sporting Chance and Ch. Hillstead Sweet Dreams to their credit, Derek and Carol Biggs also have two in Ch. Truffles of Holy Cross and Ch. Holy Cross Reet Petite, and Mr and Mrs Brian

Lusundy Sally-Anne (1991). (Photo by David Dalton.)

Squire have been very much in evidence with their Kimgarwyns, having just taken Ch. Kimgarwyn Marksman to the upper house.

Professional Handlers

Often the subject of criticism, professional handlers have, and continue to play, an important role in our world of show dogs. Much can be learned from these professionals and I have watched and listened to many of the greats over the years.

Arthur Wade was one of the best handlers of both Sealyhams and West Highland White Terriers and he made many champions, both pre- and post-war. He was probably the first person to trim down the coat to the degree we now accept as commonplace. George Barr likewise handled with great skill.

Of the post-war handlers, the late Len Pearson made the breed virtually his own. In the seventeen years he handled them, Mr Pearson made up fifty-two West Highland White Terrier champions. Ch. Shiningcliff Storm, bred by Mrs Finch, was the first in 1949 and many of the top fanciers of the day were soon beating a path to his door. Wolvey, Calluna, Cruben, Shiningcliff, Kendrum, Sollershot and many more kennels were his clients. Of his charges, Ch. Mark of Old Trooper won Best of Breed at Cruft's in both 1951 and 1952. Ch. Staplands Shepherd was another outstanding dog in the same year, and Ch. Slitrig Sachet won the Terrier group at LKA in 1962. Having been involved with the breed since 1929, when he bought his first West Highland White Terrier, he finally got around to making up a champion for himself in 1964 with Ch. Snowcliff Spring Song. He first judged our breed in 1962 and awarded breed CCs thirteen times, reaching the pinnacle of his judging career in 1973 at Cruft's.

Fred Sills has handled more than a hundred champions in all breeds, and well into double figures in our breed alone. Ch. Sarmac Heathstream Drummer Boy won twelve CCs and was Best Terrier at Chester in 1972. Five Famechecks are amongst his tally, as are Ch. Lorell Last Legacy who was Best of Breed at Cruft's in 1970, and the Champions Checkbar Tommy Quite Right, Checkbar Donsie Kythe

Ch. Snowcliff Spring Song (1964). (Photo by C.M. Cooke.)

Ch. Haweswalton Stormtrooper (1985). (Photo by Chris Kernick.)

and Checkbar Remony Rye. Mr Sills is a well-known character all over the world and his knowledge and expertise as a handler and judge of many breeds is much sought after. With the relaxation of the unwritten rule concerning judging by professional handlers, Mr Sills now awards CCs in our breed and is also a Terrier Group judge.

Ernest Sharpe has made up many champions in the breed. In conversation on a shared journey, recently Mr Sharpe told me that, in his opinion, the best West Highland White Terrier he ever handled was Ch. Millburn Mandy (1974). But by far and away the top winner and the one that springs to everyone's mind is Ch. Glenalwyne Sonny Boy, owned by Mrs Jeanette Herbert. Under Mr Sharpe's care and guidance, this dog became a champion in 1975, and then went on a spree of winning that would end with the accumulation of thirty-three CCs (a breed record until Ch. Olac Moonpilot came along). He was Best of Breed at Cruft's and top-winning male in the breed in 1975, top-winning West Highland White Terrier in 1976 and 1977, Top Terrier 1976 and fourth top-winning dog all breeds in 1977. Mr Sharpe always had the dog looking immaculate and, like so many of his charges in various breeds, was a credit to the man's skill and dedication.

Francis Rundle has handled a number of our breed to their titles. Ch. Furzeleigh Last Edition (1974) was a lovely bitch, bred and owned by John Hodsoll. Possibly the best remembered is Ch. Whitebriar Jonfair (1970), bred by Mrs Beer and owned once again

239

Ch. Cregneash Crusader seen with the author after winning the
Terrier Group at Border Union in 1987. (Photo by David J. Lindsay.)

by Mr Hodsoll, who won a double handful of CCs and was Reserve
Best in Show at the National Terrier Show in 1973.

Frank Kellett concentrates very much on other terrier breeds for
which he is renowned, but has presented a few West Highland
White Terriers in his time. Notably he handled Ch. Rotella Mighty
Miss to win her third CC, when I was unable to attend the show,
and in the same circumstances he also won a CC with my Ch.
Rotella Mighty Mike.

During my own brief fling as a handler, I was fortunate enough to
guide Ch. Ashgate Donna to her title and the award of Top Bitch in
the breed 1987, for Mr and Mrs Thomas and Heather Cery. And in
the same year, I handled Ch. Cregneash Crusader for Stuart and
Denise Limb. This dog had a twelve-day show career, winning three
CCs, three Best of Breeds, a Reserve Terrier Group at Three Coun-
ties and a Terrier Group at Border Union, before retiring mid-year as
Top West Highland White Terrier. In 1989, Ch. Hazlan Silver Knight
of Sarmac was runner-up Top Dog in the breed to Ch. Olac Moonpi-

Geoff Corish showing Ch. Angus of Furzeleigh in 1984. (Photo by Chris Kernick.)

lot, and Ch. Silver Lady of Sarmac gained her title at the age of eight, after a very short show career.

For many years now, Geoff Corish has been an ever-present handler of our breed. Starting as a young lad, Mr Corish has to be admired for the skill and professionalism he displays in his handling of many breeds. Having made up his own West Highland White Terrier bitch, Ch. Sealaw Selena in 1970, he has to date steered a total of twenty-nine dogs to their titles in our breed alone. He handled the first West Highland White Terrier to win Best in Show at Cruft's in 1976 with Ch. Dianthus Buttons, and has since repeated this win with the Llasa Apso Ch. Saxonsprings Hackensack. In 1980, Ch. Furzeleigh Startrek was handled to Best in Show at Paignton for owner John Hodsoll and, in the same year, Mrs De Terry's bitch Ch. Grierson's Fancy was Best of Breed at Cruft's. Ch. Angus of Furzeleigh won ten CCs altogether in 1984/5. In 1991, Mr Corish made up Ch. Gyllie of Drummersdale for Mrs Nellie Wright. This dog went on to claim the accolade of Top Winner in the breed 1991. Geoff seems to make a habit of being first, in more ways than one: he was also the first professional handler to award CCs whilst still active in the profession, and also the first again to judge Best in Show All Breeds as he did at Darlington 1991.

241

West Highland White Terriers Abroad

Europe and Scandinavia

In Scandinavia, and particularly in Sweden, none has done more for the breed than Mrs Birgitta Hasselgren with her famous Tweed kennel. Her breeding is based very much on Birkfell lines and the list of Tweed champions is a long one. Champions Tweed Tartan Maid, Tweed Texas Ranger, Tweed Take by Storm, Tweed Tartan Caledonier and Birkfell Storm Song are but a few. Mrs Britta Roos-Borjeson's Bushey's kennel has had tremendous success: Ch. Bushey's Magic Storm and Ch. Bushey's Major Storm lead the charge.

The Smash kennel of Mrs Louise Westerberg is having great successes with her Smash × Lasara breeding. In all, the kennel has produced nine champions, with Sw. Ch. Smash Scallywag being Top Dog 1989 and his son Ch. Smash Turbo winning Best of Breed at the Swedish Club Show in 1989 and 1991. Other principal Swedish kennels, too numerous to mention individually, include Miss Suzanne Birberg's Match, Mrs Hultgren's Pajazzo, Mrs Johannson's Giggles, Mrs Inger Marius's Glencheck and Mr and Mrs Norlander's Season.

In Norway, Mr Anthonisen and his Black Horn kennel always seem to have a good one. My Ch. Rotella Mighty Mike did well for him, winning Best in Show at the Swedish Club Show. Juha Smolander from Finland is a regular visitor to these shores and has done very well in his native land and abroad, handling Ch. Pajazzo Mona Lisa to Best in Show at the Swedish Club Show in 1990. Having a personal knowledge of Sweden in particular, I must say that at the highest level, the quality of the dogs is second to none and the trimming and presentation is quite outstanding.

The breed has many European strongholds. In France, Miss K. Round with her Champernoune kennel has been riding high. Mrs Breton Des Loys (Delbrett) and Mrs Le Pape (De Walescot) are also in evidence there. John O'Brien's newly founded kennel of imported Famechecks are beginning to make their mark, most notably Famecheck Sea Urchin and Famecheck Paratrooper. All the O'Brien charges are handled by young Michelle Gray from England.

Jesus Pastor campaigns the breed all over Europe and particularly in his native Spain. At present, he is doing very well with Eng. Ch. Ashgate Connel.

Eng. Int. and Dutch Ch. Lasara Love All (1986). (Photo by David Dalton.)

Ch. Phlurry of Highstile with four of his offspring: Ch. Caithness Clan Coquette, Ch. Caithness Pot Shot Peter Pan, Ch. Caithness Clan Caressive and Ch. Caithness Personality Pebbledash.

In Italy, Irene Gaslini's Italian Ch. Pajazzo Hoolabandoola is the top-winning West Highland White Terrier with many Best in Show wins to his credit.

Jane (Hanneke) Kabel, with her Llasara kennel, has carried on in her native Holland much as she left off when in partnership with Mrs Barbara Graham in the UK. Her UK Ch. Lasara Love All has added the Dutch and international titles to his name and helped to make Llasara Holland's Top Kennel All Breeds in 1988. Lia Meerwijk's Caithness kennel was named after Ashgate Caithness, who was one of two bitch puppies bought in from the UK as foundation stock; the other was Phlurry of Highstile. Both did well winning several CCs, but it was Ch. Phlurry of Highstile who stole the show becoming a Dutch, German and international champion. She is behind all the Caithness stock of today, and her first litter by Dutch and Int. Ch. Poolmist Pimento contained three more champions.

Mrs Lillian Brown (formerly Olsen), Mrs Inge Marie Ravn, Mrs Ellen Jacob, Mrs Joan Dan and Lise Christfort are some of the principal breeders and exhibitors who keep the flag flying in Denmark. Mrs Brown has been an active specialist in the breed for many years and now, along with the husband Kevin (who some may remember as a fresh-faced lad from his handling days in the UK), successfully campaigns several terrier breeds in Europe. Mrs Brown handled, amongst others, Ch. Teddy Trouble to his title in the 1970s. In 1982 and 1985, her multi-champion, Ch. Purston Primadonna, was Top West Highland White Terrier in Denmark. Mrs Inge Marie Ravn always seems to have a top-quality dog in the ring and has built up an impressive record over the years. Mrs Ellen Jacob is another dedicated fancier formerly under the White Clover banner, which has now been changed to Scotsween. Mrs Jacob supplied two bitches by the multi-champion, Ch. Rotella Royal Standard, who became the foundation stock of the Sonderdalen kennel. The Sonderdalens of Mrs Joan Dan have had great success in the last few years, notably the top-winning bitch team in 1990 of Ch. Sonderdalen Stephanie and Ch. Sonderdalen Jackielina. Nord. and Int. Ch. Smash I am Sparkling joined the Westie-White kennel of Lisa Christfort after a fantastic career in Scandinavia. He has carried on to win the title World Winner 1989, West Highland White Terrier of the Year and Number Two Terrier of the Year 1990.

The breed is also strong in Germany, and exhibitors come from many countries to show their dogs. Hartmut J. Bolle and his wife, Pauline Bolle-Mead, started their Montrose kennel in 1975 when

The multi-Ch. Purston Primadonna going Best in Show at eleven years of age.

they were resident in the UK. Since returning to Germany, they have done well with their English imports Int. Ger. VDH. Ch. Seacrill Sporting Chance at Highstile and Ch. Smart Alec at Highstile as well as their home-bred Ch. Montrose Quite Right, Ch. Montrose Dimple and Ch. Montrose Paladins Lass. Dr Wilfried, Elke and Britta Peper's Peppermint is another very successful kennel. Their Ch. Peppermint Florence won just about every title available with several notable Best in Shows and other top awards to her credit. Ch. Peppermint Drum Major won twelve CACIBs, many groups and two Best in Shows.

USA and Canada

In the USA and Canada, the breed is enormously popular. The distances involved in showing are so great that professional handlers are much used and, in the context of this book, deserve a special

245

mention. The writer would need another book to pay full compliment to all the fanciers, so what follows is a summary.

The late Mrs Daniell-Jenkins was a great supporter of the breed for many years with her Of the Rouge kennel and kept the flag flying in Canada and in her raids across the border.

In the USA, there has been an unparalleled rise in the popularity of our breed over the years. Imports have always played their part and many from England have done exceptionally well. Ch. Kiltie and Ch. Glenmohr Model were two of the earliest to cross the Atlantic. Ch. Scotia Chief became a US champion in 1914 and was followed by many of the early Childwicks. Greenwich Cairn Fern, Greenwich Chief and Greenwich White Crys all became champions in 1914, and Miss Claudia Phelps had many home-bred champions between 1918 and 1929 with her Rosstor kennels, helping to establish the breed in its formative years. Before the Second World War, many of the top English kennels sent stock. There were six US Cooden champions between 1932 and 1936 alone. Mrs Pacey sent over twenty Wolveys to gain their US titles, and Dr and Mrs Russell also sent some of their best Crubens.

Mrs Eppley's Ch. Wolvey Pattern of Edgerstoune was a Best in Show winner, as was the Canadian-bred Ch. Ursa Highland Major

Eng. and Am. Ch. Wolvey Philippa of Clairdene (1956). (Photo by Thomas Fall.)

seven times over for owner Perry Chadwick in the 1940s and 1950s. Miss B. Worcester's Ch. Cruben Dextor set new heights in the 1950s, and for the same owners Ch. Symmetra Snip won three Best in Shows in 1960 with a notable one at the All Terrier Montgomery County Show.

Mrs Barbara Keenan's Wishing Well kennel was originally started by Mrs Keenan and her mother Mrs Florence Worcester. The kennel flourished, obtaining some of the best English stock and, after her marriage to the late Henry Sayers (a great handler and terrier man), the success continued unabated. One of the many Wishing Well charges, Ch. Elfinbrook Simon won twelve Best in Shows in both 1961 and 1962. He went on to sire fifty-six American champions. Simon was also the first West Highland White Terrier to win Best in Show at Westminster, which had a dramatic effect on the surging popularity of the breed countrywide. The Wishing Wells are one of the most celebrated kennels in America and continue their success up to the present time. Of the many great dogs they have housed in the past, besides Ch. Elfinbrook Simon, are Ch. Rainsborowe Redvers, Ch. Famecheck Platinum, Ch. Lymehills Birkfell Soltice and Ch. Kristajen Krackerjack.

Jim Sanders started his Pagan kennel in 1977 with the help of the late David Ogg and much of the stock was Pillerton based. US Ch. Pagan Prince of Mauradoon and US Ch. Pagan Witch were but two from this highly successful kennel. Mr Sanders gave up showing and breeding in 1987, but keeps an interest and is currently second vice-president of the West Highland White Terrier Club of California.

The O' the Ridge kennel must have had a pleasant surprise when their Ch. Heritage Farms Jenny Jump-Up stopped being a brood-bitch and started being a show dog aged five years. Handled by Landis Hirstein in 1979, with a show career that lasted little over a year, she broke all records for a bitch, winning four All Breed Best in Shows, twenty Terrier Groups and seventy-seven Best of Breeds.

Mrs Neoma Eberhardt had her first home-bred champion in Am., Can. and Mex. Ch. Kirk O' the Glen Merryhart, who was the dam of four champions, including Am., Can. and Mex. Ch. Merryhart Pettipants, the first home-bred by Ch. Elfinbrook Simon. Am., Can. and Mex. Ch. Merryhart Sound Off won the National Roving Speciality in 1975 and was the dam of another four champions. Ch. Finearte Dove's Beau was brought from England and sired four champions. The widely acclaimed dog Am., Can., and Mex. Ch.

Am. and Can. Ch. Merryhart Honest John (1974), sired twenty-six champions. (Photo by Ludwig.)

Merryhart Aspen Able sired yet another thirteen champions. The list is seemingly endless from this tremendously successful kennel. In all, the Merryhart kennel was responsible for seventy-seven champions in just over fourteen years. Mr and Mrs Eberhardt have now turned their attention to judging. Mr Eberhardt judged the National Show at Montgomery in 1977, while Mrs Eberhardt judges the Terrier Group and half the Toy Group.

Before moving on to the present day, this review would not be complete without paying some respect to two (of the many) great handlers, George Ward and Cliff Hallmark. Both artists in their work, they made up countless champions in a variety of breeds and were frequent visitors to Great Britain. On behalf of the 'Wigtown' kennels of Mrs B.G. Frame, Mr Ward handled Ch. Purston Pinmoney Pedlar to a record forty-eight Best in Show wins.

Today, there are many kennels that are housing top winners, but what follows is a fairly random selection of some of the notables.

George Wright has handled a number of dogs to their titles for

Robert and Mrs Martha Black who own the Lockmede prefix. Mr Wright is currently doing well with the English import Ch. Ashgate Alistair of Trewen for Mrs Black and partner Angeline F. Austin. The Linwood kennel of Delta and Clark Champney of Ohio has had great success with its Olac imports and others. Joanne and Jaimi Glodek's Am. and Ber. Ch. Mac-Ken-Char's Irish Navigator was a multiple Best in Show winner for them in the 1980s, and they are very much in evidence these days with BJ's Madam Mac-Ken-Char amongst others. Hal and Maura Heubel have made up many champions in their Bel-West kennel. Ch. Holyrood's Hootman O' Sheely Bay was the No. 1 West Highland White Terrier in 1990 and has continued his winning ways in 1991 for the Manley kennel owners Dr James and Elizabeth Boso. Presented by Mark and Sally George he was Best of Breed at the Great Western Terrier Specialities Show in June 1991. Neil and Barbara Stoll have many American and Canadian champions in their Glenbrier kennel. Gary Gabriel and Florence MacMillan are currently riding high with their L'Esprit clan. In 1989, Am. Ch. Waterford of Wyndam was No. 1 in the breed, and they have campaigned the great Swedish import Nor. and Am. Ch. Tweed Take by Storm to nineteen Best in Show wins. Mary and Geoff Charles started off with Ch. Craigty's Something Special as the foundation bitch for their Glenfinnan kennel, and special she proved to be in producing nine champions. They are currently doing very well with Am. and Can. Ch. Glenfinnan's Special Brew, who at nine years of age still looks the part. Mrs Mona Berkowitz's English import Am. Ch. Haweswalton Aladin is a group winner and maintains the high traditions of the Momarv kennel. This dog has been taken to the heights by ace handler Wood Wornall. Co-owned by Kathy Kompare and Nancy Spelke, and handled by Nancy, Ch. Kilkerran Quintessence is a multiple Best in Show winner. At the time of writing, this dog stands as the nation's No. 1 West Highland White Terrier.

As you can see, the little Highlander is now very popular in all corners of the globe. It has taken just over eighty years, great dedication, intelligent and thoughtful breeding and a lot of hard work for our breed to come this far. My hopes are that in another eighty years, we may all be able to hold the breed in the same high esteem it currently enjoys.

Appendix 1

Standard of Points as Adopted by The West Highland White Terrier Club of England
(*circa* 1908)

No. 1 The General Appearance of the West Highland White Terrier is that of a small, game, hardy-looking Terrier, possessed with no small amount of self esteem, with a varminty appearance, strongly built, deep in chest and back ribs, straight back and powerful quarters on muscular legs, and exhibiting in a marked degree a great combination of strength and activity. The coat should be about 2½ inches long, white in colour, hard, with plenty of soft undercoat with no tendency to wave or curl. The tail should be as straight as possible and carried not too gaily, and covered with hard hair, but not bushy. The skull should not be too broad, being in proportion to the powerful jaws. The ears shall be as small and sharp-pointed as possible, and carried tightly up, and must be absolutely erect. The eyes of moderate size, dark hazel in colour, widely placed, with a sharp, bright, intelligent expression. The muzzle should not be too long, powerful, and gradually tapering towards the nose. The nose, roof of mouth, and pads of feet distinctly black in colour.

No. 2 Colour   Pure white; any other colour objectionable.

No. 3 Coat   Very important, and seldom seen to perfection; must be double-coated. The outer coat is about 2 inches long, and free from any curl. The under coat, which resembles fur, is short, soft and close. Open coats are objectionable.

No. 4 Size   Dogs to weigh from 14 to 18 lbs, and bitches from 12 to 16 lbs, and measure from 8 to 12 inches at the shoulder.

No. 5 Skull   Should not be too narrow, being in proportion to his

250

powerful jaw, not too long, slightly domed, and gradually tapering to the eyes, between which there should be a slight indentation or stop, eyebrows heavy, head and neck thickly coated with hair.

No. 6 Eyes   Widely set apart, medium in size, dark hazel in colour, slightly sunk in the head, sharp and intelligent, which looking from under the heavy eyebrows give a piercing look. Full eyes and also light coloured eyes are very objectionable.

No. 7 Muzzle   Should be nearly equal in length to the rest of the skull, powerful and gradually tapering towards the nose, which should be fairly wide. The jaws level and powerful, the teeth square or evenly met, well set and large for the size of the dog. The nose should be distinctly black in colour.

No. 8 Ears   Small, erect, carried tightly up, and terminating in a sharp point. The hair of them should be short, smooth (velvety), and free from any fringe at the top. Round pointed, broad, and large ears are very objectionable, also ears too heavily coated with hair.

No. 9 Neck   Muscular and nicely set on sloping shoulders.

No. 10 Chest   Very deep, with breadth in proportion to size of dog.

No. 11 Body   Compact, straight back, ribs deep and well arched in the upper half of ribs, presenting a flattish side appearance, loins broad and strong, hindquarters strong, muscular and wide across the top.

No. 12 Legs and Feet   Both fore and hind legs should be short and muscular. The shoulder-blades should be comparatively broad, and well sloped backwards. The points of the shoulder-blades should be closely knitted into the backbone, so that very little movement of them should be noticeable when the dog is walking. The elbow should be close to the body both when moving or standing, thus causing the foreleg to be well placed in under the shoulder. The forelegs should be short and thickly covered with short hard hair. The hind legs should be short and sinewy. The thighs very muscular and not too wide apart. The hocks bent and well set in under the body, so as to be fairly close to each other either when standing, walking, or trotting. The forefeet are larger than the hind ones, are round, proportionate in size, strong, thickly padded, and covered with short hard hair. The hind feet are smaller and thickly padded. The under surface of the pads of feet and all the nails should be distinctly black in colour. Cow hocks detract from the general appearance. Straight or weak hocks, both kinds, are undesirable, and should be guarded against.

No. 13 Tail Five or 6 inches long, covered with hard hairs, no feather, as straight as possible, carried gaily, but not curled over the back. A long tail is objectionable. On no account should tails be docked, *vide* K.C. Rule VI, Appendix II.

No. 14 Movement Should be free, straight and easy all round, in front the leg should be freely extended forward by the shoulder. The hind movement should be free, strong and close. The hocks should be freely flexed and drawn in close under the body, so that when moving off the foot the body is thrown or pushed forward with some force. Stiff stilty movement behind is very objectionable.

Faults

No. 1 Coat Any silkiness, wave, or tendency to curl is a serious blemish, as is also an open coat, and black, grey, or wheaten hairs.

No. 2 Size Any specimens under the minimum weight, or above the maximum weight are objectionable.

No. 3 Eyes Full or light coloured.

No. 4 Ears Round-pointed, drop, semi-erect, also ears too heavily covered with hair.

No. 5 Muzzle Either under or over shot and defective teeth.

Appendix 2

Useful Addresses

The Kennel Club of Great Britain
Clarges Street
London W1Y 8AB

The West Highland White
   Terrier Club
Hon. Sec. Mrs J. Herbert
Glenalwyne
Lee Brae
Galashiels TD1 1QR

The West Highland White
   Terrier Club of England
Hon. Sec. Mrs J. Abbey
7 Pottery Lane
Woodlesford
Leeds LS26 8PH

Southern West Highland White
   Terrier Club
Hon. Sec. Mrs S. Hooper
Three Ashes Cottage
North Cadbury
Yeovil
Somerset

The West Highland White
   Terrier Club of Northern
   Ireland
Hon. Sec. Mrs M. Johnston
24 Corkhill Road
Seskinore
Co. Tyrone
Northern Ireland BT78 2PW

The American Kennel Club
51 Madison Avenue
New York
NY 10010

West Highland White Terrier
   Club of America
Hon. Sec. Miss Susan Napady
c/o 27426 Mountain Meadow
   Road
Escondido
California
CA 92026

San Francisco Bay West
   Highland White Terrier Club
Hon. Sec. Marjorie Conway
7404 North Paula
Clovis
California
CA 93612

Further Reading

Beynon, J.W.H., Fisher, Alex, and Wilson, Peggy, *The Cairn Terrier*, Popular Dogs Publishing Co. Ltd (Revised edition, 1988)

Boorer, Wendy, *Dog Care*, Hamlyn (1970)

Buckley, Holland, *The West Highland White Terrier*, The Illustrated Kennel News Co. Ltd (1911)

Corbett, Thomas, *The Dog Breeders Textbook*, Our Dogs Publishing Co. Ltd (1952)

Croxton Smith OBE, Arthur, *About Our Dogs*, Ward Lock & Co. Ltd (1931)

de Bairacli Levy, Juliette, *The Complete Herbal Book for the Dog*, Faber and Faber Ltd (1955)

Dennis, D. Mary, *The West Highland White Terrier*, Popular Dogs Publishing Co. Ltd (1967)

Frankling, Eleanor, *Practical Dog Breeding and Genetics*, Popular Dogs Publishing Co. Ltd (1961)

Harding Cox, Major, *Dogs of Today*, A & C Black Ltd (1935)

Harmer, Hilary, *Dogs and How to Breed Them*, Clark, Doble & Brendon Ltd (1968)

Hubbard, Clifford L.B., *Dogs in Britain*, Macmillan & Co. Ltd (1948)

Hutchinson, Walter (Ed.), *Hutchinson's Popular & Illustrated Dog Encyclopaedia* (1934)

Leighton, Robert, *Cassell's New Book of The Dog*, Cassell (1906)

Marvin, John T., *The Complete West Highland White Terrier*, Howell Book House Inc. (1961)

Pacey, May, *West Highland White Terriers*, W. & G. Foyle Ltd (1963)

Index

636.   Wright, Roger
76
WRI   West Highland white terriers
$39.95   *00477 5408*